James Bromfield

Lower Britanny and the Bible There

Its Priests and People, also Notes on Religious and Civil Liberty in France

James Bromfield

Lower Britanny and the Bible There
Its Priests and People, also Notes on Religious and Civil Liberty in France

ISBN/EAN: 9783337094737

Printed in Europe, USA, Canada, Australia, Japan

Cover: Foto ©Lupo / pixelio.de

More available books at **www.hansebooks.com**

LOWER BRITANNY

AND THE BIBLE THERE:

ITS PRIESTS AND PEOPLE.

ALSO

NOTES ON RELIGIOUS AND CIVIL LIBERTY IN FRANCE.

BY

JAMES BROMFIELD,

AUTHOR OF 'BRITANNY AND THE BIBLE,' 'THE CHASE IN BRITANNY,'
'CLERY'S NARRATIVE OF LOUIS XVL,' ETC.

LONDON:
LONGMAN, GREEN, LONGMAN, ROBERTS, & GREEN.
1863.

PREFACE.

IN laying this book before the Public, I have but few remarks to make.

I regret that the Bible does not occupy the whole of the work; but the fault is not mine, for unfortunately it occupies as yet but a small comparative space in Britanny.

I have, however, added some observations on the state of religious and civil liberty in France generally; and as those who venerate the Bible are naturally anxious both for its spread and for the protection of its worshippers, I trust that such remarks may not be unacceptable.

Religious and civil liberty form part of the same body, and when one is wounded the other feels the stroke. Englishmen are practically ignorant of the capricious cruelties of arbitrary power, and long may they remain so; but it is well that they should be enlightened upon them in theory, instead of in practice. It is when the former means of knowledge has been wanting, that the latter often arrives.

For those parts which are savoured with what some may think an obtrusive liberalism or an exuberant patriotism, I make no apology. The fault (if any) has been one of position — that I have been resident in France, and have felt the sting of what I complain of. To those who censure me, I recommend reflection and a sojourn on the spot; it is probable that, with these helps, they will ere long think differently, and value England and her institutions more highly than perchance they do now. Foreign residence is as good for grumblers as for dyspeptics. Home privileges and comforts are doubly valued abroad.

If I am thought to speak harshly of certain individuals of another creed and nation, I can only reply, that I do ' nothing extenuate, nor set down aught *in malice.*' I merely relate what I have seen, read, heard, and thought; and I do so in the conviction that a good humoured statement of what a man considers to be the truth is always beneficial, and that when men speak their minds freely, and with temper, good will certainly arise out of it.

I send this book forth in my own name. My former work on a similar subject was written while I was resident in Britanny (as, indeed, were many parts of the present work), and was published during the same period; and as I took the liberty of speaking my mind plainly on public men and things in France, and we were then under the *coup d'état* régime, I should, in all probability, very soon have been requested (more *or less* politely) to quit the country, had I been known as the author. I was therefore obliged to write under an assumed name, and I chose the name of *I. Hope,* as at once my motto and my chief characteristic.

I have added the remarks on the French Emperor as an act of justice, and of satisfaction to my own mind, considering what I had written in my former work; and I leave them to the varying appreciation of my readers.

National prejudices are fast disappearing before the Spirit of the Age, and the frequent intercommunication of people of different countries. Englishmen and Frenchmen no longer *hate* each other *as such*; but there is yet much to do before they will regard each other *as friends.* Let Frenchmen grant to their Protestant countrymen the equal rights in all things which their laws confer *in theory,* and let Englishmen acknowledge that England has been honourably and liberally treated *even by a Napoleon Bonaparte,* and an important progress will have been made; and a little good-humoured but free criticism, on these and similar matters, can (it seems to me) do nothing but good to all parties concerned.

I trust that this work may in some degree help on the Great Cause of Religious and Civil Liberty which I have near at heart; my object will then be amply attained, and I shall be more than compensated for such censure, misconception, and ill-natured remark as those who appeal to Public opinion must naturally expect.

But, while memory lasts, nothing can rob me of the recollection of the many happy hours I have passed in preparing and writing the pages which follow, and which will soon be scattered far and wide, like the leaves of Autumn which are now fast flying over the landscape before me.

And therefore to all my readers (and may they be many!) I bid a friendly *adieu!*

J. B.

LLANBADOC : *Dec.* 1, 1862.

Errata.

Page 34, line 4, *for* twenty-five years *read* eighteen years.

„   40,   „ 28,   „   more than a hundred thousand Bibles *read* more than a million Bibles.

„   42,   „ 34,   „   Souvestre *read* Ricou.

CONTENTS.

CHAPTER I.

CHAPTER II.

CHAPTER III.

CHAPTER IV.

LOWER BRITANNY, AND THE
BIBLE THERE.

———o◦¦◦⧓◦◦———

CHAPTER I.

SINCE I last wrote on 'Britanny and the Bible'* many
years have elapsed. With the progress of time we
might reasonably have expected progress in all things;
but I am sorry to say I can only record a slow progress
of the Bible in Britanny, as far as we can judge by outward appearances. Still, there *is* progress, especially
of late.

Until a very recent period, the net had been drawn
tighter and tighter still, and, instead of progress, there
seemed almost a retrogression. Bible circulation was
wholly prohibited in one department, and impeded and
harassed in the others ; the sale of religious works of a
Protestant tendency was nearly stopped ; *colportage* was
become almost impossible; all attempts to open schools
were summarily defeated ; and friends of the cause
were everywhere discouraged and cast down. Romanism

* Published in 1852 by Longman & Co.

B

alone was flourishing, and its professors triumphant and smiling.

The tide of religious progress seemed to have receded. As sometimes happens on the sea shore, the wave retires from the shining pebbles, and makes us think that the tide has reached its highest point and has turned. But wait. To make up, as it were, for a momentary retreat, the waters return in greater strength, devour greedily the beach, hide from our view the stone we had set to mark what we had thought was the turning point, and force us, unwillingly, to retire.

The progress of the reformation shows us many periods of this kind, when the work was apparently stopped, and when its friends thought themselves deserted and forgotten. But this, *their* weakness, was God's opportunity, and almost before they had time to lament their want of faith, the cause was again advancing with rapid strides, refreshed by the short halt, and stronger than ever.

And so it will be, I believe, with Britanny. Let no one do such despite to the Great Controller of events, as to suppose that He will ever abandon the work which He has commenced, though He may from time to time try the faith and courage of those who are engaged in carrying it on. Let His servants and instruments keep steady in their dependence on Him, and ere long the mists which lately covered, and even now obscure, the view, will clear away, and they will see that even while they were the most despondent and fearful, the work was progressing the most surely. Without a deep and solid foundation no building can stand, and yet while the stones of it are being carefully laid the work is still unseen by passers-by. So let us hope and believe it is with Britanny and the Bible, and therefore let no one be discouraged by what he may read in these pages, but let him consider the nature of the work, and hope and believe constantly in the good times which are coming.

Besides, there *is* a certain amount of progress to be actually seen, when all is added together. If we look at the state of things now and compare it with, say ten years back, there is a decided advance to be noted—many new places of worship opened, and zealous ministers filling them — great increase in the distribution of the Scriptures — considerable addition to the Protestant population — and all this in spite of every obstacle and hindrance which the subtlety of man could devise. What would it have been had the Bible work had ' a clear stage,' if, with the various impediments before it, it has still surmounted them all, and advanced as it has? and we may be sure that these obstacles will not be always there; times flow as well as ebb in this world of change, and after the lowest often comes the highest tide. And in France, that country of reaction, nothing is constant long, not even oppression and persecution; and when, after a long 'winter of discontent,' the sun shines out anew, and vegetation clothes the earth with its green mantle, its vigorous growth will be in proportion to the time during which its strength and energies were apparently idle but really collecting themselves, and we shall enjoy the glorious summer all the more for the hard winter we have endured, and happily, at last, have left behind us as a thing of the past.

To suppose that distribution of the Scriptures goes on well in the teeth of government influence exerted to the contrary, is to suppose an absurdity. Government influence is great, and when exerted openly and without scruple, it is a formidable antagonist. There can be no doubt that the effect of it in Britanny has been to damp the zeal and clog the efforts of many, and until very recently the priests had succeeded in their object, and almost entirely stopped the circulation of the Scriptures. But I fully believe that there are great numbers, especially of country people, who retain their former interest in the subject, perhaps with an increased zeal arising from repression; and who, the pressure removed, will pursue their enquiries with renewed ardour. And let not those Englishmen who support the missions in this country be discouraged at the small present results, and think of withdrawing their support. Even if the missionaries should do no more (and they most certainly do much more), they at least serve as rallying points to the few converts who remain, and they are ready again to take the field when the gate is opened; meanwhile, without noise or notice, they encourage the despondent and keep the flock together.

The results must be asked for at a future day; for the present the balancing of the books should be deferred. Now that the storm is upon them, it is unkind to ask them to sit down and uncloak; but it is even now clearing away, and when the sun shines and they are dried by the wind, they will be better able to give an account of their labours.

I have often felt surprise that the societies having missionaries in France do not more frequently depute members to visit them. It would be of great service. It would encourage the ministers and promote the objects of the mission. As bystanders see sometimes more of the game than the players, so strangers with new views may often see or suggest what has escaped the notice of an old resident, and may create a new activity. For myself, I think that the rule which usually prevails among Dissenters, in moving their ministers about from place to place, may be aptly applied to missionaries, unless in peculiar cases. Long residence has a tendency to cause apathy and contracted views; sometimes, too, family ties and personal interests rise up and impede usefulness. A missionary should have but one end before him—*the Mission*—and towards this he should turn at all times with undivided attention and energy. According to the proverb, 'new brooms sweep clean,' and a new man will often open up channels which had gradually become clogged and filled up, at the same time that he arrives clear of the connections, and prejudices perchance, which have surrounded his predecessor.

One thing is certain, that a missionary abroad has a most responsible, difficult, and delicate office, and one for which but a select *few* are *really* capable. According to his capacities he will do good, either great or small; but, with the best motives, he may often fall into errors which others may see and amend, and therefore an occasional overlooking is always desirable as regards the objects of the mission, while to the missionary himself it would be an encouragement and a stimulus to exertion.

Colportage too had been almost impossible. It was useless to ask for an authorisation to sell religious tracts, and to do so without one was extremely difficult under the new law regulating colportage. By it, not only must the colporteur carry his list with him, so that it may be compared with the authorisation which he also carries about him; but also each separate work must be stamped with a special stamp easily to be recognised, or in default it might be seized and confiscated. This rendered clandestine colportage well-nigh impracticable.

For myself I continue of the same opinion which I have held from the beginning, that the most worthy course is to distribute the Bible openly and freely, and in case of seizure to try the question before the court of appeal at Paris. No direct decision has ever taken place on the point, and it is generally allowed that the Bible can only be legally forbidden by a *very strained* application of the law, which was never *intended* to apply to it. At present the government performs the act, and escapes the public shame of it; but it would be worth an effort, and a costly one, either to rescue the Bible from their clutches, or to fix upon them the ignominy of proscribing it.

The government of France, reckless as it has shown itself of national opinion, is highly sensitive to the opinion of Europe, and of England in particular, and would not enter lightly upon a course which would at once offend the religious feelings and shock the reason of both Protestant Europe and America. The true policy in such a case is courage; but, alas! that quality, i.e. the moral part of it, has in a degree flown from Frenchmen. Fear, fear of this or that, fear of what *may* happen, fear of something indefinable and indescribable, this clothed in specious words and bearing a reasonable exterior, has been in many cases too powerful an opponent to contend with ; and ' the impracticable English,' as we are called, are left to chew the cud in a glorious minority, and invoke foreign Hampdens in vain.

To my knowledge the case was some time since placed before an eminent and excellent Protestant advocate in Paris, and he advised, as every advocate whose reputa-

tion was concerned would advise, that it was a dangerous course, and that the parties must wait. An enemy's
counsel exactly—' a lion in the path.' The case is not
one of law for a counsel's opinion ; it is to be decided
by common sense, zeal in the good cause, and a good
purse, and I do wonder that none of my stout countrymen have tried it, as so many of them unite these
conditions.

As to a Frenchman standing up alone voluntarily to
oppose the government, it is a rarity — a thing almost
out of nature. Nature made him gregarious, and he
acts best in masses, the consequence of which is that
thousands oppose the law at the same moment, and
thence arises a revolution. In England revolutions
have been slowly brought about by the successive
action of individual opposition ; in France, generally,
no one does anything until all do it together, hence
a sudden and violent convulsion, often without corre-
sponding results.

The priests continue as actively occupied as ever in
detecting and suppressing any tendency towards Protestantism, and do not hesitate about means, when desirous
of reclaiming a strayed member of their flock. A
singular proof of this lately came under my personal
knowledge. A Breton woman became convinced of the
unsoundness of the Romanist religion which she professed. She had not attended the services of any Protestant minister ; it was the result entirely of her own
feelings. Having for some time entertained free notions
of Romanism, she was viewed as a doubtful, not to say
mauvais sujet by the priest, who threatened her so
severely in the confessional, that she gave up attending.
He then followed her to her house, and used all possible
means to induce her to be quiet, but without effect.

At this period she became known to a Protestant minister, to whom she stated her case, and from whom she received advice and comfort. The fury of the priest redoubled at this. He and her brother charged the Protestant minister with every kind of improper motive towards her, and the brother threatened to murder her if she continued to see him. But nothing daunted, the young woman (she was only twenty-five years of age) persisted.

The priest said nothing more, but practised a new manœuvre, which does more credit to his ingenuity and zeal for his church than to his honesty. He endeavoured to prove *that she was mad*, and procured the attendance of the doctor of a neighbouring madhouse to state the fact. This gentleman came over from some distance to see the patient, but fortunately he was an honest man. Instead of a woman out of her senses, he found a person calm, well informed, arguing with self-possession with the priest, and refuting his positions. He was astonished, and declined having anything to do with the matter, and the poor woman was spared this injustice, for had she once been placed in the lunatic hospital, we should never have heard of her again. Meanwhile, however, they give out that she is mad, to deprive Protestantism of the honour of a sane convert, and impute all kinds of criminal motives to the Protestant minister who stood by her in her troubles.

We little think, when we read of conversions, how much trial and mental suffering is implied in the word, in a country like Britanny, where the great majority are opposed to the religion of the convert, and where all worldly interests and motives are against the change; but though unnoticed by us, they are duly noted by Another, and will one day be recompensed with full measure.

It is a curious fact, which deserves mention, and one which, like Pandora's box, has hope at the bottom, that whenever great changes have occurred in the government of France, the demand for the Holy Scriptures has been increased in Britanny. In 1848, the year of the last revolution but one, the distribution of the Bible in Britanny was increased by about one-third, and during the autumn preceding the *coup d'état*, which to all intents and purposes was a revolution also, and when men's minds were full of apprehension of a bodeful future, and quaking with fear, there was again an increased demand for the Bible. And remember that no Bibles were *given*, all were *bonâ fide sold*, and that to Bretons, men who are fond of money, and never buy a thing without wanting it.

This is a clear proof of the repressive effect of government and priestly opposition.

When the political machine works smoothly and easily, pressure is exerted on all parts equally, dislocations and deviations are at once perceived, and instantly remedied. Then is the heyday of prefectorial *surveillance*. Then are showered down instructions to *maires* and *sous-préfets* to be active, and to look sharp after all who are suspected of an exuberant Protestantism; then the very *maires* and *sous-préfets* themselves find themselves looked up smartly by the head ecclesiastics of their *arrondissement*, in case they are not sufficiently zealous, and get a taste of that unpleasant dish, the government *cold shoulder*, during a short sojourn on the north side of the *préfet's* countenance; then are issued extra instructions to *gensdarmes* to dodge and dog *colporteurs* and Protestant ministers; and despatches, reports, and autocratic missives from headquarters, rain down quick and fast.

Then, too, Holy Mother Church lays aside her weeds and *deshabille*, and stalks forth in all her bravery. The confessional is worked at high pressure, the pulpits and sounding-boards groan and crack under the eloquence of the preachers; in all places the priesthood appear with beaver cocked and rampant air, and may be heard with loud tones bearing down heavily upon the timid and hesitating questioner; episcopal charges are frequent, bold, and decided, like those of the heavy brigade at Waterloo; all things proclaim the sun in the zenith, and the Church basking thereunder. And as a natural consequence of this worrying by the shepherds, sheep who are not favourites retire to their hiding-places, or meekly lie down at the shepherds' feet, hoping by submission to avert the blow, and the shepherds have the field all to themselves.

But let the political sky be troubled, and this scene is changed. The governors have then so much fear for their own safety that they almost wholly forget the governed, and no longer pay them those amiable little attentions they once did. So the poor sheep venture to look out a little for themselves, and again browse in the forbidden pastures without fear of sword or crosier, and indulge their several tastes for this herb or that without scruple, and, as is natural, use the moment with all diligence to make up for lost time. Thus the devices of the shepherds come to nought, after all, in the long run; as one great effect of their vigilance in harassing their flock, and keeping them on low diet, is a strengthened feeling of independence and an increased appetite.

In all this is ground for hope, as it proves the real desires of the people when left to themselves. And, after all, the opposition of the Government will not be everlasting. Man may propose, but God disposes; and the time is certain to arrive when the strong-looking walls built up by the so-called great ones of the earth to keep out the truth will all be thrown down, as were the walls of Jericho, and all their boasted artifices be swept away as cobwebs.

It also shows clearly the success of past labours, although that success was not visible at the time, and was perhaps despaired of. As in all the other operations of Providence, time is required for *this* work. The strong and stubborn soil of the human heart cannot at once bear a crop; it must be well drained, broken up, and prepared; weeds must be rooted out, and stones and rubbish got rid of; the seed must be sown carefully and in due season, and then left to the fertilizing hand of Providence, for it is He alone who can give the increase. And in like manner as, despite wind and storm, the seed germinates and fulfils its task in tranquillity, so the word of God, once sown, never dies. War may sweep over and devastate a country, civil strife and persecution may agitate and deface it, its very foundations may be shaken and upheaved by revolutions; yet all these will have their season and their end, and in the calm that will at last ensue, the seed will appear peacefully above the surface, and the desert blossom as the rose.

But until lately the bleak north wind has blown fiercely upon Protestantism in Britanny. The distribution of the Scriptures had been almost wholly prohibited, and colportage had almost ceased. Not that those to whom the work was confided folded their arms and did nothing; but they were driven to various devices in order to arrive at their object, and they did all these things under menace and fear of the law. Some carried

boxes of various wares, and a few Testaments stowed
away in a secret place, to comply with a casual demand;
others walked through the country ostensibly as ordinary travellers, but charged with the same valuable
freight; but all were evaders of the law, all were in the
same perpetual fear of detection and of punishment
when detected.   Bible distribution, in fact, was lowered
to the level of poaching or smuggling.

Little think the good people of England, who read
their Bibles in peace by their firesides and give it
openly where they choose, that within a short day's
journey from them is a country where until lately the
Bible was denounced more eagerly than the most
obscene book, and its distribution was visited with
pains and penalties.   And this may happen again at
any moment.

I know that calls on the purses of benevolent Englishmen are numerous as the sea sand, but I do believe that
no one of the various claims has more to recommend it
than the work of evangelisation in Britanny.   And,
happily, English charity and liberality are expansive as
the air we breathe.   Who does not feel that they act as
the lightning conductors, and that in the day when God
has chastised other nations the storm has passed over
our heads without bursting, and has discharged its fury
elsewhere.   And who does not also feel, by experience,
that in extending the circle of his charities he has in
fact extended the circle of his blessings, and that the
money he has given liberally to alleviate the distress of
others has procured a rich return of benefit and consola-
tion for himself?

Soon after the *coup d'état* an old law was revived,
under which books coming from England were only to
be allowed entry into France at certain ports therein

named, where they were to be carefully examined. This was, of course, done at the instigation of the ecclesiastical Romish authorities, as a sort of literary quarantine to prevent the spread to France of the contagion of heresy. I was very nearly suffering under the law myself. I had procured from England some Bibles and religious works for distribution in Britanny, to which a kind friend in Shropshire had made a notable addition, and they were brought over by a lady as part of her luggage. Unfortunately they had been placed at the top of the trunk, and therefore were visible at the first opening. I endeavoured to get the examining officer to take an estimate of the contents of the whole lot, but he said he must open some of the trunks to enable him to judge, and as ill luck would have it, he laid his hand on the one where the books were, as a signal to his men to open it. I, however, managed to divert his attention to something else for the moment, and told the men to open another, which they did, and as it contained nothing but clothes, it was all right. He then touched the old one again. ' And what is in this?' I replied, ' Oh ! a general lot of things ; you know ladies carry all sorts,' at which he smiled and passed on, and the books escaped seizure.

A minister of my acquaintance also wanted to publish some Bible stories in Breton, and he thought he would embellish them with woodcuts to make them more attractive, and so he procured the types in England. They were sent viâ Boulogne, but their nature being discovered, an enormous duty, amounting to a prohibition, was placed on them, and they had to be returned to England. Then another mode was tried to get them into France, which failed also, and I do not think they have ever been made use of at all. Such are some of the difficulties attending getting the Bible into Britanny.

As to getting Protestant books printed in Britanny, it is next to impossible. In the first place, I do not know a single Protestant printer in Lower Britanny. Then all printers are obliged to take out a license, and I only wish beer-shop keepers in England were under half as strict a control as are Breton printers. First, they must get the license (*if they can*) from the authorities, who have an entire discretion in the matter, and may refuse the application on the elastic ground, which cannot be confuted, that there are already enough printers in the place; and if the Préfet *chooses to think so*, you can no more make him alter his opinion than you can make a horse drink. Then they are liable at any moment to have their license withdrawn and their shop closed, without reason assigned; in other words, to have their means of living suspended, and to be utterly ruined. Coupled with this, they are obliged to furnish the Préfet, previous to general publication, with two copies of every work in the press, which he peruses, and either allows or prohibits as he chooses; and all this at his sole will and pleasure, without law and without appeal. 'T is wonderful that anything like a good sized well-conditioned fish ever escapes all these obstacles and comes to table.

In a word, Protestantism has been chilled and discouraged everywhere; difficulties are raised to its exercise, and barrier succeeds to barrier, showing an active but concealed enemy constantly at work; its professors are excluded as much as may be from the honours of the state, and are viewed coldly by the authorities; in fact, without being openly and boldly persecuted, it is stifled and opposed as much as possible. The process is one well known to the *humane* ratcatcher. No lives taken—oh! certainly not, nothing so cruel as that—but continual barking of dogs and tinkling of ferret bells, stopping holes everywhere, suspicious-looking morsels laid in curious places, and perpetual watching; under the effect of all which the vermin are starved, frightened, or worried to death, or else commit suicide, or otherwise retire from the scene: *and so you get rid of them.*

The little *Bulletin Évangélique*, to which I shall shortly allude, will be an additional proof of what I say to any one who will take it in. We had the greatest difficulty in getting it printed at all, as there was no Protestant printer to be had, and the Catholic ones would not undertake it. At last one was found to do the work, but he made us pay most heavily for it, and turned it out in such a miserable shabby state as to make one blush for one's offspring, exposed as it is on a material which in England would be called cap or curl paper. If he had meant to ticket Protestantism as a pauper he could not have done better, and every writer in it has to eat his monthly portion of literary dirt, as a Persian might say, in seeing his signature on such a scurvy surface of whitey-brown.

It may easily be imagined how all these obstacles and restrictions emasculate the literature of the country. Controversy, whether religious or political, which is the very life of a free state; investigation and exposure of abuses, leading to their remedy; reflections on government and its subordinates, certain to fall to the ground unheeded if unmerited; holding up to public contempt profligacy or imbecility in power, or boldly pleading the cause of the poor and the oppressed; in a word, that free play of mind expressed in writing which, if worthless, dies of itself, and if true, strengthens and ennobles;

all this is utterly forbidden in Britanny; and the
printing press is either the direct organ of the Government, or else pours forth a tepid current of platitude
and inanity—or, it may be, a fetid stream, redolent of
half-disclosed vice.

And what is the state of that country which thus
fetters or thrusts aside the Scriptures, and treats all religious teaching derived therefrom as superfluous or
tending to error? Does it give a preference to other
sects of earnest religionists, or to other views of practical religion? Does it soar high into the deep blue of
philosophy, and despise the more homely and vulgar
trodden regions of mere practice, or is it generally indifferent to the subject and insensible to its importance?
Each of these elements has its share in the solution, but
the one lastly named is that which contains the colouring
matter and gives character to the whole. For, disguise
it as we may—clothe it as we can in coats of divers
colours—let Romanists boast of the devotion of their
worshippers, and French philosophers vaunt the enlightenment of their disciples—the truth remains, and
forces itself on our notice, that Roman Catholic France
and all its provinces, speaking of it in the mass and
generally, is a nation of sceptics. Not that they deny
the existence of a God—I would by no means impute
that to them. The French nation possesses too much
reason and instruction, the great writers who from age
to age have prepared and directed the public mind have
been too intellectual and too advanced in knowledge, to
be atheists; for it is only ' *the fool* who says in his
heart there is no God.' But beyond the bare acknowledgement of the great principle of a Deity they seem to
me to have made little progress. The Deity being admitted, each enclothes Him with functions after his own

guise, as of old the Pagans dressed their idols according to their own tastes; and the result is a sort of human divinity with qualities varying according to the capacity of the constructor—benignant towards the frailties *he* indulges in, severe only against those *he* has no mind to: a God of earth, and not of heaven. Subscription to His revealed will as a rule of action is spurned with contempt, or neglected from ignorance; religious controversy treated with a scornful or pitying shrug as 'ridiculous'—for, 'after all, what is truth?'—or put aside as dangerous, for 'it may lead to error.' But anything like a practical confession of God's existence, and an earnest seeking out and following after His will in the conduct of life, is, I fear, rare in Catholic France.

I know that village churches in Britanny, and town ones, too, are crowded with worshippers on *fête* days and on Sundays. I know that religious processions are almost endless, and their gaudy pageantry bowed to and saluted by thousands; but that is no argument against me when I also know that nineteen-twentieths of the church-goers are ignorant of the nature and language of the service, and that crowds equal to those who throng the processions would assemble to see an exhibition of fireworks or mountebanks. The masses, i.e. the prayers in church, are all in Latin, a dead language unknown to ninety-nine out of a hundred of every congregation. How, then, can they by any *possibility* be benefited by it, except on the supposition of the priest praying for all? There is no joining in the meaning with heart and voice, as in our English churches; but all is either sealed up in muteness, or is mumbled in a tongue unknown, and therefore devoid of meaning.

As for sermons, they are only occasional; but the churches in towns are usually very large, in which

c

case they are heard only by a few; and in the small village churches they are only given seldom, and in Britanny they are often in French, to keep up, I suppose, the preference for an unknown tongue. And sermons in a Romish country-are but in general poor things. Where the right of private judgement is denied much doctrinal discussion is not to be expected; but even doctrinal statement is rare, and its place is supplied by declamation and appeals to feeling in favor of the Virgin and Holy Mother Church. I remember hearing one celebrated preacher, and his sermon was wholly composed of eulogies of certain favourite local saints; nor was there in the whole sermon more than one Bible citation — 'one morsel of bread to that intolerable quantity of sack.' Another far-famed itinerant, a jesuit, drew vast crowds, and was really worth hearing — *as a wit or jester*, for he scattered *bon mots* and Joe Millers in profusion, and many of his periods were closed amid peals of laughter; but of religious doctrine and teaching there was nothing whatever, and nothing even approaching to it.

What can, therefore, be expected, where Bibles and religious works are repressed, where serious enquiry is kept down or misdirected, where pulpits pour out chaff chiefly, and not like the winnowing machine which retains the wheat — how can we, under such circumstances, expect religious feelings, or a life regulated by religion? as soon expect a crop after sowing the husks, or look for figs from thistles.

Therefore, *and most naturally*, a religious French man of a respectable position is a decided rarity. I say a 'French *man* of respectable position,' advisedly, because women crowd the churches, and the poor go in considerable numbers. As to the presence of the women I leave its explanation to others, but it is generally admitted that they are more devotional than men, more susceptible of appeals to feeling than men, and more liable to priestly influence — probably, too, such meaner motives as want of occupation, love of seeing and being seen, disposition to talk to friends and hear the news, may not be wholly without force, as in other countries.

As to the *poor* people, I do believe that a certain general feeling of devotion takes many of them to church, and it is sad to think that that feeling must be often unsatisfied. For how can it *possibly* be satisfied with a service in Latin—an unknown tongue? One day I said to my cook, ' Do you understand the prayers at mass?' ' Oh! yes, monsieur, perfectly well.' ' Ah! then, you know Latin,' I observed. ' Certainly, monsieur, I can read Latin easily.' ' *Certes*,' thought I, 'my *cuisinière* is a learned woman ; I shall pay her more deference in future.' However, I pursued the topic. ' You can read Latin, you say ; doubtless you understand it well ; where did you learn it?' ' Oh! no, monsieur, I did not say I *understood* Latin. I said I could *read* it ; and, *ma foi!* I can do that easily enough.' And I found she meant that she could *read*, i.e. spell out and pronounce the words only, knowing nothing whatever of their meaning.

But talk to Breton gentlemen, merchants, and shop-keepers, of religion, and you will soon see what progress it has made with *them*. Not one in twenty thinks it worth talking about at all. Perhaps you may prevail upon them so far to entertain the subject as to talk of it for five minutes — but ' *mon cher ami, comme vous êtes drôle — est ce que vous me prenez pour un dévot?* or, ' You cannot be serious in giving real importance to

such matters.'   Or, 'Ma foi! I know nothing about it,
nor ever shall.'   If they are philosophical, they stand on
their lofty tower and look down disdainfully on what
they call the Babel strife below. 'What folly thus fighting for nothing, beating the air after an *ignis fatuus*.
But so it has been and will ever be.   Fight dog, fight
wolf—kill each other and the world will be better for it.'

I know one man, a person of good natural disposition
and sentiments and a certain degree of education, with
whom I had considerable discussion, but invariably, when
I pushed him hard with Scriptural proofs, he would
say '*ah! mais que voulez-vous?*   If we are to begin
arguing from Scripture we may arrive at anything.'
The doctrine of the sole and infallible teaching of that
phantom, the church, was so firmly rooted in his mind
as to have quite destroyed his idea of independent
judgement on such matters.   He would often say, 'I
am not *au courant* to those passages, but I am sure
they have all been explained by the church in our favour,
and I leave them to better heads than mine,' and would
thus dismiss the matter as of no *personal* concern.

Another man of my acquaintance, and a worthy man
too,—now alas! no more — would often remark to me,
'What serious fellows you Protestants are, especially
you English ones; you are always in earnest; *c'est très
bien* for some things, but as to religion what *can* we
know about it?   It is all in the vague; and if we talk
about it from now to eternity, we can be none the
wiser.   For my part I look upon it thus: We move in
a circle, and when we have got round it we begin
again.   There is nothing new, no progress, no goal,
events repeat themselves, and we must do as well as we
can.'   'But,' I would say to him, 'Even supposing this
to be true of the material world as a system, what does

that signify? The important question for you is what
is your part in it as an individual?—for instance, is
there not a future state *as a fact*? Of what nature will
it be, and what effect will our life now have upon our
life then, according to what revelation teaches us, and
which is all open before you?' '*Ah! par exemple*, that
is hard to say; but suppose there is one, what then?'
'Why, if there is one, you are acting most foolishly to
make no enquiries about it. If, in an affair of this life,
I were to act as foolishly, you would most certainly
condemn me to the mad-house.' '*Ah! mon bon ami*,
there you are again, always *au sérieux*. No! rely on
it, we live in a circle,' &c., &c.; and so on with his
miserable patched up theory, out of which it was as
impossible to extract him as to pat a snail out of its
shell.

In the great body of French Romanists of the
middle and upper classes religion seems a mere name,
useful and necessary, perhaps, as a name, to signify and
ticket a party or a subject, but less interesting than a
dried specimen in a museum, or any other strange relic
of past ages. As a theory or debateable ground to
sharpen wit upon, in a harmless way, as of old knights
tilted with blunted spears, it may amuse or at least be
tolerated; but it is absurd, not to say ill-bred and
detestable, to discuss it with so much heat and earnestness. For, after all, say they, what *can* men *know*
about the future? Look how the matter stands. One
upholds this theory, another that; one burns his brother
in all Christian love and charity forsooth! another, like
a fool, submits to be burned sooner than bend to
authorities better informed than himself. How unworthy all this of sensible practical men. '*Bah!
revenons à nos moutons.*'

And what is there so difficult to deal with as this
spirit of light sceptical indifference ?   It is related that
when the Jesuits first went to China they were delighted
with the new phase of mind which they found there.
The Chinese doctors disputed and discussed, easily and
fluently, in good humour and with all courtesy.   The
good fathers wrote home in ecstasies—that the people
were polished and civil, and that the work was sure to
prosper.   But they were, for once, mistaken.   After
weeks of talk they found no advance beyond courtesy
and civility, and at length discovered that the Chinese
were supremely indifferent on the subject as a practical
one, and *therefore* had toyed and sported so pleasantly
with it.   No ! give me anything rather than polite
indifference.   With a stout, courageous, cut-and-thrust
opponent you have always a chance, for the same spirit
which makes him fight well will make him yield nobly;
with the man who runs away you have also a chance,
for he may be a being of impulse, and may take a
sudden turn and run into your arms ; even with your
scientific, logical, dried-up disputant, you are not
without hope that, screwed up in a syllogism, he may
surrender at discretion ; — but with the man who
good-humouredly and smilingly dallies and skips about
the subject, making a hit here and receiving one gaily
there, until at last he looks at his watch and says, with
a bow, that it is time to say adieu, hope is banished.

I often think, when reflecting on the present religious
aspect of Britanny, of the vision of the dry bones.
There they lay in that drear valley, whitening the earth
for many a ghastly league, and there they would have
remained for ages, cold and lifeless, dull to the gaze
and deadening to the heart of the beholder.   But God's
spirit breathed upon them, and in a moment the scene

was changed! Bone joined to bone, sinew clung to sinew, blanched and eyeless sculls grew suddenly instinct with life, the body so long dissevered sprang up again warm and united, and, instead of an inanimate mass, appeared a mighty living army. And so it will be here. At present, humanly speaking, all has been dead; apparently 'the first dark day of nothingness' has arrived, and hope has fled away; but, as the blackest hours of the night are those which most nearly precede the coming day, so even at this moment may the Spirit be preparing for His divine mission, and ere long the descending air may rustle among the trees, the precursor of a mental resurrection as wonderful and unlooked for as that viewed in the prophet's vision.

Let us then hope always—hope ever.

CHAPTER II.

'BULLETIN ÉVANGÉLIQUE' — M. LE FOURDREY — TROUBLE WITH
PRÉFET — SUPPRESSION OF 'BULLETIN' — EXTREME INTOLERANCE
— SOCIETY FOR GENERAL INTERESTS OF PROTESTANTISM IN
BRITANNY — ITS PROGRESS AND WORKING.

IN 'Britanny and the Bible,' p. 88, I allude to the
establishment of 'The Society for the General
Interests of Protestantism in Lower Britanny.' In
connection with that Society a religious periodical was
started, called *Le Bulletin Évangélique*, for Britanny.
The chief editor was the Rev. M. Le Fourdrey, the Protestant pastor of Brest, and certain other ministers and
Protestant friends contributed articles from time to
time. But M. Le Fourdrey was the life and soul of the
publication. And let me here express my sense of the
debt which the English friends of the Protestant cause
in Britanny owe to him, on this and other accounts.
Without his help the *Bulletin* could not have been carried on, and therefore he steadily gave his attention to
the work, and devoted to it time which he snatched
from other and manifold occupations. And the duties of
an editor of a periodical are always irksome enough,
but in Britanny are doubly so. Articles written in
English must be translated into French, or if written
in French by Englishmen, errors must be corrected,
and the whole carefully looked over, lest aught should
be contained hurtful to French feelings, or strange to
French modes of thought. Then an eye must always

be kept open as to the legality of this or that, and the
law of the press well conned over and kept in mind ;
the authorities must be corresponded with ; subscribers'
letters replied to ; correspondents stirred up ; in fact,
there are a host of minor and mechanical difficulties,
all annoying to a man every moment of whose time is
employed, but which M. Le Fourdrey met with an un-
varying steadiness, good temper, and tact, which deserves our warmest thanks.   Let us not forget, too, the
liberal-minded and most efficient support which he
ever gave to English missionary ministers — a support
which, had it been given grudgingly and sparingly,
would have prevented much of their present usefulness,
and whose coming into the country might have caused,
very naturally, in the mind of a man constituted otherwise than M. Le Fourdrey, feelings of jealousy and
dislike.   But his nature excluded such sentiments, and
warmly holding out the right hand of fellowship to
them, he kept it constantly extended ; and I have no
hesitation in saying, that his aid most materially assisted in establishing them, and also in increasing their
present means of doing good.   Should M. Le Fourdrey
ever visit England, I trust that these facts will be remembered with practical gratitude, and that his name
will be a ready passport wherever he may present
himself.*

To return to the *Bulletin.*   It was established after
much cogitation, and finally launched by the Society
above named.   We might have imagined that, situated

* Since the above was written M. Le Fourdrey's death has taken
place, an immense loss to the cause in Britanny.   He is succeeded by
M. Chabal, an excellent man, and who also superintends the *Bulletin*,
as chief editor, at Brest.   M. Le Fourdrey leaves behind him a widow
and a daughter (Madame Caradec) to lament his loss.

as Brest is, at the very extremity of France, the slight glimmering of light which this little star might give would pass unnoticed by the Argus eyes of the authorities. We might have thought that, speaking abstractedly, there was nothing unreasonable, nothing objectionable, in the fact that the Protestants of Britanny should wish to have a periodical of their own, which should express their own sentiments and views, seeing that the Romanists of the country enjoyed that privilege to its full extent. In a country professing equal care of all religions, there seemed nothing *à priori* extraordinary, that as one was allowed to speak, another should cease being silent, and should speak also.

But Protestants must not reason, at least they must prune their logic before coming to France.' Reason, it would seem, is not immutable; it is one thing here and another there; and in all these foregone conjectures and assumptions, we should have been committing the common error of ' reckoning without the host.'

The first number was printed, and, according to law, two copies were sent by the printer to the Sous-Préfet of Brest, for his approbation. It is probable that a small bomb-shell would have caused less confusion than did these little rolls of paper. ' These Protestants, then, have the audacity to print their *Bulletin*—here in Finistère' (aptly called the world's end); *qual infamia!* *qual picardia!* as Borrow would have said; ' but we will see.' Thereupon immediate movement to the Préfet, report on report followed, however, by *a shot* in the shape of a prefectorial decree thus laconically couched : ' In virtue of the discretionary powers entrusted to me, I forbid the publication of the journal of which a copy has been submitted to me.'

The Préfet was wise in his generation : 'act first,
reason afterwards ;' the thing is *to stop* the *Bulletin.*
' Leave me alone to justify my acts in due time.' Therefore he gave no reasons ; and in sooth, the thing would
have been difficult, for we are bold to say that sucking
doves might have produced the articles in the number
impounded, so mild and harmless was their tenor.   The
law on the press having made the Préfet the supreme
judge without appeal in all such matters, the editors of
the *Bulletin* were forced to stand by, and thus see their
firstborn die before their eyes by a violent death.   Not,
however, without complaint ; and for the honour of
England, and as a proof that Englishmen are not called
' grumblers' for nothing, I am bound to award the palm
to my countrymen on this occasion for having out-
growled even themselves.   Great was their indignation, expressed and understood ; and had some one on the moment
proposed an instant sack of the prefectorial *bureau,* I
believe it would have been carried with acclamation.

Soon afterwards appeared the new law for regulating
the public press, and it gave hope for the *Bulletin.*   By
a certain clause in it, it is provided that the Préfet's
power shall only apply to journals treating of politics,
or matters of social economy.   This was probably as a
concession to Roman Catholic publications, but in opening the door for them the *Bulletin,* being small, slipped
out also ; hastily, however, and in fear of leaving its
tail in the door joint.

The editors, therefore, took heart of grace, and decided to publish again and run all chances, and, in case
of being once more stopped by the Préfet, to try the
question before the courts, as to whether, being a *religious* journal, he had any power in the matter.   No. I.,
therefore, appeared without asking for the sanction of

the Préfet, the editor contenting himself with merely
notifying the fact of its publication, and No. II. soon
followed. All articles or allusions of a political character
were carefully pruned out by the editor, so as to fit it
to the standard ; and indeed it seemed quite a pattern
number.

But he saw not as saw the Préfet. With an instinc-
tive sagacity which in general belongs only to the lower
animals, the latter at once detected what had escaped
the innocence of M. Le Fourdrey. The plague spot was
evident ; let me fumigate the subject, and present it to
my readers.

Behold the atrocity! It is an extract from the English
journal, the *Record*, and runs as follows : — ' On the first
Sunday in February last, five persons abjured the *errors*
of Romanism, in the Free Church of the Canongate, in
Edinburgh.' Nothing very extraordinary here you will
say ; nothing infectious or dangerous ; or, at least, if any
are alarmed by it, as nervousness sometimes produces
disorder, let them shut their eyes, or take a tonic immediately.

But what says the Préfet and his council. 'What
insolence! these Protestants, with their little flimsy
journal, to come under our very beards, and talk of the
" *errors* " of Romanism ! This is too bad ; we must
stop it *sur le champ*, or no one can say what will follow ;' and accordingly the editor received the following
' *avertissement* from authority : '—

' Sir, — The Sous-Préfet of Brest has sent me two
' copies of the *Bulletin Évangélique* published by you.
' I read in this work, page 22 : " The first Monday in
' February five persons abjured the errors of Catholicism
' in the Free Church of the Canongate in Edinburgh." In
' giving you an acknowledgement of the declaration made

' by you of the foundation of your paper, I only con-
' formed to the law, which did not allow me to prevent
' its publication. But the law gives me the right to stop
' the publication, if it becomes an instrument of trouble,
' and I shall use this right if you give me occasion. The
' article which I have above cited shows a tendency on
' your part to attack a religion which is in an immense
' majority in this country, and is of a nature to cause a
' controversy which I judge dangerous. I give you
' notice, Sir, that if you do not absolutely abstain from
' all allusions of this kind, I shall not hesitate to apply
' to you the power with which I am armed.

> ' I am, &c.,
> ' RICHARD, Préfet of Finistère.'

And this is a country in which equal religious rights are
granted by the constitution *to all!* Monsieur le Préfet,
then, is clearly infringing the constitution, *or else* the
constitution is waste paper. But, perhaps, in so polished
a nation, it is forbidden to apply epithets in controversy ;
and justice, who delights in holding the scales evenly,
will not allow a license to Protestants which she forbids
to Catholics when speaking of Protestants. A good
rule this, though somewhat over-refined : and how is it
carried out ? Simply by allowing Catholics to expend
the vocabulary of abuse upon Protestants, without a
remark being made upon them.

I will not swell out this book by hashing up what I
have said in ' Britanny and the Bible,' pp. 35, 37, 42,
et seq., but will merely say that if I am told that the
expressions and epithets of ' robber, thief, liar, perjured,
bigamist, libertine, fornicator, drunkard,' &c., do not
exceed the limits of polite argument, the information is
new to me ; and that such expressions, with all their
variations, are applied by Romanist controversialists

towards Protestants I have now the books *in my hands*
to prove, and again refer to my former work.

And this scandalous abuse is suffered to circulate in
public schools, and is patronised by priests, and distributed among 'the faithful'·to enlighten their minds,
without observation or check; while the word '*error,*'
applied in a Protestant journal, and merely copied from
another, calls down all the terrors of the law upon·the
man who employs it. What prostitution of *justice* is
this! Better erase the word from the language than
thus barefacedly misapply it. 'What word could be used
more tender than " error?"' as Girardin, the able editor
of the *Presse* observed, in alluding to the circumstance.
' Unless we are to be denied altogether the practice and
theory of discussion, we are at a loss to see how a better
or less offensive word than "error" could be made use
of.'   But the truth is, Protestants must bear all as they
can, and must thank their stars it is no worse. *Heretics,*
on the soil of Catholic France, have no right to be
recognised *at all.*

M. Le Fourdrey replied to the Préfet in a worthy
manner, defended the use of the word 'error,' and
claimed the same liberty of discussion as was granted to
the Romanists; in fact, wrote an admirable exposition
of the whole subject, which could not be replied to. He
had afterwards an interview with the Préfet, who complained heavily that his letter had been *published* in
the Paris papers, and showed that general soreness, which
confirmed what I heard from another quarter, that he
had probably been well rated by the government for the
' blunder' he had committed — a thing politically worse
than a 'crime.' He had been so anxious to strike that
he had struck in the wrong place, and injured his friends.

Since then, the *Bulletin* has gone on steadily, and

without attack. Its present circulation is about 250, which, considering the small body of Protestants in Lower Britanny, is very satisfactory, and it certainly unites the friends of the cause, and interests them generally, and so does good. I receive it regularly every month for a subscription of 2s. 6d. a year, and any friends of Protestantism in Britanny may receive it equally on sending me their names and addresses, and a year's subscription.

The Society for the *General Interests of Protestantism* also goes on well. Its committee hold quarterly meetings in different parts of the country, when information is given on all points connected with the cause, and to judge from the numerous audience, much interest is excited. At the last meeting, at Brest, which continued for three days, excellent sermons were preached by the different ministers present, and collections made after each sermon for the benefit of the Society; and, as a proof of the continued feeling in favour of the work, we may add that the last collection, at which it might have been expected that the purses of those who attended were wearied, was the largest of the series. The Society has established an agent at Brest, under the superintendence and with the aid of the minister there, and by his agency it is hoped much good may be done. It has also relieved some cases of very pressing necessity among the Protestants, and supports and keeps alive the *Bulletin.*

With larger funds it would do much more good, and it is hoped English friends will support it. Some have already done so, and by their aid, and that of others resident in the country, the Society may commence bravely the campaign for another year. Unlooked-for support has been given to it from many quarters, as gratifying as it was unexpected, showing that the want was a real one.

To those who kindly responded to the appeal made by me in 'Britanny and the Bible,' I return my sincere thanks, and I can assure them that their money has been wisely expended; and to those who have not yet contributed to it, I beg again to mention its claims, and to ask their aid. Any sums remitted to me, under cover to Messrs. Longman, for that purpose, will be gratefully received, and immediately handed over to the Society. The Society embraces all the Protestants in the country, except those who, from indifference to the cause, or narrow views of the unity which should exist among Christians, have stood aloof; and let us hope that the minds of the former may be warmed, and of the latter liberalised and enlarged, so as to concur with their brethren in such a good and practical object.

CHAPTER III.

DURING the summer I had occasion to go into Lower Britanny, which comprises the Departments of Finistère, Morbihan, the Côtes du Nord, and Île et Vilaine, and travelled to Brest, by way of Quimper. Quimper is the chief town of Finistère, beautifully situated on a river, and with many attractions, as a place of residence for Englishmen.

It is very delightful to meet with fellow labourers in a foreign land! The heart warms, and the hand advances to grasp that of a countryman, especially when he is of a kind sympathetic with ourselves. My old friend Mr. Williams, the Protestant minister at Quimper, received me with all that warm kindness and hospitality which is part of his nature, and which at once goes to the heart and opens it. He gave me many interesting details as to the work now going on in the country, its difficulties and discouragements. And how great are those difficulties? They who sit easily at home, dozing through life, sipping its pleasures, enjoying its comforts; their worship unfettered, their liberties guaranteed; without anxiety for the present or fear for the future,

D

how little can they conceive of the lives and hardships
of others!

Mr. Williams, for instance, has been minister at
Quimper for some twenty-five years, and has difficulties
of all kinds to contend with—open opposition of the
authorities—covert stratagems of the priests—the
natural rudeness and ignorance of the people—prejudices against him as a stranger—hatred of him as a
Protestant—the language (Breton) hard to be understood—few zealous supporters, many lukewarm ones;
and all these real obstacles met by him with a hopeful-
ness and zeal which it is wonderful is not more conta-
gious than it seems to be. And he has no ample revenue
to support him. His income is of the smallest, and yet
he makes head against life and its burdens with cheerful-
ness, and supports and brings up creditably his excellent
wife and family. He is one of a sort rarely to be met
with, and deserves every help which can be given to
him.

I was extremely pleased with the chapel at Quimper.
It is a neat stone edifice, with minister's house attached, and has been built with a taste, good judgement, and economy, which do credit to its designers.
There are two pretty painted windows, a gallery, an
instrument to accompany the singers, and all that is
needed in such an edifice. The ten commandments and
the creed are on large tables, handsomely and legibly
printed, so that you may read them from all parts of
the chapel. The importance of this in a Roman Catholic
country is great. As is well known, the Romanists leave
out the second commandment forbidding image worship,
and make up the number of the ten commandments by
dividing the tenth into two parts; it is therefore very
desirable to place the real text before them.

I myself know two Romanists, now converted to Protestantism, who date their conversion, i.e., the first step towards it, from seeing the ten commandments in a Protestant chapel. They were surprised at the novel terms in which the second commandment appeared, surprise caused increased attention, attention led to consideration and enquiry, and in the end they became Protestants.

In England almost all places of worship are provided with the ten commandments, unless they are too poor to procure them. In France all *should* have them, and generally it is the case, but I have noticed otherwise, and all exceptions are to be much regretted; and I cannot imagine that those English societies who have established chapels in France, would be satisfied if they learnt that their chapels were unprovided with legible impressions of the tables of the law. And yet it is in one of these chapels that I remarked the omission in question. There was a small printed form, placed where it was almost useless, but no tables legibly printed, so as to strike the eye of everyone who might enter.

I have heard objections made to the tables on the ground, that men might be misled into supposing that the whole of religion was there contained; but, besides other answers to this objection, it may be met by adding to the ten commandments the summary of the law given by our Saviour in the New Testament, and in the two series, taken together, all our duties may be said to be comprised. Where possible, it is very desirable to have the creed added also. This deprives Romanists of their grand objection as to the disunion of Protestants. The creed of the French Protestant Church is identical in words with our Apostles' creed in the English Church,

save that it substitutes ' *Universal* Church ' for '*Catholic*
Church;' that is, it uses the Latin instead of the Greek
word, for each word expresses the same idea; and, as in
a Roman Catholic country, the latter word, ' Catholic,'
would be likely to lead to error, it is judicious to use
the word ' Universal' instead.

The Church and mission at Quimper is supported by
the Calvinistic Methodists; and it will be pleasing to
that body to know that their efforts are producing good
effects, and that their station at Quimper is so well conducted.   As to great *present* fruits we must be content
with little for the moment. The work of evangelisation
is necessarily slow, but the harvest will arrive when we
least expect it; and it is certain that nothing will be
reaped, unless the ground be previously sowed and
tilled diligently.

Mr. Williams has distinguished himself as a contro-
versialist.   He has published several little works, and
recently ' *La Basse Bretagne et le Pays de Galles,*'
Paris, Meyreuis, 1860, price two francs, which is very
deserving of perusal.   The Count de Villemarquè in a
work written by him, entitled ' *Contes Populaires des
Anciens Bretons,*' in speaking of Wales had said much
of the way in which Protestantism had deteriorated
that country.   In particular vol. ii. p. 287, ' the Protestant sects which divide and *dcpoetise* this unhappy
country have deprived these feasts (fairs and wakes) of
all their religious character.'   In another place he
speaks of the ancient games of Wales being replaced by
drinking bouts, and generally he alludes to Wales as a
country which has been in every way lowered in the
moral scale by the adoption of the reformed religion.

Mr. Williams as a Welshman and a Breton missionary
felt that these assertions required a reply, and he has

made one by the work above mentioned, and I think the Count has little reason to be satisfied with the result. Mr. Williams shows that Wales had an independent Church of its own, centuries before the visit of Augustine, and that it preserved its independence for many ages until finally overwhelmed by the power of Rome during the dark ages. When Augustine had his celebrated interview with the Welsh bishops at Bangor on the Dee, hoping to make them acknowledge the supremacy of Rome, the bishop who replied to him used these memorable words, ' We will never admit the pretended rights of Roman ambition any more than those of Saxon tyranny; we owe to the pope, it is true, the submission of *brotherly charity*, the same as to all Christians; but as to the submission of *obedience*, we owe it only to God, and after Him to our venerable head (*surveillant*) the Bishop of Caerleon on Uske.' *

Mr. Williams then shows the happy results which the Protestant sects, of which M. Villemarquè laments the existence, have produced in Wales. During the seventeenth and eighteenth centuries, but for the existence of these same ' sects,' Wales would have been little less than a heathen country. The Church of England, speaking generally, was then in a miserable state of Arianism and inactivity, chiefly concerned in politics or tithe taking, only feeling an interest in the flock at the time of the annual shearing, and being then very disagreeably active ; and the interior of Wales — in particular the mountainous portion of it — was left almost wholly to its own devices. The few bishops seem to have chiefly stayed at home in their cathedral towns, or else to have attended the House of Lords in

* *Histoire de la Conquête de l'Angleterre par les Normands*, vol. i. pp. 94, 95.

London; and the poor clergy with their livings, or rather
starvings, which (shame to say it) *even now* are in
many cases under 50*l.* a year, eked out their subsistence
by such occupations as were most convenient to them,
from farming to selling commodities of various kinds,
and, as I have heard, down to shopkeeping, or lower
still, *keeping an inn!* This was the period when the
parson was asked to dine in the servants' hall, and
only drank and hunted with the squire occasionally as
a great honour; a period we look back on with horror
and pain, but which it is well to look back upon now and
then to draw therefrom its moral, and exhibit and test the
practical and innate 'divinity' of the Church of England
so loudly claimed by the High Church party in this day.

I consider that religion owes a deep debt of gratitude
to Dissent for having in some degree occupied these
waste places, and there lighted and kept alive the lamp
of Protestant and Christian truth; and I concern myself
little whether the form of worship was in all or any
points conformable with the rubric, or the doctrine
preached according to the thirty-nine articles. I thank
God that the light was kept burning *at all*, and am
indifferent as to the chemical analysis of the oil that
fed it; enough for me that its light saved numbers
from perishing eternally.

The state of the Church of England is bad enough
in Wales even in our own day, but it is not in the
state it was. Yet its revenues are still wretchedly
inadequate to its wants. Still there are numerous
'starvings' under 50*l.* a year, requiring two to be joined
together to make even a poor living; the effect of which
generally is, to have only one service on Sunday instead of
two, and the consequence of all which is to have a much
lower class of clergymen than is to be seen elsewhere.

Doubtless there are great difficulties in the way of re-
forming this state of things, and the tithes being chiefly
in the hands of laymen is one great difficulty, and the
question of patronage, or proper nomination to livings,
is another ; but I never yet knew anything about which
there was no difficulty.

What is sorely wanted in both England and Wales,
is a better distribution of the revenues of the Church.
I should like to see them more equally distributed; the
hills reduced in height and the valleys raised. I would
not reduce all to a dead level of uniformity, but I
should like to see such reductions made, and such
useless places abolished, as would enable every working
incumbent to have enough to live respectably upon
(say 200*l.* a year at least), and it is a shame and a
scandal that such is not the case. Our feelings would
then no longer be outraged by seeing advertisements asking for cast-off clothes, ' not too much worn,' for ' poor
pious clergymen ' and their families; advertisements
the reading of which is likely, one would think, to
cause an unpleasant feeling of fulness in the head to
plethoric and philanthropic pluralists, and which fulness one would not regret, if it eased itself by emptying
their pockets.

As to the Church Commission ' for the relief of spiritual destitution in populous places,' with its outlays
on bishops' *extra* coachhouses and stables, and bishops'
flower-gardens, and restorations of cathedrals, and re-
building canons' houses, and so forth; and its expenses
of management, amounting to 20 per cent. on the gross
revenue of 160,000*l.* a year, it is nothing less than a
system of high-actioned clerical jobbery, which should
be at once abolished, and something better substituted
in its place.

When I think of these and many similar abuses, and
the many useless portions of the outward framework of
the Church of England, I think that it is not 'Church
Defence Associations' which are wanted, so much as
'Church *Reform* Associations,' and I am surprised that
the lower clergy do not turn their attention to the subject, and agitate it actively. Well acquainted as they are
with the practical defects of the system under which
they live, and in many cases almost *starve*, and asso-
ciated by common ties of origin with the middle classes
of society, the laity in general would, I believe, look
with sympathy and confidence upon a plan of reform
emanating from *them*, the working-bees in the hive,
and would be well disposed to support it with their
influence. As to any effectual reform in the general
distribution of Church revenues coming from Church
Lords (so miscalled) who want great revenues to support their state, and from dignitaries in high places, it
is, I fear, vain to expect it, nor would it be worth much,
probably, if it did come.

But to return to Mr. Williams' book. He there shows
the religious activity of these 'unhappy sects' of which
M. Villemarqué deplores the existence, how they have
covered the country with 2,370 places of worship, how
the idea of the Bible Society, that most noble effort
of active Christianity in modern times, was first conceived and put into practice by a Welshman, Mr. Charles
of Bala, and that, since then, more than a hundred thousand Bibles and New Testaments have been printed in
Welsh for circulation in the country. Mr. Williams also
shows that the idea of translating the New Testament
into Breton was also due to a Welshman, the Rev.
David Jones, who was sent into Britanny to enquire
on the subject, and who employed Lègonidec to do it

at the expense of the English Bible Society. And very curiously, at the time this was done, in 1827, so cold was the reception given to it in Britanny by the priests and people, that almost the whole edition was finally sold *in Wales*, which, by the way, is a strong proof of the close connection subsisting between the language, &c. of the two countries.

I may add here, that the MS. of the Old Testament, translated into Breton by Lègonidec, has also been for a long time in the hands of the Bible Society in London, and will perhaps be published ere long for distribution in Britanny. I hope that it may be well received there, better than was the New Testament by a *curé* in the diocese of Quimper, mentioned by Mr. Williams, who, on the colporteur offering him one, immediately bought up all he had—*and burned them.* Let us also hope that the translation will not be altered by Breton priests, as was done by the priest of Vannes, in his work, 'The Life of Christ,' quoted by Mr. Williams (page 62), who for the words in the 33rd verse of the 10th chapter of St. Mark, 'And shall deliver Him *to the Gentiles*,' substituted 'And shall deliver Him to the *Huguenots*,' or Protestants !

But I refer my readers to Mr. Williams' book, which can be procured through any London bookseller, and I think they will agree with me, that it contains much valuable information in a very lively and agreeable style. The latter portion is composed of a controversial dialogue between Mr. Williams and a priest, in which the *tu quoque* argument is used with such a quiet irony, and keen appreciation of the subject, as is but seldom met with; and though, in this case, the supposed priest is but a man of straw, I am well assured, from an intimate acquaintance with Mr. Williams, that

he would deal in an equally trenchant way with one
who was a living specimen, and clothed in 'buckram' or
bombazine.

At Morlaix, some forty-five miles from Quimper, there
is much activity also, and many signs of religious progress.

Mr. Jenkins, who has ministered there for nearly
thirty years, has rendered great services to the good
cause. He is a Baptist missionary, sent to the Bretons
by the Baptist Missionary Society, and has a chapel in
Morlaix, where there are services in Breton and also in
French. But it is more especially to the adjacent
country that his labours are directed, and there he is
carrying on a very important work. He celebrates religious worship here and there, as may be required,
superintends certain movements of an educational kind
in various localities, and directs matters generally with
great zeal, prudence, and good judgement. He is fully
acquainted with all the circumstances of the country,
from his long residence in it; and, from being an excellent French and Breton scholar, is well fitted for the
work he carries on. He it was who revised Légonidec's
translation of the New Testament into Breton for the
Bible Society, of which 8,000 copies have been distributed, and a new edition is now preparing, and soon
to be issued, of 6,000 copies more. And can all these
copies of God's word remain void? Impossible.

It may be interesting to observe that Ricou, the well-
known Breton poet, who died a Protestant, gave some
assistance to Mr. Jenkins in this work. It is also
worthy of remark, that the two most remarkable Breton
poets and writers of our own age, Souvestre and Ricou,
became converts to Protestantism, and died in that communion. Souvestre was buried (at his own particular

request) by Mr. Jenkins, with whom he had long been
intimate. These are distinguished fruits of the Bible
in Britanny, which should not be forgotten.

Mr. Jenkins also has colporteurs at work, and in 1861
he distributed by their means not less than 700 copies
of the Breton New Testament. This is the greatest
quantity that has ever yet been distributed in a single
year, and it represents a vast amount of labour on the
part of Mr. Jenkins and his cooperators.

Morlaix is a thriving town of some 15,000 inhabitants,
situate on a tidal river, about eight or nine miles from
the sea, the sail from which is one of the most beautiful
things of the sort I have ever seen. The railway from
Paris to Brest passes through it, and it has considerable
commerce. Small ships ascend the river and discharge
their cargoes on the quays, and give the place a lively
bustling appearance. Steamboats run between Havre
and Morlaix, and between Morlaix and Bordeaux, at
short intervals. I often have wondered that Englishmen do not go there in greater numbers, for, as it is,
the English population is limited to some half-a-dozen
families ; and I cordially recommend it to anyone seeking an economical and agreeable place of abode in
Britanny.

I know that I shall always regard it with affection. I
lived near to it for some years, during which I co-
operated cordially with Mr. Jenkins, Mr. Williams, and
others, now alas ! no more, in various Protestant works
which were then going forward ; and I look back upon
those years as amongst the happiest ones of my life in
many respects.

The country around Morlaix is extremely picturesque,
and offers many points of interest to the painter, the
geologist, and the antiquarian. There has been a very

notable advance there in all things since I last wrote
upon it. A lover of antiquities would, perhaps, sigh
over the destruction of many of the beautiful old,
half-timbered houses, with quaint devices adorning the
corbels, with stories projecting one above another like
the stern of a three-decker, which formerly abounded
in its streets, and of which some few specimens still
remain; but in the place of the narrow streets, almost
deprived of light by the upper stories of the houses
nearly touching each other, there are now broad and
airy ones, and people gain in health and comfort what
they lose in other ways.

There are also many other signs of progress. An
agricultural society is established at Morlaix, of which
the good effects are visible in the improved state of
agriculture, and the improved breeds of useful animals.
Annual meetings are held, and prizes given for best
oxen, cows, pigs, fowls, corn, butter, cultivation, &c.
Draining, too, is coming into more general use. When
it was first introduced, some twelve years back, what
difficulties it had to encounter! The draining-pipe was
regarded as the new road to ruin. There was a great
deal of irrigation practised in the neighbourhood, and,
like everything else, it was on the most primitive plan,
i.e., the water was brought on to the meadow, or probably brought itself there, and was left to itself to get
off as it best could. Now, I believe, it is a principle of
irrigation, as of commerce, that the circulation to be
profitable must be rapid, and that water should be quick
on and quick off, so continually bringing and leaving
behind it its fertilising qualities. But this was too quick
for Britanny, so farmers shook their heads by the score,
and said it was ruining the meadows to under-drain
them, that they would all dry up and become baked like

brick-fields, and that nothing should induce them to try it.

At that period I was a member of the Morlaix Agricultural Society, and one of a committee appointed on the subject of draining, and therefore I had various opportunities of ascertaining the almost impossibility of getting a new idea into the head of an '*entêtê Breton;*' and life being, unfortunately, of very limited duration, we should not have made much progress before the end of all things, had we rested on argument alone. So an enterprising member of the society undertook to drain a marsh of his own, which had been an excellent place for snipe; and he executed his work on the best principles, and in an admirable manner, and there it was to be seen of all—'*oculis subjecta fidelibus.*' Then the thing began to take—it is useless arguing with a fact—and draining slowly commenced. A tile-making machine was obtained from the Government, which liberally encourages such improvements, and there is now a considerable movement in that direction.

But what retards agricultural improvements is the excessive subdivision of property, and consequent want of capital. What can be done in this way in a country where I have seen an acre of land subdivided into forty distinct properties, and one of these might possibly give birth to half a dozen subdivisions more. The law of primogeniture is by no means wholly good, but its opposite is as bad. The golden mean must lie somewhere between them, one would imagine.

So in other directions also, is improvement to be seen. We do not now see so many of the long-legged scarecrows which mock you with the name of pig, with heads like greyhounds, and, for that matter, almost as fleet, and ears like those of young elephants. I shall not forget what happened to me, à *propos* of those long ears. I was objecting to the large ears of an animal I was looking at. But said the owner, 'Why object to large ears. They are excellent things, and I always look out for them? Is there a better dish than pigs' ears?' *Je vous demande un peu.'* So pigs were kept for the *ears.* A couple of hundred-weight of flesh sacrificed for the sake of one dainty dish! It seems epicurism can exist in a high degree where civilisation is low, and this almost equals the famous peacocks' tongue pie of Heliogabalus. It reminded me of the way of getting roast pig in China. A sow and her interesting progeny were unhappily destroyed by a fire, which burnt down their dwelling place. The poor owner, lamenting, walks round the ruins, and is inconsolable, when suddenly he smells a most savoury smell. He follows his nose, and at length stands like a well-trained pointer opposite the cause of the scent; his mouth waters; and his fingers naturally move towards it, and he touches it — 't is hot as fire, and the burnt finger naturally seeks the mouth to soothe its pain — but ah! what pleasure does the palate receive; 't is like the creation of a new sense! With a long-drawn respiration, the process is renewed, and repeated till appetite is satisfied, and the Chinese no longer regretted his piglings. Thenceforth, as the historian says, pigsties were blazing in all directions, until some one, wiser than the others, found out the more economical culinary process of preparing 'roast pig' at the home fire.

I doubt not but that pigs of an improved English breed would now be as eagerly sought as they were formerly contemptuously rejected.

The same is the case with oxen and cows. The Breton cow has of late been introduced into England, and is a

beautiful and very productive animal, remarkably small,
but giving, for her size and keep, a large quantity of
excellent and very rich *buttery* milk. They are, however, more suited to a wild and rocky than a fertile
country, as they jump about like sheep, pick the sweet
grass from between the gorze bushes, and feed where
others would starve, and that seems to me their great
excellence. Importers must make a pretty handsome
profit on them, I should fancy, selling them at from
15*l.* to 20*l.* each, and not giving more than from 5*l.* to
8*l.* for them in Britanny. Indeed, I have bought them
for much less than 5*l.*, and the freight, I believe, is only
about 1*l.* a-piece.

In fowls, too, there is a great improvement. Formerly they were almost as small as Bantams, from continually crossing and breeding *in and in;* but this is
now altered for the better.

When first a direct commerce between Morlaix and
England was opened, in 1851, by a steamboat, called
the 'Grand Turk,' from Southampton, lots of eggs were
sent over from Britanny for sale. It seems that, to prevent loss of time, egg-merchants have rings of different
sizes to measure eggs with, and they pay according to
size ; but these little Breton eggs were smaller than the
ringmaker had ever thought possible,—for they all went
easily through the smallest ring, and, of course, fetched
only the very smallest price. Since then, fowl-shows have
been commenced and prizes given for good breeds, and
there has been quite a '*furore*' among amateurs. I knew
one Breton gentleman who gave 125 francs for a couple
of Brahma fowls, and 100 francs for Crèvecœurs. The
latter is a most excellent French breed, of the same good
qualities as our Dorking, but, I think, in many points
superior to them, especially in the size of their eggs,

which are extremely large, averaging nearly three ounces, which anyone can ascertain to be large by weighing an ordinary egg. So that now, I dare say, Morlaix eggs will be found worthy of the largest ring, and Morlaix fowls be sought for by English gastronomes.

All these are signs of progress in the good town of Morlaix and its environs, and it is well deserving of notice to anyone seeking a residence abroad. It is not everywhere you can meet with a Protestant place of worship attended by an English minister like Mr. Jenkins. As to his being a Baptist, he never obtrudes his opinions where they are not sought for. I for one thought little about it, and regarded him only as a good Protestant Christian, whose ministrations in a foreign land I was most happy to enjoy; and where I find those points, I find what I am well content with.

When we find these signs of material progress we may hope that religious progress is going on also. Hitherto the priests and fanatics have had the country almost all to themselves; but I trust this is coming to an end.

There can be no doubt but that, when all the progress is summed up, the country is far behind every other part of France; yet to hear priests and certain of the religious *dilettanti* speak of it, you would think it was the very pearl and essence of the nation; so much devotion to throne and altar—such obedience to Mother Church and her servants—or, as I should say, masters. O that all France were the same, they say, and then we should have a glorious time of it! They say nothing of the drunkenness which exists there to such a dreadful extent as I have seen nowhere else; of the violence which prevails, as is shown by the calendar of crime; of the gross ignorance of the people, as is shown by the statistics of

education in France, and in which Britanny, and Finistère especially, figure at the bottom of the list. They
ignore all these patent facts, and foolishly hold up Britanny as a model of the effects of the Romish system.
Priests in general do not reason, and do not allow others
to reason; and of course reasoning has no proper place
in an infallible despotic church, and therefore is very
consistently shut up in prison or turned out of doors.
But I should have thought they would not have been *so
foolish* as to hold up poor Britanny for a model.

In mentioning the attractions of Morlaix as a place of
residence, I must not pass over the shooting and fishing
in the neighbourhood, which are generally recommen-
dations to an Englishman, as healthy and agreeable
amusements. I enjoyed both one and the other for
many years. Of game, there are partridges, hares, woodcocks and snipe, rabbits, quails, and wild-fowl, in fair
quantity, to the good sportsman who will work for his
game; for it is not a country for the *battue*. A chance
wolf and wild boar is to be found, too, here and there.
There are a few salmon rivers, and plenty of trout in
the smaller streams and mountain lakes; indeed, in one
of the latter I enjoyed the best trout-fishing I ever had
in my life, or I believe ever shall have.

But for all this I must refer my readers to 'The Chase
in Britanny,' written by me, and published by Messrs.
Longman and Co.

At Rennes, a Protestant minister, Mr. Vermeil, has
arrived within the last four years, and is attentively
listened to by a large congregation, and has a pretty
little chapel. That is a great step in advance.

Every fresh Protestant chapel opened in Britanny is
as a fresh beacon holding aloft the light of truth, and
warning unwary travellers of the rocks and sandbanks of

E

Rome. It constitutes a fresh centre, round which new
forces accumulate against the common enemy; and, provided that it is founded on the doctrines of Protestant
Christianity, it is, in my opinion, of minor importance
to what denomination it belongs.

The mere denominational divisions of Protestant
Christians are of little comparative consequence, so
long as they agree in the essential body of Christian
truth. The outward form or shape imposed on that
body I regard as the mere clothing; and I should as
soon think of quarrelling with a friend about the cut
of his coat, as I should of separating myself from a
brother Christian on account of his form of worship
differing from my own, much as I may and do prefer it.

In England we are great formalists in many things,
and in religious worship among others. I respect and
reverence the Church of England, of which I am a sincere member. She has in many ways supported and
advanced the cause of Christian truth, and especially by
keeping up a good standard of doctrine, and by great
recent missionary zeal and efforts. As 'a congregation
of faithful men,' she has had, and will yet have, a prominent part in the history of the Church of Christ, but
there are also other, and I trust many other, 'congre-
gations of faithful men,' who are not unworthy of being
her associates in the great work; and I look forward to
the time when the union of all such will become more
complete, and when each will give to the other, in this
world, the right hand of Christian fellowship, and all
will dwell together in unity.

But meanwhile the Church of England has much to
do in the way of amending herself, and in casting away
the many weights and hindrances which impair her
activity and mar her usefulness, in order that she may

be ready, and not behind in the race; and she has not
lived through so many ages without contracting some
of the rust of age, and some of the corruptions of past
times still cast a shadow over her; and I deem those to
be her best friends who seek to clear away the one, and
endeavour to remove her from the influence of the other.
Let her not, therefore, be exclusive in her claims or
arrogant in her pretensions, for the house in which she
dwells is but of man's building; and the tendency of
the age is against all exclusive establishments, whether
civil or religious, which cannot justify themselves by
their public utility, and by their fitness for the place
they fill.

CHAPTER IV.

IN the department of the *Côte du Nord* there are also signs of life among the Bretons, and enough may be seen to show that the word of God, which has been distributed there by various agencies, especially that of Mr. Jenkins, has not been unproductive. Indeed, how could it ever be so? God's word never returns void, but does its work; and I believe fully that the ground there has been prepared in a manner which will one day show itself in a very rapid germination of the seed, and an abundant crop.

There is a district there with which I am well acquainted, not far from Guingamp. Perhaps there is, or rather was, not a portion of earth's surface more intensely Romanist than was the part of the country in question, and, as the natural consequence, it was intensely ignorant. The people are as completely under the priestly yoke as were the Spaniards in the time of Philip II., and obey them as implicitly as if their directions were revelations from heaven. It was there that the attempt to murder Mr. Jenkins took place which I have narrated in 'Britanny and the Bible,' p. 60 — an attempt which, but for active aid, would apparently have succeeded: and the people are noted for their savage manners and ferocity—stabbing, for instance, with the knife, a practice not usual in Britanny. Well, even in that very district has God's word found its way, and with great success. Mr. Jenkins, aided by some good men and women, who, having arrived at a knowledge of the truth themselves, have been naturally desirous to extend it to others, has established a system of teaching there, and the New Testaments he and others have distributed are already leavening the previously inert mass.

Under the law as to education in France, no one can open a school without the license of the Academic Council in each department; and this Council being generally composed of say four Romanists, including the Bishop, and one Protestant, and voting by a majority, the chance of a license being granted to a Protestant is infinitesimally small. But it was thought that you might go round and give lessons here and there to a few children without being considered to 'hold a school,' and so a trusty agent went about from one place to another, teaching half a dozen children here and half a dozen there to read; the lesson-book being the New Testament.

The authorities, however, who always awake speedily when called upon by the priests, soon began to look sharp, and a system of espionage was organised, under which, one fine morning, as the mistress was giving her lessons to some few children, the door opened, and in walked the *Maire*, in his tricoloured scarf, followed by the inevitable *gendarmes*, as if there was a riot to be quelled.

The effect was magical on the scholars, who bolted in an instant, and gave themselves a holiday, and a *procès verbal*, or formal account, was there and then drawn up, signed, verified, and transmitted to .head-quarters, the effect of which was that the poor woman was in due time tried and fined 400 francs, and threatened with worse if she did it again.

But as there are other ways of getting into a house than at the door, wits were again set to work, and it was arranged that, instead of the scholars coming to her, she should go to them, by which she would do the work safely, though not so quickly, as before. And so began the *leçons à domicile*, which have ever since been carried on, and by which she and others enter twice as many houses as they did before, and teach twice as many children; and up to this time this has been the happy result of the interference of the authorities.

We may well say that the word of God will not be bound. Compress it here, it extends itself there; banish it from one place, it takes strong root in another. Borrow was imprisoned for preaching and selling Bibles in the streets of Madrid, and, lo! he preaches and sells immediately *in the prison*, so that the priests exclaimed that 'this was worse than ever,' as the thieves were such a numerous and active class, and always held together.

The neighbourhood I have just spoken of had originally been one vast forest, full of Druidical remains, and there were still large woods in it, where the wolf and the wild boar inhabit. In fact, the wood at the back of my house was called 'Wolves' Wood,' and the following curious thing happened there during my residence:—A countrywoman was going to town to buy something with which to fill an empty bag she carried with her, when, in passing through this wood, she heard a squealing snarling sound. She followed the sound up to its source, which proved to be a wolf's *earth* or bed, and in it lay, nice and warm, but in a very quarrelsome

mood, *seven* young wolf-cubs. Now the worthy dame
knew that each cub was worth five francs to her, as the
authorities give that sum for every wolf-cub, and, being
a true Breton, and regarding five francs as something to
run a risk for, she at once threw down her bag, and,
catching one little Master or Miss *Loup* after another
by the scruff of the neck, pitched it into the bag; and
having finally bagged them all and tied up the sack's
mouth, threw the lively burden over her shoulder
and went on her way rejoicing, and with all kind of
musical honours, no doubt. It was a happy thing for
the brave dame that old Mrs. Wolf had had to make a
wide circuit that morning to get a dainty bit for the
family breakfast, or perhaps had wasted time in a
gossip with an old friend about the lamentable scarcity
of mutton and beef; for had she found out in time the
way her house had been ravished in her absence, she
would as surely have scented the robber out and break-
fasted on human flesh that day, as, luckily for the good
dame, she happened not to do it. But the bold housewife was meanwhile at the town gate only three miles
off, and there she went direct to an English furrier who I
knew very well, and turned out her seven little wolfies
'all alive oh!' on his floor, snarling, biting, struggling,
and fighting, to his great surprise, as may be imagined.
They were about as large as kittens of six weeks old,
and with skins like moles. She got the reward all
right, and well deserved it, and I ultimately got three
of the skins, with which I covered my game-bag, the
little tails hanging down before and looking very
picturesque.

I have just met with a proof of the silent but effectual working of the distribution of the Scriptures in
Britanny, which may serve to console those who think

that it is getting on slowly. I had been shooting
woodcocks in a very wild part of the country. The
woodcock is a *connoisseur* in scenery, and always chooses
his abode in the most secluded spots where hill and dale
meet, and give him the flowing streams and marshy
ground he delights in. The day grew more and more
unfavourable, till at last the rain poured down and
forced me to think of shelter, and, instead of a good
furze bush, I was most happy to see at a little distance
a mill, to which I betook myself as quickly as I could.
The Breton mills are primitive-looking affairs, like most
other things in Britanny — generally small one-storied
cottages, with the wheel at one end and the dwelling at
the other, and grinding just enough corn to supply the
wants of the immediate neighbourhood. The miller
gave me a friendly welcome, and I soon got into the
chimney corner with my dogs, and began to talk with
him. He had seen military service, like so many of his
countrymen, and had many strange stories to tell. He
told me, too, how glad he was that wolves were less
numerous than they had been; 'for,' said he, 'I have
had them as thick as bees about the mill, and have not
liked to go out; and, besides, it kept away my customers. Often in winter I used to see them by threes
and fours together on the top of the hill there, peering
down upon me and the mill with a nasty hungry look,
which was not at all pleasant; and *nom d'un chien!* it
would never do for an old soldier to be killed and eaten
by wolves. I, however, used to catch one every now and
then in a trap I made, and got twenty-five francs for
his skin; though when he got in he used to make such a
din that he brought all his comrades round him, and I
never dared to go to him and settle him until chance
brought a neighbour this way, and then we went

together.' At last he said to me, 'Am't you a Protestant?' I replied I was. 'Wait a bit, then, and I'll
show you something which will please you.' So he
went up into some dark corner and returned with a dirty
worn-out Breton New Testament, and said, ' There,
autrou (or sir), is the best book I ever read in my
life.' I was surprised and pleased, as may be imagined;
and this was the history of the matter.

The poor man had long, it seems, disliked Romanism; he had had real yearnings after a better system,
and had complied reluctantly with the various forms
imposed by the priests. He had heard of New Testaments being sold and colported here and there, and
had at length procured one and read it carefully, and,
as he said, prayerfully. He soon found that he had
got what he wanted. ' Then,' said he, ' I began to
think of making it known to my friends and neighbours.' So he spoke of it first to one and then to
another, and they came from time to time to the mill,
and he read it to them; and they all talked and thought
about it. At length periodical meetings were arranged,
and once a week some few came regularly to him, and
they all enjoyed the reading of God's word in their
own simple way. And thus a little congregation of
faithful men grew up in that remote valley, all drawing
water for themselves from the pure spring of the
Gospel. They needed no learned commentators to
obscure by laborious criticism what was before clear,
and no priests to interpret authoritatively that Word
which was given freely to all; each man got what
satisfied his own mind, and cleared up the doubts and
mists which had previously hung round him. Happily, the essential truths of religion are few and simple,
and easily learnt by one who seeks them in earnest; for,

were it not so, what would become of the ignorant and simple-minded? When the rain cleared away I parted from the miller with regret, and have never heard of him more.

This little incident will show how the distribution of the Scriptures is silently working. There is no parade, no loud announcement of converts. The Temple is rising in silence, and as if without hands being employed in the building; but its foundations are sure, and there will be one day a glorious superstructure. This miller did not call himself a Protestant, but he was one in reality. He had long since ceased confession, and went rarely to mass, but in process of time, and as his own feelings would dictate, he would cease it also, and become openly a Protester against the errors of Rome. And, doubtless, there are thousands of such cases in Britanny; and therefore I say, let no one be faint-hearted, but let all wait and hope.

We have just had at Guingamp the fête of the Immaculate Conception, expressing the joy of the Romish Church at that dogma being henceforth incorporated in the creed of that Church as an essential truth. The fête was celebrated with the usual pomp and pageantry. Ten or twelve bishops attended and a whole army of priests, and a grand mass was celebrated in the open air, at which an ugly old image of the Virgin, looking like a block of charred wood, but dressed gaily and quite *à la mode,* was the 'cynosure of neighbouring eyes.' The poor ignorant people regarded the miserable image with avidity, knelt to it with fervour, and prayed to it with all the earnestness they could give.*

* A very good account of the religious *fête* days of Britanny, is given by a little book, entitled *Recollections of Britanny in Prose and Verse,* published by James Blackwood, London, price 2*s.* 6*d.*

And yet this is not *image-worship!* it is offensive to
'ears polite' even to name the word — but what else is
it? And how can it be otherwise than a breach of the
second commandment, which expressly forbids anyone
to 'bow down' to any graven image. This applies to
the act of bowing down, without reference to anything
else, and the people and the priests *do* 'bow down.' Where
is the loophole of escape here for a plain man? For
instance, I had a niche I wanted to fill up in my house
staircase, and I put into it an old wooden figure I had
found in my cellar, and my servants said it was St. Barbe
or St. Anne, and 'bowed down' to it every time they
passed it. Here was the act as a sign of adoration. Was
this no breach of the second commandment? But, in
fact, Romanists admit the fact, and get over it, by
omitting that portion of the second commandment in
their decalogue, and making up the 'tale' by cutting the
tenth into two parts.

It may seem strange, but in some sort I rejoiced to
witness this incorporation into the *infallible* creed of
Rome of this *new* doctrine. Even the strong camel is
at last overweighted by a straw, and falls; and as I
earnestly desire the fall of the Romish system, I look
upon all addition to its burdens with satisfaction.

And this is, in truth, a very notable addition! It is
indeed something to witness, in this nineteenth century since the age of the great founder of our faith, who
laid the bases of essential truth once for all, the addition of a *brand new essential* doctrine. True that the
Council of Trent and other councils had been so considerate as to give dates to many essential truths, and
so enable us to celebrate their birthdays, and have
proof of their human origin; but time effaces memory
so fast, that the dates were beginning to be lost in the

haze of the past, and the doctrines to have a respectable
antiquity about them — at any rate there was haze
enough to puzzle those whose sight was weak, and to
enable bold seers to speculate on what they said *they*
could see.

But here we have no ground for mistake or doubt;
and infallible Rome in this our own time, and despite
objections from her own adherents, decrees the addition
to the already long list of essential truths, of this one
of the Immaculate Conception of the Virgin Mary — a
mere figment of human invention, unsupported by a
single line or word of Scripture. And yet this is a so-
called *infallible* Church! has never erred, although it
never did this great act before; and never can err,
although it now for the first time establishes this truth
as essential, without bringing forward a single word of
Scripture in its support! It is to rest upon Rome's decree — the Pope's *ipse dixit*. Let us thank heaven
that the Pope's *ipse dixit* is worth so little. Ours is
an age of fact and proof, and not of *ipse dixit*.

I have often thought how striking a proof there is of
the way in which God works out his own purposes by
means of the weakness or pride of man, in the decree of
the Council of Trent establishing the infallibility of the
Romish Church. The Reformation was then acquiring
great proportions in Germany and elsewhere, men's
minds were everywhere working, the mass was heaving
uneasily, and no one seemed to be able to say what
would be the end. Rome trembled to her very foundations, and doubtless numerous were the secret councils
and conclaves, and profound the cogitations of learned
and subtle doctors, on the best means of arresting the
movement. At last a means is found, and all hail it
with delight : it is the impregnable cuirass which shall

for ever guard the sacred bosom of the Church from these heavy blows. And so with great pomp the Romish Church is decreed *infallible*, and many accept the defence and dismiss fear from their minds; and this heavy armour, forged and welded by mere frail humanity, is put on, and is to defy every weapon for all future time. But the breast-plate has proved so unwieldy as fatally to encumber the wearer, and it will inevitably weigh him down to earth and stifle him.

It reminds us of the heavy armour of the mediæval knights, which has passed away, being found useless against the improved weapons of modern warfare; and so, in like manner, this cumbrous doctrine of infallibility is useless against the march of modern civilisation and enlightenment. Men's minds revolt from the idea of infallibility in any institution of human origin like this one *dating from Trent in* 1560; and they will revolt more and more; and the Romish Church, shut up in its iron case, can but shake its head angrily and look on in impotence; and so the shield forged to paralyse the attacks of Luther will only serve to drag Rome down to ruin.

CHAPTER V

PRIESTLY POWER IN BRITANNY — JESUITS — LORIENT AND M.
PLANTA — PROPOSED NEW CHAPEL THERE — NANTES AND M.
VAURIGAUD — FRENCH PROTESTANTS AND THEIR EFFORTS —
THE POOR IN BRITANNY AND THEIR SUFFERINGS — NO POOR-
LAW IN FRANCE.

I HAVE recently had the subject of priestly power in Britanny brought home to me in a very palpable and disagreeable way. I had taken the chateau I lived in by the year, at the rent of 300 francs, or £12, a sum sounding small in English ears, but which, according to the value of things in Britanny, was a full rent — indeed, probably rather more than would have been paid by any real native, for Bretons love the chink of English money so much as to get out of us all they possibly can; and as they have an innate talent for bargaining, Englishmen generally leave a good deal of their loose money behind them in passing through Britanny. As I am disposed to make the best of any place I may live in, I had made many small embellishments here and there, so much so as to receive various visits from my neighbours in order to see my improvements. My landlady also indulged in sundry compliments on the subject, à mon adresse, as they say, and all went on very smoothly and pleasantly until the end of the year approached. I then thought it well, as a matter of form, to express my intention of remaining another year, and the landlady said she would gladly allow it.

A short time after, however, she called on me and said, with a good deal of embarrassment, that she had reflected on the subject, and should have no objection to my remaining, as she had already intimated, but that I must pay *double rent*, or 600 francs. I was astonished at this, as was natural, and tried in vain to show her the unfairness of her conduct; but it is ill arguing with a Breton who has made up his or her mind. 600 francs was the figure, neither more nor less, and I must pay it or pack up. I felt I was ill-used, and therefore, as soon as I could, I did pack up and depart, and Madame never ceased expressing her regret at losing so good a tenant, although all the while it was her act which made her lose me.

I felt there was something I could not make out; but one day her brother let the cat out of the bag, and explained the matter very simply. As thus:—Madame was a *dévote*, and, of course, had a father-confessor, the priest of the parish, who was—as many Breton priests are—fanatic and violent. He had, it seems, paid my wife and myself the compliment of preaching against us, and had stated that it was a shame to see Huguenots in the parish, but a profanation to have them installed in the chateau which had been inhabited by so many generations of good Catholics. He warned servants not to live with us, and threatened them with non-absolution if they did—advised his flock to have no dealings with us—in fact, drew round us a very tight *cordon sanitaire*, the effect of which would have been, but for the Breton *auri sacra fames* which almost balances his fear of the priesthood, to starve us out of the country. As it was, however, with ready money and high prices we managed to get on.

But his *grand coup* was in reserve. Finding his

previous manœuvres fail, he called one day on our proprietor, and rated her soundly for the evil act she was permitting, put in play all his resources, natural and supernatural, and, in fact, brought her to the point of agreeing to do something. But then came in Plutus and his attractions, for she, too, loved money like all her race, and so, probably, did the priest. Suppose, suggested Plutus, that, instead of sending your tenant away, you first try to make a little more money out of him — a happy thought! and so she agreed *to double my rent*, and I have little doubt she and the priest divided the money between them.

He was a thrifty man was that priest, and looked well after his ' rights.' I remember, one day about Easter, meeting him in the fields, dressed in his best, and followed by two men with sacks half filled. He was collecting his ' Easter dues ' in kind, and had a motley collection of them. I heard of his going into a cottage hard by, and where a poor woman had nought but a hen, and this he had the coolness to ask for. But it was almost the poor woman's living, and she fought hard with his reverence for the '*pauvre poule*,' and finally saved her, on condition, however, of giving up all her eggs ! Rather close shaving of the flock this !

I had a very ludicrous meeting with him on another day, on the high road. He was riding and I walking, and as he approached me I noticed his pony zig-zagging across the road in a strange style, making regular tacks, as if beating up against the wind. The priest, good man, did not spare the stick, but nothing could keep the animal's head straight, and every now and then he made a dead stop; and in this guise we approached each other. I could not help laughing, and I dare say he would think that the pony would not pass a heretic, being, as he doubtless was, a good Roman Catholic beast.

There are a good many Jesuits in Britanny, and they are, as usual, much disliked by the 'regular' priests. In fact, France was never so full of Jesuits as at the present moment, and yet, strange to say, by law they have no right to be in France at all, as I believe that the law expelling them has never been repealed. I fear that the Gallican party in the French Roman Catholic Church, I mean that party which upholds the right of the French Church against the encroachments of the *Romish* Church, is almost destroyed. Certain it is that Jesuits, the very heart and essence of the Ultramontane party, abound everywhere.

There are lay members, or of the '*robe courte*,' as it is called, and I have known some. One, in particular, I was in some sort intimate with. He was a very clever man, with a wonderful memory and power of speech; and his close and accurate acquaintance with the state of the English Church, not only in England but in our colonies, was most surprising. It so happens that I am nearly connected with one of our colonies, New Zealand, and therefore I was able to 'check' his conversation upon that head by my own knowledge, and yet I found that he was at least as well, if not better, up than myself in all which related to Church matters there. The movements of the High Church party in England were subjects of especial interest to him, as might naturally be expected, and he said he looked forward to more and more conversions, or, as I should call them, ' perversions,' until England returned again to the bosom of Rome. I always told him not to delude himself, and mistake the isolated acts of a few individuals, whose temperament was unsuited to

F

the free air of Protestantism, for the tendencies of a
people.

When I see water flowing up hill, I shall begin to
see a chance of any other impossibility happening; till
then I shall feel tranquil. Englishmen have not read
history and the Bible for nothing. It is well for England's future that she was Romanist in times past, and
she is not a dog to 'return to her vomit.'

At Lorient there is decided movement and activity
in religious matters. Mr. Planta, a Swiss minister,
supported by the same society which supports Mr.
Williams, is labouring there with great zeal and activity,
and is effecting a notable work, for he is a devoted and
able man. The authorities, too, at Lorient are liberal
and tolerant, and have shown a favorable spirit towards
Mr. Planta. For instance, they have allowed him to
celebrate weekly worship in one of the halls of the
mairie; a very great act of condesension on their part,
and due in some degree, I doubt not, to their opinion
of Mr. Planta himself. They have also allowed the
society '*des intérêts généraux*' of Protestantism to
hold an occasional meeting in the same *salle,* and on one
occasion upwards of 300 persons attended one of the
meetings. There is a large floating population of Protestants at Lorient, composed of sailors and workmen
in the dockyards, so that Mr. Planta has a large
congregation.

He has also held public discussions with Romish
priests and others, and sustained his part with much
ability; and is altogether a very valuable man. He is
now engaged in getting the means of building a Protestant chapel at Lorient, to which end he is applying
to well-disposed people to help him with donations; and
from my knowledge of the circumstances I can say that

any such donations for that purpose would be well
bestowed. They might be sent either to the Rev. Mr.
Planta, Ministre Protestant, Lorient, or to Messrs.
Longman, under cover to myself, and I will undertake
to forward them to their destination.

At Nantes, as well, are many signs of life, and vigorous life too. The name of Nantes recalls many things
to the mind, especially the massacres there in 1793, and
the revocation of the Edict issued from there, and which
revocation was apparently the death-blow of French Protestantism. Nantes is the chief town of the department of
the *Loire Inférieure*, and a place of importance. There
used to be a Protestant church in a very bad quarter of
the town, and altogether unworthy of the congregation, but in 1855 a new and handsome building was
opened, which is by far the largest and most sightly of
any of the Protestant churches in Britanny. Mr.
Vaurigard was then and is now the minister, and is
a man of high quality in every way. He is *Président
du Consistoire* of the district, or diocese of Nantes.
In all cases of emergency he has been ready to fight in
the van, and has done very much to uphold the good
cause in Britanny.

From all this it will be seen that the Bible, in spite
of all the opposition of the government and the priests,
is not without many witnesses in Britanny. Let all
who are interested in the work pray that God's special
blessing may be poured out upon the workers there,
and let every human help at the same time be given to
them that can be given, for they well deserve it.

I fear that some of the sentiments I expressed in
' Britanny and the Bible,' as to the apathy of French
Protestants, have been misconstrued, and have given
pain to many good men to whom they were not intended

to apply.   It is in truth difficult for an Englishman to
look on the subject with French eyes, and to speak the
truth without giving offence.   We in free England,
unfettered by an overbearing government, with all our
political and religious rights guaranteed to us and in
full exercise, able to conceive thoughts and express or
act upon them as seems to us good, can form only an
inadequate idea of the state of things in France, which
is so totally the opposite of this.   French liberty is so
hedged in and watched, so ' cabined, cribbed, and confined,' that none but spirits of a high and ardent nature
venture to assert themselves; and the average mass of
men, even good men, who compose the multitude, are
unable to cope with the difficulties; and more or less
reluctantly succumb to them.   Some have tried to act
and have been defeated, some are fearful of trying,
though glad to see others do it, and so in effect a very
different state of mind in face of difficulties prevails to
that which an Englishman is accustomed to.   It is hard
to accuse them of apathy, when it is rather the deadening effect of the system they live under; and we
should pity and not blame them.   Yet we *must* speak
what we consider the truth if we speak at all.

The same ' *amende honorable* ' I should also wish to
make as to my remarks on French christian liberality,
which I know hurt the feelings of many excellent and
liberal Frenchmen, and of course *to all such* they do
not apply.   But I do insist that there is no comparison
between the real liberality towards religious objects
of the two nations; and I do not think I overstate the
matter if I say that one third of the amount raised by
voluntary effort for the support of Protestant religious
objects in France comes from English pockets, either
in England or in France.   I know well that in any

project for building new churches, &c., one of the
first steps taken is to organize a deputation to proceed to England to collect money ; and I believe
such efforts always succeed, and I trust always will ;
though it is only fair to let the fact be stated and
admitted. And what church or chapel in England was
ever built by such means?—i.e., by money collected in
France, even in infinitesimal sums? I am sorry to
have hurt the feelings of anyone among the many
excellent men I have known in France, but I cannot
consent to place French liberality in such matters on
the same level with English ; and yet I am much disposed to think that the average amount of savings
annually realised by individuals is greater in France,
with respect to incomes of equal amount, than in England. If this be so, then the amount contributed to
religious objects might be greater than it is. Riches
are not so much positive as comparative, i.e., it is the
proportion of expenses to revenue which makes a man
rich, and I decidedly think that Englishmen generally
are less economical than Frenchmen, and do not calculate ‘ ways and means ’ so well.

It is a very common subject of remark by a Frenchman, that England neglects her duties towards the poor ;
and yet how unfounded is the remark ! But, unfounded
or not, it is an idea which will never be eradicated from
the French mind. Because our public papers, which
publish all things, occasionally publish one of those
appalling cases of starvation which from time to time
occur in London or elsewhere, they jump to the conclusion that our poor are horribly neglected. But what
are the facts ? why, that England, with half the amount
of poor which France has, pays, I believe, twice the
amount towards their support which France does, — so

making four times as great a provision for each poor
individual. If France had newspapers like we have —
if every small town had its public eye and ear and
mouthpiece, as we have in England, under the influence
of which if almost a sparrow falls it is duly noted down
—the cases of death from starvation in France would be
counted by scores. I feel no doubt whatever of the fact,
judging from what I have seen in Britanny.

In England, come what may, the law gives the poor
man *a right* to relief, independently of all private charity;
and I say that the English system of Poor Laws, faulty
as it is in various points of administration and detail, is
still a noble national act of charity, to which no other
nation on earth can offer a parallel ; for what other state
or nation can show an annual sum of 8,000,000*l.* a year
given *by law* to the poor ? And as to public charities
of all kinds — almshouses, hospitals, asylums, refuges,
reformatories, dispensaries, coal-clubs, soup-kitchens,
clothing-clubs, lying-in charities, Dorcas meetings, and
other similar societies of every alphabetical initial letter,
and of as many or more sorts than the mind can conceive
—to say nothing of the million acts of private benevolence — I feel confident that in these we outdo France,
or any other nation, in the proportion of two to one.

And yet the poor exist, and even die in our streets !
And the poor always *will* exist and be with us, and now
and then men *will* die in the streets through exceptional
circumstances ; but whenever such cases do occur, they
are held up to public notice, and the blame is brought
home to the parties deserving of it. It is not that the poor
are neglected, but that we live as it were under a micro-
scope, which detects the slightest flaw and exposes it.

I was in Britanny during the winter of 1853-4, which
was extremely severe. The ordinary sources of labour

were soon exhausted, and the roads were thronged with
haggard, hollow-eyed, scarce-living skeletons, whom it
wrung the heart to look at. It was impossible to prevent begging in troops, for a third of the population
were beggars — and meanwhile, let us remember, no
Poor Law, as in England.

Soon some died. The authorities then exerted themselves in every way; but there being no legal means of
obtaining money — i. e. no *poor-rate*, they could not do
much. In the parish or commune in which I lived, a
public meeting was held, and the poor were apportioned
among those who were *willing* to support them. But
all were not willing. We had three given to us, whom
we supported during the winter as well as we could.
I knew one generous family, of the old noblesse, who
took in thirty, and had them all at rack and manger.
But many stood aloof and took none.

That was indeed a fearful winter. I remember seeing
the tracks about turnip-fields, made by the poor starving
creatures who went to and fro and fed themselves with
the raw turnips; and it was dreadful to meet at every
turn poor famishing scarecrows, whose looks told all
their sad story. Now in England this never could have
happened — thanks to our Poor Law. It is, therefore,
most unfair to charge England with neglect upon this
head, as compared with France.

The poor showed great fortitude during this hard
winter, but, of course, small crimes were abundant, for
nature returns to her normal state when misery passes
certain limits. The stealing of wood, among other
things, was universal. One morning I was walking in
my shrubbery, when I heard an unusual noise, and
looking about I espied a man seated high up in a oak-
tree, deliberately sawing off a large bough. I shouted

to him, and as the best means of alarming him which
presented itself to my mind, I put my walking-stick to
my shoulder as a gun, levelled it at him, and called out
that I should shoot him if he did not come down. And
he certainly did come down *by the run*, for almost in a
second, and before I could get to the tree, he was at
the bottom and off. As our wood had been regularly
plundered in this way, I wanted to make an example
of one of the plunderers, so I started after him. After
a short chase, in which the man did wonders considering that he wore sabots, or wooden shoes, I caught him,
but I could not hold him, and he started again, and I
also. Then he lost a shoe, and I caught him again, but
he being stronger than I was, he got loose again, and I
should never have ran into him at all but that he
missed his footing and fell headlong into a heap of
briars, out of which he could not get. I then had him ;
but as we were each of us pumped out, we could do
nothing at first. When he got his wind, and free from
the briars, he came out, and I collared him and said I
would have him put in prison for what he had been doing;
but he begged so hard, and promised so well, that I at
length let him off, on condition that he would promise
never to come to the wood again, which he did, with
many asseverations — *à la mode de Bretagne.* So he
went off with a torrent of thanks, but soon turning
round, he said, '*Monsieur, n'a pas un vieux pantalon
a donner?*' ('Monsieur hasn't got an old pair of
trousers to give away, has he?') I couldn't help laughing heartily at his coolness. We had been in regular
conflict, and hard at it, glaring mutually like two wild
animals, now up and now down, as might be. I had let
him off very easily as I thought, and, after all, to ask me for
an old pair of trousers! 'Twas French to the backbone.

CHAPTER VI

BREST AND M. CHABAL — SIR ANTHONY PERRIER — PROPOSED
NEW CHAPEL AT BREST — DOCKYARDS — FRENCH NAVAL AFFAIRS
— NAVAL SCHOOL — NAVAL HOSPITAL — THE BAGNE OR PRISON
— JESUIT MIRACLE THERE — THE PROTESTANT PRISONER.

THE greatest number of Protestants in Finistère are
to be found at Brest. Some are French, others
have been attracted there from other countries by.busi-
ness, and the rest by the *agrémens* it offers as a place
of residence. In truth there are few towns which
present such claims as Brest.

In itself the town is exceedingly clean and well built,
and with one of the finest promenades in the world.
Taken in connection with the splendid bay, which is
unrivalled in Europe, I know nothing equal to the
Cours d'Ajot, and I have heard those who have travelled more widely than I have done confirm this
opinion. The promenade is of considerable length,
and runs alongside of the bay, and while it constantly
offers a most charming view to the lounger, he is sheltered from the sun by the noble trees which line it, and
is refreshed by the cool sea-breezes. The adjacent
country is undulated, and very picturesque and rich,
and the people have a high character for hospitality; a
character which, from experience, I can pronounce to
be well merited, as I have nowhere in Britanny found
such cordiality as there. Hospitality is well classed
among the Christian virtues, and doubtless affinity of
religion is a strong motive power to its exercise, but

whether owing to this, or to the air or the soil, there
seems some special virtue of this kind at Brest.

There is also much to interest anyone who takes an
interest in the distribution of the Scriptures, and the
spread of religious knowledge.   The large floating
population, as we may call it, consisting of regiments
in garrison and ships in port—these, combined with the
criminals in the *bagne*, or prison, present a vast mass
of material which continually comes and goes, and,
counting by opportunity, gives a larger population in
ten years than most towns in France.   The Rev. M.
Chabal is the Protestant minister there, and has a well
attended chapel.   M. Le Fourdrey, late the excellent
pastor there, was the first Protestant minister in Finis-
terre who was recognised and paid by the State.   He
ministered at Brest for upwards of twenty years, and
during that time laboured hard to enlighten the people,
and with success.   He was a Frenchman, but spoke
English fluently, and was much respected by all, authorities included, and may be considered the chief restorer
of Protestantism in Finistère.

In addition to this, England is most happy in her
consul at Brest, for Sir Anthony Perrier is all that
could be wished to represent our national interests.
He, and his family also, give a helping hand to every
religious and philanthropic work, and assist powerfully in cementing and increasing the Protestant body
in those parts.   For example is better than precept,
and when we see a man discharging every public and
private duty in an admirable manner, we not only
respect and love *him*, but are insensibly drawn towards
the principles he professes, and disposed to respect and
perhaps to adopt them.

At one period the authorities at Brest were exceedingly well disposed towards a full religious toleration, but that was in the reign of Louis Philippe, and things have changed for the worse since that period, though they are now improving again. On one occasion (I think the anniversary of some important event in Louis-Philippe's life), M. Le Fourdrey was greatly surprised, but much pleased, by the presence in his little chapel of all the great authorities of the town ' en grand tenue;' and individual men in power also occasionally attended the service. I fear that religious conviction had not much to do with all this, which probably was just the mechanical motion of the flower which follows the sun, and Louis Philippe was liberal in such matters; and now, times being changed, and Romanism very rampant until lately, I fancy the authorities would be almost as likely to enter a lazaretto.

M. Chabal, the successor of M. Le Fourdrey, has been enabled to see the happy issue of the project for building a new chapel at Brest, which M. Le F. conceived, and there is every probability that it will soon be commenced. The Government have recently granted 25,000fr. towards this purpose, and the municipality have granted 20,000fr. also; liberal aid has also been given by the Protestants of the locality and friends elsewhere, but more money is still wanted, and any sums for the furthering of this excellent object would be received with thanks by the Rev. M. Chabal, Brest, Finistère.

The dockyard at Brest is extremely interesting and worthy of inspection, but it is difficult to be admitted there; in fact, strictly speaking, admission was impossible, unless by *special* order of the Minister of the Marine at Paris. Of late, however, it has been difficult, not to say impossible, even with a special order, and, some time ago, even the Duke of Rutland, who was then at Brest, was refused permission to enter.

This jealousy is very absurd and needless. Any information really wanted can always be obtained, despite of bolts and bars; and as to piracy of improvements, &c., there is little of that sort to take away which would benefit Englishmen. We have probably all which is to be found at Brest at our own Portsmouth and Plymouth, *and more*; why, therefore, make a fuss about nothing. But this feeling seems generally prevalent. I mean the feeling that while *we* are going ahead rapidly, other nations are standing still; whereas, in this time of rapid intercommunication, no new invention long remains the exclusive property of any one people which has a real aptitude for it. The Americans possess this notion so strongly, as to look down upon other countries as almost out of sight; the French, and doubtless ourselves, are not without it. For myself, I have visited the Brest dockyard frequently without any permission, as a supposed Frenchman and in company with Frenchmen, and I have also seen our English dockyards, and while I allow Brest to be well worth visiting I should say that we have nothing to fear on that subject. At Portsmouth, I believe, is to be found all which exists at Brest, *plus* the biscuit-works and the block-works, though, on the first *coup d'œil*, Brest dockyard is superior, owing to the whole being together, for, being in the form of an amphitheatre, it is visible at one view.

Everything at Brest is certainly well kept and in good order. I have often visited the works where they finish or repair steam engines—for, in fact, none have been actually made there, as the government prefers to employ private enterprise—and there I saw the giant slave which we prize so much in England in full activity; for, as with us, steam did everything. Drilling, planing, sawing, boring, lifting, moving about, hammering, everywhere was the modern Briaræus in full life. In one place you saw a plate of iron half an inch thick cut through like a board of dough at a pastrycook's, in another the boring machine passed easily and smoothly through some apparently soft material but which turned out to be iron also; here a gigantic hammer split a bulkhead or cracked a nut with equal facility, and there a great plane worked out slices and shavings of the same metal thinner and more delicate than were ever cut at Vauxhall. On the one side was nature with her mineral treasures rich and valuable but obdurate and hard to win, on the other was art brought to perfection wooing and successfully vanquishing all opposition, and producing so to say impossible results. .

Whatever *may have been* the inferiority of the French in the application and management of steam, it is certain that their inferiority is gradually disappearing. In this as in other things study and use will do much, for between nations of equal intelligence there cannot be any natural inaptitude for a given pursuit, and France has for many years encouraged every attempt of her own people to cultivate a further acquaintance with the steam engine. For some time the French government have employed none but Frenchmen on board their steam navy, with very rare exceptions, although at first the engineers were generally English; and nowhere are Englishmen to be now found save on steam vessels of commerce.

There is great activity in the dockyards, many vessels refitting, and others on the stocks; and the place resounds with the hum and noise of labour. The port is very convenient and has vast natural advantages. It is

in fact a deep creek, which runs up into the country for
say a league, and has throughout sufficient depth of
water to float a ship of the largest size. As it flows into
the bay it is of course impossible to get to it by water
save by entering the bay and passing all the forts,
though on the land side it is much more accessible.
On the sides of this creek the rock has been worked away
nearly to a level, so as to form a large space on which,
and on the sides of which, stand the workshops, ma-
gazines, slips, and all else pertaining to the navy. The
two sides of the creek are now connected by a noble
bridge.   .

Brest is the only port of France which has preserved
its virginity, having never fallen into the hands of any
foreign power, or ever been visited by a sudden *coup
de main.* In the life of Lord Exmouth it is stated,
however, that he (then Sir E. Pellew) had an intention
to make an attempt with his frigate squadron, not with
the view of a sustained attack but rather as a sailor's
dash to do much mischief in a short time and destroy
the *prestige* of the place; but our cautious Board of
preventive service at the Admiralty would not allow
him. This was a pity, as he was not a man to undertake what he could not probably accomplish; but it is
not the only brilliant exploit which the 'old ladies in
London,' as Jack used to call them, have nipped in
the bud.

Depend on it that something of a striking kind will
be wanted in the next war, whenever it may come, to
reduce the confidence of the French navy. Nor is it to
be wondered at. They see themselves in possession of a
splendid fleet, and have few opportunities of seeing and
inspecting British ships, and few sailors of the present
day have been actually opposed to us in fight. Then

they do not consider that they have been so often
beaten as *we* think — accounts differ, and each side believes his own story.   Indeed, in the opinion of many
Frenchmen we had the worst of it during the last war,
at any rate as to our merchant marine; and this is
probable, as we had *ten* merchant ships for every *one* of
theirs, and had therefore more to lose.   That their
privateers were numerous and profitable is certain, as
many of the opulent families in the coast towns of
Britanny made their present fortunes by privateering,
and probably their children would like to try it again.

Only last week I had a striking instance of the
different light in which a naval battle can be viewed
on opposite sides of the Channel.   What Englishman
does not know well and his heart still burn at the
remembrance of 'the glorious first of June,' when Lord
Howe broke the line of the French fleet and captured
six line-of-battle ships, and all this with an inferior
force, and certain members of that force not doing
their duty.   Well! glorious as the victory was to *us*,
there are Frenchmen, and those naval officers, who
claim it as equally glorious to *them*.   I happened to
mention Ushant, or *Ouessant* as it is called in France,
and my friend, a lieutenant in the French navy, said,
'Ah! the English were well brushed there.'   'Well
brushed,' I replied; 'then it was themselves that did
it.'   'But,' said he, 'you do not mean to say that you
gained the battle ?'   'Yes! I do, most decidedly; and
the proof of it is that at the end of it six of your line-
of-battle ships remained in our hands, and none of ours
were captured by you.'   This he could not believe, and
appealed to another French gentleman on the subject,
who said he did not know the exact particulars.

And thus it is with a large proportion of what we

count as victories — such as the actions of Sir R. Calder
and Sir R. Strahan, and many others. But it was too
bad to claim 'the glorious first of June,' so often sung,
toasted, and poetised. Of course there is no doubt,
(no room for it) as to Trafalgar and the Nile, but then
they attribute them only to Nelson's great talents, and
say that such a man only comes once in a century, and
that next time it will be *their* turn to have a Nelson.
These considerations may, perhaps, serve to show to
Master John that it is possible he may place himself
at too high a valuation.

I was much pleased with the naval school at Brest.
It is held in an old three-decker, moored in the bay,
and is an institution for supplying the navy with
officers. Young men are sent to it as to a school,
and the terms are 600 francs a year. For this sum
they are taught all the branches of a complete naval
education, as well as boarded, lodged, and clothed.
There is also a yacht attached in which they make
voyages, often long ones, to learn navigation and the
handling of a ship under sail; and in this yacht they
went up the Thames to Woolwich a short time since,
and were highly pleased with what they saw there,
though, owing to some misapprehension of the Government orders, it is said, they were not admitted to see
the whole of the arsenal. There are from 80 to 100
youths at the school, including many of the high
noblesse; and, with similar institutions at Toulon and
Cherbourg, we may imagine that France will soon have
a well instructed and capable force of naval officers,
who learn their duties afloat and not on a carpet.

One thing amused me there, as illustrating the doctrine of equality, which in many things has taken so
firm a hold on the French people. Ever since the great

revolution it has prevailed largely, and despite the Empire and its tyranny, and the Bourbons and their feudality and pride, it has survived and still flourishes. In the naval school the cadets are of two classes — of *one* and *two* years' standing — and no contact or intercourse of any kind is allowed. Though confined within the same narrow wooden walls, they seldom see or speak to each other. One class has the larboard, and the other the starboard side of the maindeck, properly partitioned off by bulkheads, and when one class goes on deck to breathe the fresh air, the other remains below. The reason given me for this was that when the boys were together it was found that the elder ones domineered over the younger — in other words, *fagged* them; and this being contrary to all notions of equality, they were separated.

I have no wish to defend the system of fagging when practised in the extreme, but I maintain that within limits it does good. If my Lord A— or the Marquis of B— has to run errands, prepare lunch, or bring out the tea and coffee for their 'tyrant,' who may be a lawyer's, a merchant's, or even a shopkeeper's son, the lordlings learn a useful lesson or two by the way, besides merely making coffee or arranging the table. They learn, or at least may learn, that, notwithstanding titles and privileges, they are but of the same flesh and blood as their neighbours, and that they must curb their pride and ill-tempers, a thing as necessary for high life as for low. A good thrashing from plebeian hands, or a smart punch on young nobility's head, may just come in time to check budding qualities which, once developed, would be incurable. It seems to me that permitting the practice is more republican and levelling than forbidding it, but it would appear that

G

La Jeune France is too tender for such rough towelling, and therefore its vanity is left to sprout at will.

There is in the Brest dockyard a mute but striking
register of the political changes in France, which deserves notice; that is, the state-barge in which the head
of the Government embarks when he arrives at Brest to
visit the port, &c. This particular one was built for
Napoleon the First when he was at Antwerp, and is a
very splendid affair, magnificently fitted up, gilded, and
painted, and when pulled rapidly through the water by
the twenty-four oars for which it is intended, must flash
before the eye as something regal. What changes has
it not seen in forty to fifty years ! Napoleon I.,
consul and emperor—Bourbon—Napoleon again—Bourbon — Revolution — Orleans — Revolution —Republic—
Napoleon III.— in all, *ten*—a short average for sovereign power regarded at the time as durable, not to say
everlasting. Cheap is, or should be, royalty or headship
in France — four years' purchase and a few months —
that is all ! hardly worth the strife, one might say. As
an officer told me, they have ceased altering the royal
emblems of late, as not worth the expense ; and, therefore, *n'importe* under what rule France lies, all is the
same to the state-barge, which takes it easily, and holds
to its *premier amour.* The regal crown still keeps its
place at its head, as of yore, and in the cycle of changes
will doubtless again find its lawful claimant.

Indeed, the old barge preaches a good moral—that
changes in the Government do not greatly affect the
condition of individuals. It reminds me of an old
French story. When Louis XVI. was violently taken
from his palace and placed in the Temple, and the day
of insult and outrage drew to a close, a worthy citizen,
a staunch royalist, who had been an unwilling witness of

all, retired sorrowfully to his bed, his heart broken and
his spirit bowed down to the dust. The royal person
profaned — the palace destroyed and sacked — the king
in prison — were too much; the cup of divine forbear-
ance must certainly overflow—the world was evidently
near its end. Musing painfully on this and kindred
subjects, the good man fell asleep, and slumbered soundly
until awoke in the morning by the cry of the baker with
' hot bread.' He sat up and rubbed his eyes. Was he
alive, or were the events of yesterday a dream? He
was puzzled; and yet still ' hot bread,' quite a cry of this
lower world, rung in his ears. He grew more awake,
rubbed his eyes less and his head more, and mused again:
King in prison! horrible!! dreadful!!! But still ' hot
bread! hot bread!' and his appetite arousing, and the
baker's boy impatient; and, therefore, after buying a roll
and eating it, the citizen returned to bed again, with a
new political idea in his head, namely, that kings were
not necessary to his existence, and, thought he, that he
was much less intimately connected with royalty than he
was the evening before.

There is an institution at Brest of which France may
be justly proud, and that is the Naval Hospital. I have
visited several institutions of this kind in England and
elsewhere, but I never saw anyone at all equal with this.
It is not that the size is so great—though it can receive
from 1,200 to 1,400 patients at once—but all the ac-
commodations and arrangements are so excellent. I
believe it is generally admitted that the French hospitals
are very admirable, and that England might copy from
them with advantage. At Brest everything is not only
in excellent working order, but is arranged with such
good taste and effect, as to make objects often disgusting, or at least disagreeable, positively attractive and

captivating. For instance: all the world knows the article
called 'man's tufted nightcap,' a thing apparently invented to offend the ladies and sow variance 'twixt man
and wife by its ugliness and the danger of reflecting that
ugliness on all near to it. In Brest this monstrous
article is so tastily arranged 'in stock' as to change its
character and appear like the last fashion from a Parisian
modiste! Under the same magical wand a room full of
invalids, suggesting disagreeable sights, bad smells, pain,
close air, and *ennui,* becomes an elegant and airy saloon;
tastily fitted up, draped with divers colours, and occupied
by quiet interesting-looking individuals, who might be
philosophising in bed '*more Romanorum.*' For the
convalescents there are long and well-lighted galleries,
perfectly ventilated, and looking down upon agreeable
views, in which they can lounge, chat, and smoke; and
when appetite is returning and becoming clamourous,
its demands are met by a kitchen as well appointed and
served as that of a London clubhouse. Between every
sick ward are gardens planted with shrubs and flowers,
regaling the senses, and refreshing the mind thereby;
and those who have for weeks been shut up and stewed
in a close room, with no other landscape than four walls
dotted with physic bottles, and enlivened by a monthly
nurse and her mob cap in the foreground, will easily
imagine how grateful these pleasant views must be, and
how really conducive to recovery.

Another arrangement also evinces the care which
has been taken to comply not only with every want but
with every wish in this noble institution. In Roman
Catholic countries, as is well known, prayers are offered
up in a church for the souls of the departed, and a
mass performed at which the relatives attend. In order,
however, that this ceremony may be as private as

possible, and out of respect for the feeling of the sur-
vivors, the body is taken at Brest to a chamber fitted up
as a chapel called ' *La Mortuaire*,' where the relatives
may indulge their grief unseen by others than themselves. Those who have mourned over a lost friend,
and have been obliged to do so in a rude crowd, will
best appreciate the feeling which has dictated this
arrangement. Indeed, all is admirably managed; and
others may take a lesson on the subject from the Brest
Naval Hospital. One of the surgeons told me that
they always use chloroform in painful cases, and without
fatal result as yet, and he much lauded it; though
admitting that great care was necessary in applying it.

As to the *Bagne* or prison at Brest, it is less worthy
of praise. The French, as it would seem, are strangely
backward in the treatment of their criminals. Deprived of colonies to which to transport their convicts,
we might have expected to have found a well conducted system of prison discipline. Where a nation
cannot send away its convicts but is forced to keep
them at home, the question of their reformation becomes doubly important, in order to escape the necessity of again pouring out the plague upon society. It
is not enough to seclude the criminal and to punish
him, but the endeavour should be made to reform him,
otherwise society in the long run gains little, perhaps
indeed loses, by receiving back a man steeped in crime
instead of one only accidentally vicious.

In England, as is well known, the problem of the best
mode at once to punish and amend has been long and
anxiously debated, and many lost efforts have been
made on the way to our present state. America has
also studied the matter deeply, and spared neither
trouble nor expense in the attempt at a solution, and

we may hope that the human limit of 'the best possible' has been attained, or is in the way of being so.
True, that the results are uncertain and chilling to the
warmth of the philanthropist, — for instance where we
read reports of criminals returning again and again
to the prison, — but it must needs be so. The best
system of prison discipline, of convict management,
that was ever invented and adopted, what is it at last
but a *mere human machine?*—and without the breath of
the Divine Spirit to animate the whole, we must not
expect life or motion, any more than from the steam
engine without steam.   At the same time, we know
that God works by human means, and it is clearly our
duty to use the best human means in our power, as we
use the best agricultural means to raise a crop, leaving
it to Him to give the increase.   But at Brest there
seems to be no system, and no object save the one of
gain to the State from convict industry, — the worst of
all objects, inasmuch as it is a selfish one.

The convicts live together, work together, and sleep
together, and no effectual restraint is placed upon the
principle of mutual contamination.   Oh ! the hell upon
earth of such a place — the seething cauldron of vice
and unknown crime which rages there ! What human
force could resist its boiling fetid slime, or withdraw
itself from its noxious vapours ? Like that lake ' whose
gloomy shore' undecked with life told of exhalations
ever rising, deadly and to be shunned like death, so we
may regard the mass of moral turpitude thus heaped
together and speedily fused into one common homo-
geneity of wickedness.

For there are degrees in vice as in virtue. The
swindler, the fraudulent, the pilferer, can hardly be
classed with, or be said to have reached equal depths,

with the murderer, the incendiary, or the burglar.   The youthful delinquent, thrown naked on the world, perchance the fruit of illicit pleasure, starving, without knowledge or support, unloved, uncared for, cannot be regarded as on a level with the old criminal, grown grey in vice, and perfected in crime, alas ! by age.

Yet by the undistinguishing system, or rather want of system at Brest, such inequalities are all levelled together.   Youth learns wickedness from age, age fiendishly gloats on the essays of youth; the half-corrupted soon learn to regret their incomplete state, or are forced to abandon it, and each has the Satanic pleasure of looking upon his equal in sin, and saying with delight, ' How thou art fallen.' . What barriers can a faint remorse oppose to foes like these, or how escape them ? ' Where'er I turn is hell; myself am hell.'

As I walked among the convicts, and heard the clanking of their chains, I could not help thinking that they were the victims of a barbarous carelessness, but that if expiation and circumstances could ever wash guilt away, or extenuate its colour, it should be here.   A perfect justice will estimate not the mere nominal crime which human laws class under a given category, but the proportion between temptation and resistance — between natural character and circumstances; and out of exactly similar events, may yet give a widely different verdict as between two individuals.

The convicts at Brest may well have dreaded their fate, for it *is* dreadful.   They are generally chained together night and day — they work at the hardest labor in all weathers — at night they lie on a mere board, without mattress, by lots of fourteen, all chained to an iron rod, allowing just sufficient space for moving ; and only once a week do they change their clothes.

Added to this, their food is very poor; and all this is often *for life*! No wonder that many should prefer the guillotine.

There is a committee which recommends commutations, on reports from the superintendents; and this is the only symptom of the reformatory principle — the solitary spice of possible alleviation in their cup. But hope has a home in every heart, and could we examine even here, we should, doubtless, almost everywhere find that heavenly tenant.

It is curious to see how they hold to anything which has not merely a probability, but a possibility — *a chance* of amending their fortunes. I mentioned in my former work (see 'Britanny and the Bible,' page 44) the tour of conversion made in the Brest prison by the Jesuit preacher, and the great unfairness of the government in refusing permission to M. Le Fourdrey, the Protestant pastor, to preach also. I have since heard a few further particulars, which I now subjoin.

He worked miracles of conversion that Jesuit, and should have a special niche as a saint highly favored. Considering the *morale* of the prisoners, we should have expected conversion to have been difficult among them; and so it had been previous to this counterfeit Pentecost. I believe, on the average, one a year would have been about the mark. But that was in olden time, before modern inventions had accelerated the pace of all things human, and when the phenomenon of conversion by steam was unknown. For how many converts, think you, were made by this new apostle in one short fortnight among the 2,000 prisoners at Brest? A hundred, say you? Guess again. Five hundred — a thousand? Still again — do you give it up? Then I will tell you: *just* 1,600, neither more nor less — up-

wards of 100 per day! Sharp work, it must be con-
fessed, for one pair of lungs and one head — was it
not?

One is curious to know the logic he employed;
pity' the secret should be shut up in these infidel
times, for it reads like magic. Sixteen hundred in
a fortnight. Extraordinary! That is not the word.
Let us invoke Dominie Sampson, and say '*Prodigious.*'

Meanwhile, we may make one observation. In pri-
sons the sole resource to the convict, save religion, is
hope — hope that they may be pardoned — may escape
— may have their period shortened, or their punishment
commuted; hope, vague, or more or less definite —
but still hope. To this they cling under all things,
and into this crucible they resolve every circumstance
which affects them. And it is natural.

When the preaching of the Jesuit was announced,
and all were ordered to attend, ah! what hopes were
again called forth? Power of the priests — influence at head-quarters, and with the authorities; and
when conversion was held out as the act which all
ought to perform, which all who had hope beyond the
present should perform, and when this was dressed in
attractive eloquence, and, perchance, accompanied by
rhetorical flourishes and artifices — by promises of certain benefits, which low minds might construe in a
pecuniary sense, and of certain ameliorations which
sanguine ones might read in reference to their actual
lot as prisoners — when the barrier was once removed
and the road opened to free action by the standing
forth of some prisoner more deeply affected than the
rest, can we not imagine a perfect rush, a very steeple-
chase of converts? To suppose the real sincere

heartfelt conversion of 1,600 of the dregs of mankind in
a fortnight, requires a simplicity too strong for *our* day.

It may be fancied, however, that the conversion once
made was not kept hid under a bushel. From the
Univers, the great Parisian organ of the Jesuits, down
to every petty provincial grinder of news, nought was
spoken of but this crowning miracle, which proved that
the Church still possessed her ancient gifts and power;
and nothing was left undone in Brest to nail as it were
this great fact into the memories of the faithful there.

Like everything else in France, it was made the
subject of a fête. On a given day the 'sacred band,'
in number 1,600, were marched in full liberty through
the streets of Brest, with white bands, emblematic of
their purity and innocence, carrying banners and
crosses, and headed by the authorities with their insignia
and the priests with their finery, to a place where an
altar was erected, and there, with due ceremony, their
conversion was publicly celebrated by high mass, prayers, and a grand religious service.

This would be a treat to the prisoners—to breathe
fresh air for once, and would cause a lively interest
among all those sons of the faithful who looked upon
the scene, though some would wonder why so many
soldiers and policemen and convict guards were mixed
up with the people, and would be grieved to learn that
they were there to prevent the escape of these interesting, meek-looking, white-clothed converts, and to
reconduct them to the prison. But, happily for priestly
tricks, reflective people seem few in France, though
it is hoped they are growing more numerous.

And a word here. The authorities were all in the
procession, to add to its importance. Curious this, in
that France which professes equal favour, or rather equal

indifference, for all religions. When where the authorities last at any *Protestant* fête? This deponent knoweth not.

One little trait deserves especial notice, and we record it. The convicts, poor as they were, having only the few *sous* per week which they gain by their labour, were moved to wish to buy themselves crosses; and it was, so to say, a touching incident to see them give their own money for this object. *Luckily* the worthy father, or some of his troop, sold these articles— for it seems that, ever since the days of Luther and Tetzel, priests drive a little honest traffic in crosses and relics — undoubted ones of course, and 'warranted sound'— and the bargain was soon made, with a handsome discount, doubtless, on account of the great number taken — for all men will bargain. If my memory serves me rightly, the price was ten sous per cross; a small sum, but which, multiplied by 1,600, grows into 800 francs,— a large amount to come from small pockets; and many persons are ill-natured enough to say that there would be a profit to the good fathers on the transaction of at least 700 out of the above 800 francs; proving that jesuitry is really an excellent trade, and never without an eye to the main chance.

Far-sighted men these followers of Loyola, and see a 'chance,' as the Americans say, a long way off. They were in this case clever in the means employed, and we shall, perhaps, some day know what those means were, whether material or moral; but believing that miraculous powers have ceased, I can but look for something of the earth—earthy, and think of Pindar's lines on the 'Pilgrims and the Peas.' My readers, doubtless, know the story: — the Pilgrims were both ordered to visit 'Loretto's shrine,' and as a penance were to walk there

with peas in their shoes — an unpleasant addition,
bad for corns and bunions. One was stupid but honest,
and kept the hard peas in his shoes ; the other was more
clever and put the peas into his pocket, and afterwards
boiled them, returned them into the shoes well softened,
and walked easily. The clever one, by the speed of his
conversion, reminds me of these convicts.

> He saw the Virgin, soon ' peccavi' cried,
> Had his soul whitewashed all so clever ;
> Then home again he nimbly hied,
> Made fit with saints above to live for ever.

And now that the excitement is over, how much better
is the prison at Brest for this wholesale whitewashing ?
Are the convicts quieter, more orderly, obedient,
and moral ? Is there less crime and vice among them ?
Have their keepers and guardians less trouble and
difficulty with them ? All these questions were put by .
me to one of the authorities in the prison, and the
answer was, ' The chief difference I perceive is that the
convicts are more unruly and turbulent than ever.'
And so ended the miraculous Jesuit conversion at
Brest.

The number of Protestants in the prison is from seventy
to eighty only, out of 2,200 inmates, which tells well
of the morality of Protestantism. The Protestant
population of France is in the proportion of a *fifteenth*
of the general population ; and if the same proportions
held good in the prison, there would be, say 213
Protestant convicts there, instead of, say seventy-five ; in
other words, tested by these figures, Catholic immorality
is three times greater than Protestant.

There is one rule of the prison which speaks volumes
against the actual prison system, and is an additional
practical proof, if any were needed, of the constant

leaning of the government towards Romanism, in spite of all constitutional or paper theory of equality of religions. Every convict on his arrival in the prison makes a declaration of his religion, and this declaration once made, he is *never thenceforth allowed to change it* — so runs the rule. This is done to avoid all prose- lytism being attempted; but, how supremely lament- able? In a prison, above all places, religion and its supports are needed, and yet here is the only place where they are limited, and, as it may be, *denied* by the law.

For instance, suppose the case of a Romanist with commencing desires towards Protestantism — old feel- ings recalled perhaps, or new ones divinely implanted — does not the rule *deny* to such an one all outward religious help? This inexorable law *denies* him all aid in his trouble, forbids him even to call for it, and fixes him in his half-recognized errors as immutably as the grave.

This is wretched legislation! based on that philosophic principle of professed equality, but real infidel indiffer- ence, which prevails in France. It cuts short the period of probation which God allows to all, by ante-dating irre- vocably its termination, and in opposition to the Divine precept, which says that only 'where the tree *falls* so shall it lie,' it makes its mere accidental leanings final; for many *die* in prison.

Thus much against the rule in impartial theory. But the practice is tainted with the same partiality for Romanism, that real '*religion de l'Etat*,' which marks all other arrangements. If the rule were fairly carried out, all we could object would be that it carried indif- ference up to infidelity — that it was only equal injustice to each party. But in point of fact it is only carried out *as against* Protestantism. Catholics must remain Catholics, but Protestants may change if they are so disposed. Witness the conversions by the Jesuit preacher and the liberty given to all to attend his lectures, while the same liberty was denied as regarded M. Le Fourdrey. Is this conduct worthy of a great nation? to have a a law and follow it not? Can the people be expected to be better than their rulers?

There are many interesting cases among the Protestant convicts showing a sincere repentance and desire to amend; and if the indiscriminate no-system of the prison was improved, there would probably be many similar instances, who are now overwhelmed in the current of vice which surges about them. One man in particular deserves mention. He was convicted of passing bad money and has continually asserted his innocence of the crime, and *has refused a commutation* of his sentence, claiming either a free pardon or to remain in prison. He has for many years devoted the money which he accumulates by his work entirely to charitable purposes, and of late he has sold his rations of wine and even his soup in order to increase his means of doing good. The Protestant chaplain remonstrated with him, and begged him to regard his own health, which was certain to suffer from the deprivation, but the poor man replied that he was only too happy to have the power of doing good to others left to him, whatever might be the personal sacrifice to himself. This was noble charity — let us believe that it will not be without its reward.

The earnest practical religion of this man has procured for him at least the respect of his fellow prisoners, although at first he was tormented and persecuted by them beyond measure. He has said to me that no one could paint the horrible pollution of the general body

of convicts, and in proportion to their blackness would
be their feeling against one who sought the light, and
so *impliedly* reproved them. Perseverance, however,
aided from above, has carried him safely through all;
and the dark and loathsome prison is to him but as the
vestibule of a heavenly mansion.

His deeds, however, attracted the notice of Romanists,
and were a stumbling-block to them, for 'can such a
good thing come *out of Nazareth?*' However, Jesuits
are clever ; and if they cannot get over a difficulty, or
round it, have always some scheme in reserve, and in this
instance they adopted one of which we must ever admire
the boldness. They simply swallowed the difficulty —
one gulp and down with it. They stated the facts of the
case in one of their public journals, and attributed
them to a *Romanist* instead of a *Protestant* convict !
This was cool and pleasant, and saved trouble !

Capital punishments frequently occur in the prison.
This must be expected, as nothing short of the severest
means can restrain the convicts. All crimes of disobedience are promptly visited, and disobedience carried
into violent action — for instance, striking a keeper or
guardian — is followed by death. The execution
takes place with every possible solemnity, and is a
fearful spectacle. The convicts are all assembled and
ranged around the scaffold, and to suppress a revolt on
the instant, should it arise, a battalion of infantry with
loaded muskets surrounds the spot, which is also com-
manded by two guns charged with grapeshot.

On a given signal the culprit appears on the scaffold,
and the convicts are ordered to kneel down on pain of
being fired upon after the third summons, and, as if to
show their native independence and contempt of the
authority which compels them, my friend, an officer in

the dockyard, told me they generally did not comply until *the third* signal. The ruling weakness even here — pride in a prison! At length they kneel — the artillerymen with lighted matches stand ready — the battalion is at 'attention'—the criminal is bound to the plank, wheeled forward, and, *click!* the knife falls, a gush of blood, a quiver, and the fate of one more soul is settled for ever.

Compared with the guillotine, our gibbet is a clumsy instrument; witness the writhings, the struggles, even the re-hangings of the victim — rousing sympathy and pity in the spectators. The guillotine is short, sharp, and sure, and so combines all the requisites; for if human justice takes away life, she is bound to do so by the most direct method, and has no right to superadd torture to a penalty already so great.

More than this, the machine is portable and small, and not, like our huge gibbet, erected over night, and casting its huge gloomy shadow for hours over earth's surface, advertising to the idle and vicious the horrid but (to the mass) attractive spectacle of the morrow. The machine is soon constructed and soon removed — the mob has no time for fatigue or diversion — nothing to distract it from the awful sight. And cold steel, too; something fearful *there*, makes men shudder where the rope leaves them unmoved — blood also! visible and in a torrent — all unite to make a deep impression.

A friend told me that, for the half second after the head was cut off, the surface of the severed neck was of a remarkable whiteness, but which suddenly changed to deep red as the heart poured forth the volume of its last pulsation. Despite stoicism and military habits he said he was profoundly struck by the terrible sight, and that all the crowd seemed equally affected — no one speaking, all holding their breath in suspense. How different this to our English executions!

I remember seeing Greenacre hung in 1838, at Newgate, and sad was the scene. To this hour it is vividly present to me, but I was far more affected by the conduct of the crowd than of the criminal. True, that *there* before me, was a man loaded with crime going visibly into eternity, passing under my eyes, as it were, from the seen to the unseen world — but *there* were also under my eyes thousands equally bound on the same voyage — perhaps to depart on the same day, the same hour, or even the same minute, and, to judge by their behaviour, equally unprepared with the other. The chief difference was, so to say, an accidental one — the rope and gibbet were but *effects* in the picture; for some sang filthy songs — some cursed and fought — some laughed and mocked — some looked on listlessly and vacantly — some picked pockets, as I myself saw from my window — few seemed to think the matter solemn or affecting. The fiendish yell which saluted the miserable man when he emerged from the dark prison door long rang in my ears, as also the universal hiss which arose at his parting struggle, like the hailing salute from the snakes of the pit; but deeper still was my impression that our manner of executing criminals was calculated only to brutalize the beholders.

Escapes frequently occur from the Brest prison, notwithstanding the vigilance of the guards. When this occurs a cannon is fired, and then two others, to spread the alarm round the country. Gendarmes and police go out on all sides, and it is but seldom that the convict gets clear off. A reward of 100 francs is paid for his apprehension within twelve hours — a large sum in a poor country, and sufficient to put the peasants on their

H

mettle; and when the 'hunt is up' they are very active
in the chase.

It is not agreeable to live in lone places near Brest.
The escaped convicts seek such to avoid detection,
must have money to enable them to get through the
country, and are of course not burdened with scruples;
therefore robberies by them are of frequent occurrence. Some keep the high roads at night, as best for
travelling, and there are many crosses erected to mark
the spot where, sinking from the excessive fatigue for
which their stationary life in the prison has unfitted
them, these miserable men have paid the last debt of
nature. One of these escaped convicts called at the
country-house of a friend of mine, who instantly recognised him, but, as he said, his feelings revolted against
capturing or informing against him, and he gave him
a trifle and left him to his fortune.*

* The number of convicts at Brest is now greatly reduced, as the
French government have adopted the method of transportation to
Cayenne and New Caledonia as a means of disposing of part of their
criminals; and it is said to be their intention totally to abolish the
bagne as a place of criminal punishment, as soon as they have a substitute ready.

CHAPTER VII.

A N incident recently happened in our household,
illustrating the manner in which the Romish
system, as practised by priests, traffics in the religious
feelings of the people of Britanny.

My man Mark is a thorough-bred Breton, and therefore has a strong reverence for the Church, but also has,
like a true Breton, a decided love of money. I used
sometimes to say to him, in joke, that if I were to throw
a handful of *sous* in his face half of them would stick
there, so strong was the attraction existing between
him and a metallic currency.

Mark had a stepmother, who died and was buried,
and, as the priests say, went into purgatory.

This is a notion out of which the priests suck no
small advantage. Purgatory is, of course, a very unpleasant place to be in; but is nevertheless a place you
can get out of for a *consideration* paid to the aforesaid
priests, the effect of which 'consideration' is to cause
them to say a mass which opens the door for the poor
spirit and lets it out. So that the priest first gets you
into it for nothing, and then gets you out again for money;
which, of course, is a very profitable affair to him.

The price varies with the station the person held in

life, and is from 10 sous, or 5d., up to 1,000 francs, or
more. One would think that, considering the sad
sufferings said to be endured by these poor spirits in
prison, a benevolent priest would occasionally be found
to let them out without charging a fee; but I never
heard of such a case, and suppose it is against the
' usages of trade.'

Well; soon after the funeral, the priest met Mark,
and told him he ought to have a mass said to release
his mother, and Mark said he would see about it, and
asked what would be the price, and the priest said two
francs. Mark thought this a deal of money, and the
old woman was only his stepmother after all. Had it
been for a real mother ' *c'est une autre chose*,' but a
stepmother ! two francs was a deal of money. So the
matter rather hung fire.

One day the priest met him again (the man told me
this himself the day it happened), and said, ' Ah ! Mark,
your poor mother appeared to me last night ' *et elle
souffre beaucoup*.' She is in a dreadful state, and all
because you won't pay this two francs. What an un-
dutiful son you must be !' ' Well,' said Mark, ' if she
suffers so much, why don't you let her out of your own
accord ?' ' Can't do it without being paid; it's against
rule,' replied the priest. So Mark and he debated the
matter, and finally (for priests can bargain well)
Mark gave in, paid the money, and, as Dr. Eck,
the celebrated vendor of indulgences in the time of
Luther, said, as soon as the money clinked in the plate,
the soul of poor old Mary Jeanne was considered
to mount aloft straightway into Paradise.

Rome is a clever money-maker and taker—gets much,
but does not give much. In Borrow's 'Romany Rye' is a
passage, where, meeting with a Jesuit in want of money,

Borrow advises him to get money *from Rome.* This strikes the Jesuit as such a rich idea, so full of humour, that he does nothing but chuckle and laugh at it; and at last he says, ' Young man, that is the most witty remark of yours I ever heard, ' Get money *from Rome*; money *from* Rome; from *Rome*!!' And yet what becomes of it all? for it is certain an immense amount goes *to* Rome. We may as well ask what becomes of castaway pins.

I mentioned, in page 18, how the distribution of the Scriptures was working in Britanny, and I have just had another proof of this.   A man who lived near to us, named Louic, came to my house and asked to speak with my wife.   He asked if I sold Bibles, and said he wanted one.   I asked him if he was a Protestant, and he replied, ' No ; but that he had long read his Bible, which was in fact worn out;' saying which he produced it, and truly it *was* worn out, and in the service too, and not by moth and rust.   A more dog's-eared, be-thumbed, and dirty book I never saw, for cleanliness does not dwell in Britanny.

But the man had perused and reperused, and had got from it what he could get nowhere else — some satisfaction for the cravings of his soul, and some comfort in his troubles.   He had given up confession and the mass, and was marked by the priest as a black sheep; but he persevered in the path opened before him, which will, I hope, conduct him to a better country than the one he will have to leave. My wife gladly gave him a New Testament, which he was vastly pleased with; and I only regret we did not take the old dirty-faced one in return, for it would have been a curiosity.   He had obtained it from one of the colporteurs, and this is another proof of the way the Word of God is working of itself, and by slow degrees penetrating and vivifying Britanny.

I believe no one can form any approximate idea of the floods of vice and blasphemy which were poured forth in Britanny during the French Revolution, although the Romanists vaunt its people as so naturally religious and saintly. For instance, in one case the holy vessels were tied to an ass's tail, and trailed in the mud; in another a feast, characterised by the grossest debauchery, was given in the church of a small town I know in Britanny, the communion vessels were used as drinking-cups, and the table itself as a sideboard; and men, moreover, thronged the church, rivalling each other in obscenity and mockery, as if openly to defy God and brave his thunders. Certainly men may well fear the repetition of such scenes, where the very fountains of the great fiery deep seem to have been upturned to pour out their torrents upon the earth, to scathe, blast, and pollute everything upon it.

An anecdote was told me of a circumstance which happened at Morlaix, which is worth recording. One day news arrived there of some victories of the Republican armies over the Coalition. A fête was arranged, and a public dance given in the *Grande Place*. At that period the popular dance was the *Carmagnole*, a sort of *grande ronde*, in which twenty or a thousand people could equally take a part. It was, like all other republican institutions, somewhat levelling in its nature — equally practicable by, and open to, all the world. Near to the *Grande Place* flowed a small river, of some twenty yards wide, and perhaps a yard deep, and this gave occasion to the fertile brain of some democratic dancer to conceive a very ingenious and amusing plan, which was forthwith put in practice amid roars of applause.

All the *aristocrates* of the town were assembled by beat of drum, and ordered to present themselves immediately in the *Grande Place*, to take part, with cheerful faces, in the national fêtes then celebrating there, under pain of death on refusal. Accordingly few absented themselves; and all came, probably bowing and smiling, with great politeness and apparent pleasure, and took their places in the dance.

The fiddles flourished, the flageolets shrieked, the dancers shouted, screamed, and sang, and the dance swayed to and fro, a mass of animation; but a cautious observer would have remarked a gradual but suspicious approach towards the river side. On went the music, however, and if anyone did remark it, he thought little about it, or kept his thoughts to himself. Nearer and nearer drew on the dancers at each gyration, and at length the river's edge was reached. Then, with a shout, the circle broke up, and a democrat seizing an *aristocrate*, rushed with her to the river side, and, as quietly as might, or might not be, deposited her in mid-stream. Another followed, with a similar burden — another and another, until, from side to side of the current was established a line of women, at different depths, according to height and the river's bottom. There they were, the young, middle-aged, and old, the tender and the hardy, all elegantly dressed as for a fête, *standing in the river*, some ankle-deep, others up to their shoulders, and no egress allowed.

When the line was completed, men on the opposite side joined hands to the lady nearest to the bank, others pieced on to him on the dry land, the ladies were ordered to join hands in the river, and the dance recommenced, with this solitary but important difference as regarded the dancers, that the republicans all danced on *terra firma*, whereas the poor women were danced and draggled so far and back again, again and again, through the muddy river, until the malice of their tormentors was assuaged.

And this, too, to well born and well bred women, in a province of France — the nation of *gallantry, par excellence* — famed (in its own opinion) for devotion to the fair sex! Ah! if a Frenchman wants an antidote for overweening conceit, he has one close at hand, but seldom read by him — the pages of his own Revolution of 1792.

The Romish party, in particular the priests, are never weary of singing the praises of poor benighted Britanny. They hold up the devotion of the Bretons, their loyalty, their love for the ancient faith, their constancy, and an imaginative sketch of all the rest of the cardinal virtues, as something almost supernatural, and as the model for all the world to follow.

I wish the practice corresponded with the theory, but as far as my experience of ten years goes, I must say it is quite the reverse. It is difficult, for instance, to conceive equal ignorance in any other people with what prevails in most parts of Britanny; and this is not a thing to be proud of. Out of the young men of twenty-one in *Finistère*, only fifteen out of a hundred can read and write, according to the Government returns; and in the *Côte du Nord* the proportion was even smaller. The comparative value of this may be tested by the fact, that in the departments in the north of France adjoining Germany, and abounding in Protestants, the numbers of the same class who could read and write was, according to the same Government returns, seventy in each hundred. And as a consequence there is much vice and immorality. Crimes of violence, too, are far more frequent than in other parts of France, as is proved by the calendar of crime.

As to drunkenness, it is the bane of the country, and in no part of the world which I have ever seen is there the same amount of this horrible vice as in Britanny. Wherever you may be, in town or country, it forces itself upon you. Cæsar, in his Commentaries, mentions the Bretons as 'impatient of thirst' 2,000 years ago, so it seems that the tendency is of long standing.

The practice of the *goutte* of *eau de vie* is almost universal, and the quantity of vile stuff taken under the miscalled name of ' water of life,' is something wonderful. Nothing can be done without it. If you set out on a journey, or arrive at home after performing one— if you have suffered misfortune, or met with success—if you buy, sell, lend, or exchange—if you quarrel, or make it up—whatever you do, suffer, propose, or almost think of, it must be stamped by a *goutte*, or it will not pass current. It would seem as if the rule of the *goutte* was part of the religion of the country, so rigorously is it observed. I remember once remarking how many *gouttes* of brandy my guide took in a shooting excursion, and I am certain he took not less than a pint of neat *eau de vie* during the day. If constant *dropping* wears a stone, it must surely wear away flesh and spirit also.

And if I am asked, what part the priests in Britanny take to counteract this — whether they preach against it, or establish associations to check it, or show by their own abstinence their abhorrence of excess, I am bound to answer that, as far as I have heard and seen, they do nothing at all in that direction; and yet, with their influence with the peasantry, they might do almost everything.

Then swearing, or taking God's name in vain, is more common in Britanny than I ever heard it in any other

country. Its varieties and ramifications make it quite
a science; and it is so interwoven with conversation,
that it would seem impossible to get on without it.
This is not only the case with the poorer classes, but
with all, without exception either of *priests or nuns*.
I was one day talking with a *sœur* on the subject, who
warmly defended her countrywomen from the charge,
for I had said that I, a Protestant, was scandalised at
the open swearing among women of the better classes.
This she denied, with many asseverations, in particular
'*Mon Dieu*,' '*Grand Dieu*,' '*Bon Dieu*,' and other
takings of God's name in vain. I then remarked that
she was herself a swearer, and repeated her various
exclamations during the previous minute or two. She
was extremely angry with me, a Protestant and a
heretic, for calling her, a *religieuse* 'to order,' for the
breach of a commandment, which she was obliged to
admit; for ' taking God's name in vain ' is *a fact* in a
small compass; and she never was friendly to me afterwards. Her excuse was, that she meant no harm by it,
for of course she could not deny either the commandment, or the fact of its breach.

Here, again, is room for the sacred influence of the
priesthood; but if I am asked whether they exert it, I
am bound to say that, judging from what I have heard
and seen, they do not in any way interfere in the matter,
save in countenancing it by their frequent practice.

When I hear of the activity and devotion of Romish
priests in Britanny, and their anxiety to attack and
remedy social evils—when I hear of them in their extreme zeal, for instance, proposing a crusade *against
Protestantism*, I ask myself why they do not commence a crusade against prevalent bad usages at home.
There are surely evils enough to remedy *there*. Lying,

sexual vice, drunkenness, all abound in Britanny as we
have seen, each sufficient to call forth the energies of
many a Peter the Hermit; and there is also the custom of
duelling—a social evil of a deadly nature, and yet in frequent practice. The existence of duelling in Britanny
and the frequency of its occurrence, is a proof that the
country is yet only partially civilised, whatever may be
said or sung to the contrary; for duelling is undoubtedly
a relic of the very dark ages.

The duel is, in fact, the *ultima ratio* —is not only
practised but defended and glorified by the highest
authorities. Hardly a session passes in which at least
half-a-dozen honourable members of the French assembly do not amuse themselves with sword or pistol ;
and not without damage, not all ending in smoke.

Few men of ' *esprit* ' but what have fought their way
up to their position and gained a reputation at the pistol's
mouth. I know two brothers who have fought at least
twenty duels between them, and have survived, being
masters of the art—not so, alas! some of their unfortunate opponents. Within a very short period, and
within a mile from where I lived, two duels were
fought, in one of which a leg was lost by a young
man whom I used to meet frequently ; and only a week
since another duel took place between two youths whom
I know, and all these about mere trifles. Even my doctor, whose profession is to heal rather than fight, has lost
an eye by the sword of one opponent, and has shot away
the leg of another, to make matters even, I suppose.

A brace of duelling pistols is as necessary as an
umbrella, a sword as a walking-stick, and the laws
of duelling are *codified* with a scientific accuracy.

Surely there is scope here for the efforts of the
ministers of religion.

Here is a social evil of great magnitude, deplored by many, in opposition with the interests of all, and in direct collision with the Word of God, which might with great propriety and benefit be attacked; but I am told that they leave it almost wholly untouched, and no one of my acquaintance ever remembers having heard a sermon, or a pastoral allusion to the subject. Yet, what eloquence is strong enough to brand that practice by which, for an unworthy trifle—a look or gesture—the peace of families is destroyed here, and the ruin of a soul consummated hereafter.

Had real civilisation pervaded the country, it would have banished this cruel, stupid sin; men's minds, enlightened by education, religion, and reason, would have acknowledged its enormity, and by common accord have condemned it to contempt; but France seems not yet to have travelled so far on the road of real progress.

In England, happily, the custom is nearly extinct,—is more a tradition than a fact. For many years it had led a hobbling, tottering existence, was resorted to with reluctance, and was generally viewed with dislike or ridicule. The *law* was always clear on the subject—let us do that justice to it—and declared it murder; but judges charged mildly, juries, influenced by custom, would not convict, and the offenders escaped.

By degrees, however, this changed; judges became more severe, juries remained oftentimes for hours shut up in their box in difficult and painful gestation; and every man who fought a duel ran a very unpleasant chance of being hung afterwards. This was not satisfactory—there is no romance where the gibbet is included; no man of fashion would like to be hung by the help of Jack Ketch.

I well remember the case of Lieutenant Munro, whose *second* was tried for the murder of Colonel Fawcett, and it was a very near thing. I think it was Baron Gurney who tried the case, an upright man, but severe and strongly opposed to the practice; he charged very strongly, and men held their breath until the verdict was given. It was a very narrow escape.

Other causes assisted in their turn, and powerfully. Reason awoke anew to the absurdity of the practice; pulpits thundered against the *lex talionis*, and invoked religion's aid against it; elderly females joined with juveniles in a shrill and potent chorus of detestation; and the cream of the thing, and its gentlemanly *tournure*, began by degrees to vanish.

All things pointed to the speedy extirpation of duelling in England, and at last it fell ingloriously, and (alas! for the sentimentality of the thing) by the measuring-yard of a *linendraper*,—for I fully believe that the *coup de grâce* was given by poor *Mirfin* of Oxford Street, *draper and hosier.*

As thus. England is aristocractic in her habits, and duelling had always been regarded as a sort of luxury, fitting for the nobility, but too good for shopkeepers. The higher classes, therefore, almost exclusively enjoyed the privilege of destroying each other with sword and pistol; while the lower classes settled their differences by the more natural means of fist or cudgel. But the spirit of revolution, not content with the field of politics, invaded the home circle, and threatened the ancient institution of the duel. Merchants and lawyers, those classes always active in and upon ' 'change,' openly enjoyed the privilege; shopkeepers began to follow in their wake, and there seemed a probability that, ere long, the very chimneysweeps would claim the right of

killing each other *à la mode*. Universal suffrage, that
bête noire of the upper ten thousand, seemed less objectionable than universal duelling—and High Olympus
was seriously alarmed.

At this juncture arose Mirfin of Oxford Street, *draper
and hosier*, and became, Curtius-like, the saviour of
his country. Like others of his ' order,' he, too, would
fight a duel; and, unfortunately, was killed. His death
broke the charm. So long as duelling was confined to
the upper circles it was time-honoured and honourable,
' the distance lent enchantment to the view,' but practised by shopkeepers it was voted vulgar, and the
absurdity appeared in a moment. Poor Mirfin had his
revenge, and it was a noble one. If a duel was the
death of *him*, he in his turn was the death of *it*; and
on his tomb should be inscribed, ' Here lies Mirfin, who
destroyed duelling with a yard measure.'

Thanks, in a degree, I believe, to him, duelling is
now nearly obsolete, and rests harmlessly in the lumber
room, along with ladies' wooden dressing skewers and
castellated headdresses, and the pasteboard breeches of
our forefathers ;—and there *let* it rest. A friend of mine
was going from Brighton to Dieppe, when, just at the
moment of the boat leaving the pier, a man rushed on
board in haste to depart. He had little luggage, and
was in dress boots and other light clothing unfitted for
a voyage, and seemed in good spirits with all the world,
joking and laughing with those around him. There
was, however, something in his manner which was re-
pulsive to my friend, and he had no communication
with him; nor was his feeling of dislike — nay, disgust—
abated when, on landing, he discovered that he was Mr.
Johnson, the man who had killed Mirfin *that very
morning*, and who was then reeking with the blood

of the murder, and in hot hurry to escape from justice. To judge from his trifling manner he might just have left a ball, my friend said, and not the scene of a murder perpetrated by himself.

I trust that henceforth the law of England will be administered as it ought to be, and that the very next duellist brought to its bar will be *hung*; this will put to flight the last lingering remnant of the practice, and will deprive the world of the shadow of an excuse for provoking a duel. When a challenge becomes simply an invitation *to be hung*, probably few will accept it.

For the *rationale* of the practice is so perfect! A man injures you, and what do you do? You call him out, and give him the chance of shooting you *in addition*. Good common sense that, is it not? He ruins or destroys the peace of your wife or daughter, and then kindly offers you 'satisfaction,' i.e. the opportunity of being shot by him *in addition*; or else you, not having been sufficiently injured by him, *volunteer* to give him the chance of adding to it by calling him out *to shoot you* if he can. A dispute arises, followed by angry words; no solution can be found except that of producing conviction in the brain by an ounce of lead. He was no fool, who, on receiving an offer of satisfaction from a so-called 'gallant' captain who had eloped with his wife, replied, 'Thanks for your kind offer, but I shall not hazard my life for a bad woman. Keep her; and may she be better with you than she was with me.'

Truly the equity of the system is exquisite! I have often thought that to make the game a fair one, the injured party should blaze away at the other till he had wounded him; and then, having inflicted wound for wound, the amiable disputants would be on a level, and might fight on upon equal terms. I wish this plan was tried in France. I do not think duelling would long survive the treatment. Seducers, bullies, liars, are great egotists—devoted to themselves; and, with all their pretended love for the fair sex and scandal, I greatly question whether they would consider the most lovely creature who ever breathed, or the most *piquant* story which was ever invented, a recompense for the smallest injury to their own most precious skins.

But then it is a 'satisfaction.' A fine satisfaction truly!—the satisfaction of killing a fellow creature, or of sending him to grope his way through life led by a dog and a string, or to limp through it on a wooden leg; the immense satisfaction of breaking his arm or his ribs perchance, or of sending him to Bedlam a drivelling idiot; and the satisfaction of having a good chance of these benefits for ourselves. For myself, I hate wooden legs, green spectacles, and arms with hooks on the stump, but doubtless I am singular. I suppose there must be a great satisfaction somewhere, since so many people say so; but for the life of me I cannot imagine where it lies.

All reasoning on the subject is vain. You gain the argument, and lose the application; you fight victoriously, and are tripped up at the corner; you nail your opponent fast in a frame of syllogisms, or smother him under appeals to feeling, and the next moment he is before you as lively and capering as ever, with his grasshopper chirp of *Il faut se battre.*

Il faut se battre. Exactly, that is just it; the cuckoo cry of 'must,' without reason, feeling, or common sense. Away with argument, for it is not a matter of reason; keep your appeals to feeling for a softer audience; pack up and stow away your stale morality; don't talk to me of Scripture, for religion has nothing to do with it; we *will* break each others heads, *il faut se battre.* This is not cutting the knot with the sword, like Alexander, but smashing at it with the club, like the fool. And, after all, these pugnacious logicians speak the truth in one thing—it *is* useless to argue the matter with *them*: and we can only say, as Sterne said to the ass, 'I never argue with any of *your* species.'

If men must fight, if they *must* have a violent means of settling what may almost always be done amicably, let it be done with natural weapons. As says Cowper—

> A Trojan combat would be something new,
> Let Dares beat Entellus black and blue,
> Then each might show to his admiring friends,
> In honourable bumps a rich amends,
> And carry in contusions of the skull
> A satisfactory receipt in full.

I am no advocate for boxing, but I have had sufficient experience in a public school to know that an open quarrel settled on the spot causes much less malice and heartburning than a pent up and therefore enduring feud; and the man who punishes an insult at once, does but use those means with which Providence has armed him to repel aggression.

To those who object to the natural mode, and ask for a better substitute for the sword and pistol than the fist, I would propose a Court of Honour. The French have a council of *prud'hommes* to decide matters of trade, why not have a council of *brav'hommes* to decide matters of honour? Character would be safe in their keeping—reputation is not like a herring, which is best when *smoke* dried, though when damaged it of course needs to be *cured.* All that is required is for a certain

I

number of men of high standing and character to agree to submit to such a tribunal, and the mass would eagerly take refuge in it; for no one can possibly be benefited by the present system save the gunsmiths and Curtis and Harvey.

Already the French army have adopted an approach to this principle. Curious that the army, and that one notorious for high courage, should preach peace to civilians: but it shows that the duel is considered simply as a nuisance, and no proof or effect of bravery. In the army each regiment has a council, before which all quarrels are laid, and which decides whether they shall be amicably arranged or shall go further; and I am told that almost all are stopped on the way. Let this principle be carried further still, and the power be given to arrange *all* cases amicably; and the thing is done. Let the councils have power not only to decree apology, but damages also, if they see fit. Let their decrees be published, and have a judicial power, and the world would soon recognise their utility and support them with its public opinion.

By the way, what has become of the English association of eminent men, civil and military, who some few years ago entered into a mutual engagement not to fight duels? I have not heard anything of it of late, but I hope it is not dissolved. If alive, it should give some note of its existence, and might carry out the idea I am now suggesting, and send a circular to The O'Donoghue and Sir Robert Peel, asking for their adhesion.

I have said nothing of the question in a religious point of view, as almost needless, but what says the Bible as to it? Ridicule, contempt, and sarcasm would seem enough to combat so absurd and cruel a custom, but to complete the circle, what says the Bible? Is the matter treated doubtfully, or is any hole left by which human ingenuity can escape?   No! sternly and in few words speaks the Law, and by the command, 'Thou shalt do no murder,' briefly decides the question.

But, says some small casuist, 'What *is* murder?' Murder is the act of killing another with the *intention* to do so.   Apply this to duelling.   Either the parties go out with the intention of killing each other, or not. If they *have* this intention, they are clearly murderers; if they have it *not*, they are self-convicted of a stupid farce.   On one horn of the dilemma they must be impaled, let us hope it may be on the latter.   But suppose they have not the murderer's intention, and yet *kill*, are they guiltless?   What says the *New* Testament? There we find the commandment repeated in a new form, 'Thou shalt not *kill*,' as if to meet the case in question; and how, between these two authorities, can the duellist escape?   The last authority closes the dis-cussion.

As to arguments in favour of the practice drawn from honour, custom, feeling, &c., all these are powerless before the great authority we have cited.   If *that* speaks, all others must be silent, and may be disregarded.

It is singular, and proves the wisdom of that apothegm of Lord Bacon, 'Men reason from reading and expe-rience, and act from *custom*,' that, notwithstanding that duelling is thus condemned by revelation, reason, and feeling, yet it still exists, and is occasionally had re-course to.   How is this?   We often see an ugly object, an unsightly tree, a ragged wall, offending our eyes and annoying us year after year, causing growlings and threats innumerable; and yet, because it will require more than our mere personal effort to overthrow it, we are content to grumble indolently, but to do nothing

more. At length, our humour being on that day more
acrid than usual, the wind blowing from the east, and
the daily paper having miscarried, or a favourite horse
having been just thrown down by the groom, we boil
over, call in our neighbours, set to work vigorously,
destroy the nuisance, and then look about and breathe
freely, and wonder we had not done it before.

So with duelling. If our French neighbours will
only use their eyes and their tongues, and pull well and
pull together—examine and attack the principle and
practice in question boldly and openly, without fear or
favour, they will find it but a giant in pasteboard, all
hollow within, which will crumble under their hands ;
and, without waiting for the final *coup de grâce* from
linendraper's yard measure, or chimney-sweeper's brush,
will expire, all naturally, from want of life.

What France seems to me to want is a few more
active *practical* philanthropists. Owing to the nature
and form of their Government—paternal and patriarchal
as it is—everything is done *for* the people, and but
little *by* them. They are, therefore, in some degree
like children in leading strings, or high-bred London
dames turned out suddenly at the diggings, and told to
work. In England it is wholly different. There, in
every town, almost in every village, you find some active,
bustling, perhaps testy, impersonation of charity, who
has the direction, or is busily concerned, in every good
work. Only convince his reason that your plan is good,
and you at once gain his heart and aid, and secure a
hundred-handed coadjutor. He knows the feelings of
all his neighbours, can tell you the best way of bringing
the matter before this one and the other, weighs to an
ounce the respective merits of this plan or that; and,
while you are puzzling out your path among the clouds

of good intentions, lands you in a trice on *terra firma*, puts a road-map into your hand, and tells you how to start and when. While others are talking, he organises; and ere another has finished a general sketch, he presents you with the article cut and dried. A hundred such would go far to abolish duelling in France.

There is, however, one essential difference between the countries, viz., that *the law* of France does not consider duelling as murder, if it is fairly conducted. If there are seconds, and the principals take no undue advantage one of another, and one is killed, it is viewed as manslaughter — nothing more. In case of a duel without results, a *procès verbal* is prepared and forwarded to the authorities by the police, in order to notify the fact to them, but no further steps are taken in consequence. The law of France is therefore in some degree accessory to the custom of duelling, and does not resemble the law of England, which pronounces it to be murder; but let public opinion in France declare itself adverse, and the law will speedily be changed; and let us hope that our own time may see it.

But if asked what part the priests take as to duelling, I am constrained to reply that they seem to me to take no part at all.

The way Sunday is observed in Britanny is another proof of the small amount of religious influence actually exercised by the priesthood for the practical reformation of the people. I am quite aware that the Romish Church considers Sunday as a feast day and day of rejoicing, and not as a day of rest and religious worship; and I think it a very strong proof of the irreligious worldly character of the Romish system, that it does so. In truth it is just another illustration of the way in which it favours, instead of controlling, the evil

tendencies of human nature. But in Britanny it seems
to me that Sunday is more devoted to pleasure than in
other parts of France.

For in other parts of France the Government has
made certain steps in this direction, which are to its
honour, and deserve record ; and let us note that these
steps have been made by the *Government* as a civil
power, and in no respects by the Church. In 1856 the
French Government, by a circular addressed to the
Minister of Public Works, abolished work on Sunday
in all undertakings under Government control, save in
cases of extreme urgency. Certain *Préfets* also acted in
a similar manner. I have a *décret* of the *Préfet* of the
Yonne now before me, dated 1857, which says, ' Considering that the rest of Sunday is as necessary for the
health as for the mind of workpeople, and that it is
painful to morality and religion to see the laws of
society and tradition thus passed over,' goes on to
decree that all Government contracts and works shall
thenceforth be stopped working on Sundays. This is
all done by the civil Government, but, as yet, I have not
heard of any steps having been taken by the Church in
the same direction.

And it was high time. The desecration of Sunday
in Britanny and in France is dreadful, and every lover
of his country would do well to look to it. For, in spite
of the scorn of the scoffer, the sneer of the unbeliever,
and the subtle fine-drawn reasoning of the so-called
philosopher, God's judgements *exist* on the earth, and
are exercised upon nations as well as individuals ; and
when nations collectively sin — when general practice or
legal authority sanctions or enforces actions contrary to
the Divine will, that nation will, I believe, as certainly
be punished for its conduct as will an individual for
his sins, at the Great Day.

In Britanny, Sunday is *the* day of the week, *par excellence*, given to pleasure. If a man be somewhat devout, he goes *en déshabille* to the early mass at seven in the morning, for an hour; and having thus compounded for the duties of the day with its great Giver, he returns home, changes his *déshabille* for his Sunday best, and prepares for the promenade, the *fête champêtre*, the ball, the chase, or any other special pleasure. In fact, having given a small corner of the beginning of the day to God, in his undress, the Breton fits himself out in his best for making a worthy full-dress sacrifice of the remaining eleven-twelfths or more of the day to Mammon.

As to rest being the character of the day, it is precisely the quality absent. Many shops are open, and doing an unusually active business; men's brows are furrowed by the troubles of a ceaseless care; the pursuit of gain is in full cry everywhere; music and dancing are all around; on every side is Mammon looking prouder and gayer than usual, more attractive, and more successful. Instead of being under the Christian dispensation, it would seem as if we were under a Heathen one; and instead of being the Lord's day, it might be the feast of Bacchus or Terpsichore. And thus it arrives, that this great Divine institution for the spiritual, moral, and physical improvement of mankind—this plan so admirably calculated for the purifying of his soul and the strengthening and renewing of his body, is either only half used or is wholly cast aside and neglected, and man's natural proneness to evil again mars the benevolent will of his Maker.

We read in ancient history of a fountain in which aged and diseased persons were dipped, and such were the wonderful virtues of the water that the sufferers immediately regained all their youthful beauty and

vigour. And we are not surprised to learn that the
fountain was crowded—that multitudes surrounded it on
all sides, waiting each one his turn, and that many had
summoned the last remnant of their surviving forces to
carry them there, and had died, alas! on its very steps.
And yet *here* is an institution, as beneficent and life-
giving in its effects on our moral nature as were the
healing waters to the physical body, and it is passed by
with indifference, or contemptuously rejected; and the
golden streams, marked only by a slender belt of green
round their margin, waste themselves in the desert they
were intended to fertilize. Romanism has something to
answer for here, also, or Scripture is devoid of meaning.

I do not advocate a Judaical observance of the
Sunday; on the contrary, I reject it. I draw my
reasons for its observance from the New Testament, and
not the Old, and consider that 'The Sabbath was made
for man, and not man for the Sabbath.' I think it is
to be subordinate to the moral and physical wants and
condition of man. But all Christian nations are, I
think, agreed that the day should have a more or less
sacred character, and that the two characteristics of
repose and *religious worship* especially belong to it;
but Rome, giving way to, and drawing support by
ministering to, the pleasures of the world, has so
reduced these characteristics as to make them almost
wholly disappear.

I think that those who place the observance of the
Sunday on Judaical grounds—that is, on the grounds
disclosed in the Old Testament—do harm to the cause
of the due observance of the day. The arguments
drawn from that source seem, in my humble opinion, so
poor, and capable of such an easy refutation, as to prejudice the cause generally; and as it is an institution of such high value in every point of view, it is

desirable that its justification should be based on firm
and irrefragable foundations.

The minute and rigorous strictness of the Jewish rites
offends the spirit of Christian liberty, and is impracticable and impossible to carry out in the age we live in.
Why, therefore, encumber the ground and impede progress by an adherence to obsolete views intended for a
past age and for a peculiar people ? As a sharer in the
Christian dispensation I draw my reasons from the New
Testament—from the precepts and practice of Him
whose day we call it—from the usage of the early Christians, and from those moral and physical reasons in its
favour which are visible all around it.

To *impose* upon any one an ascetical pharisaical
observance is not justified by any Christian authority I
know of; but the two marks of repose and assembling
for religious worship where we are able, stand out distinct and indelible, must be accepted by every Christian
who examines into the subject, and are sufficient to
secure the great objects of the day.

As the Archbishop of Dublin, Dr. Whateley, says:—
'It should be observed as a day of religious worship,
mental repose, and bodily rest. This is not inconsistent
with some unpaid recreation, such as libraries in the
winter, and the fields and parks in summer. Is it not
delightful to see a father and his family taking their
recreation amid the glories of God's creation on a fine
summer evening? And let the services of the Church
be made attractive and faithfully performed, and they
will be duly attended, and the day will so be dedicated
to the service and glory of God, and to the service and
use of man.' And I quite coincide with these sentiments; and as there is ample argument to justify this
view of the matter, why hazard the existence of the
whole question in the minds of many by attempting to

carry it further on grounds which are easy to controvert, and which, even if they were admitted, could never be carried into practice.

As Paley concludes his argument on the subject:—
' The conclusion of the whole inquiry is this: the assembling upon the first day of the week for the purpose of public worship and religious instruction is a law of Christianity of Divine appointment; the resting on that day from our employments longer than we are detained from them by thus assembling is to Christians an ordinance of human institution, binding now upon the conscience of every individual in a country in which a weekly rest is established for the sake of the beneficial purposes which the public and regular observance of it promotes, and recommended by the resemblance it bears to what God was pleased to make a solemn part of the law which He delivered to the people of Israel, and by its subserviency to many of the same uses.'

But when I ask what part the priesthood in Britanny take to second the efforts of the French Government to secure a better observance of Sunday, and to promote the moral and religious interests of their people in this particular, I am obliged to answer that, so far as my experience goes, they take little or no part or action, and leave the people almost wholly to themselves.

And if enthusiastic Romanists point to the people of Britanny as presenting fit models for our imitation in the moral and social virtues, I feel bound to say, judging from what I have seen and heard, that, in proportion as we *avoid* following their example in those points to which I have specially alluded, will be our value and position as a people, and our happiness and well-being as individuals.

Britanny may answer as a *warning*, but should never be our guide.

CHAPTER VIII.

THE number of convents in Britanny is still great,
and must have been enormous. Everywhere you
see the venerable relics of these buildings, more pleasing in decay than when they were inhabited, for they
are generally well situated, and always picturesque.

The conventual rigour of other days is now much
relaxed. Nuns are not now built up in stone niches for
irregularities, as was Constance in 'Marmion,' but the
discipline is still severe, and restrictive measures are
still necessary to prevent the caged birds from seeking
the open air.

By law a nun may return to the world when she
likes; but what avails the law of the legislator?—the
law of the priest is stronger far; the chains which custom and education have forged are more powerful than
all others, and hence retreat is *practically* impossible.
Occasionally an escape takes place, always by stratagem
or force; but there is no instance, which I have heard
of, of a nun being allowed to pass the outer doors because she *wished* to do so.

Not long ago there was an instance of escape from a
nunnery not far from this place. The poor girl had
managed to convey to her brother intelligence that she

was miserable, but could not get out, and desired his aid. He presented himself at the convent, and requested to see his sister, and the interview was granted, but only on condition of the Superior being present. And so far from this being considered strict, there are many convents where interviews are wholly forbidden, and where even fathers are only allowed to meet their children at a grating, with a curtain between them, allowing nothing but *the voice* to communicate from one to the other.

And doubtless this is wisely judged for the interests of the convents; for nature is strong, and many fathers, even when cold enough to allow, or even to oblige, their daughters to take the veil, would, on seeing their emaciated despondent looks, be seized with remorse, and would retake them and replace them in their home.

The brother asked his sister if she was happy; she replied, ' Perfectly so.' ' But you look ill ? ' said he. ' I have not been well, but am now better. It is nothing.' He asked her if she wished to return, and she replied, 'Not for the world.' The brother was hurt by her constraint and puzzled by the apparent contradiction, and retired thinking he had been made a dupe of.

Soon, however, another note reached him, which explained all. She said, nothing could describe the treatment she had been subjected to, to prepare her for the interview with him. The threats of the confessor, the wiles of the Superior, all had been exhausted upon her, until, yielding, she had agreed to become their instrument, and unsay what she had before said. She now besought him not to abandon her, but not again to hazard an interview, for she mistrusted herself, and dared not again encounter the treatment she had just received. This time she asked him to frame a scheme for her escape, and confiding in him and his ability to help her, she would give him a week to prepare it; and on that day week, if he would walk under a particular part of the convent wall, a stone containing a roll of paper should be cast over, naming when she would be ready.

The brother was rather confounded, but he was certain that the handwriting was that of his sister, and he determined to act upon it. He therefore took his measures, and at the appointed time walked under the wall, where speedily a stone fell down before him. This had a note attached, stating that time pressed, that she would be ready in the garden at a certain spot at a given hour of the next evening, but beseeching him, for his soul's sake, not then to fail her, for that measures were taking against her by which she would be ruined both here and hereafter, if she remained a day beyond the time fixed by her. The brother accordingly prepared a rope ladder, and with two friends, on whom he could rely, reached the rendezvous.

It was a dark and gusty night—which favoured them, and enabled them to cast their ladder and ascend it unobserved. One remained on the outside, the other mounted the wall to observe. Nothing was visible—no living being appeared. The hour sounded heavily from the turret-clock, and no noise disturbed its echoes. Their anxiety increased : was her plan discovered ? was her ruin consummated ? Maddened by the thought, he was on the point of wildly rushing to the convent and frustrating all, when suddenly from a cellar-door on a level with the earth stole a figure which, on a near approach, he recognised as his sister.

She was saved! In a moment they place her on the

ladder and she commences the ascent, when, from long
pent-up emotion, the joy of success, the dread of re-
capture, she droops and faints, and falls heavily into her
brother's arms. He essays to mount the ladder with
her, but in vain ; the rope-steps are difficult to mount
when alone, but impossible with a burden. They support her, and endeavour to restore her ; her sleep seems
eternal. At length she moves, and breathes more
quickly; she is returning to herself. Oh ! the rapture
of that moment! She raises herself, and becoming
more alive to her critical position, and more able for
exertion, she again commences the ascent, and this time
with better success. Already she has gained a few feet
from the ground, when lights are seen rapidly moving
in the convent, voices are heard, an unusual agitation
prevails.

Her brother presses her, but again she fails, and is
unable either to advance, or return and make way for him,
else perhaps he may mount above her and drag her after
him. Nor can his companion on the other side help
them, as he holds the rope, and his slightest inattention would ruin all.

On a sudden the gate opening into the garden from
the convent is violently thrown back, and a crowd of
women, with two priests, rush confusedly out, searching
on all sides for the lost one, but blinded by the darkness, and as yet not perceiving her. The imminence of
the danger restores her, and she, by a supreme effort,
reaches the top of the wall. Just as this has been
effected the pursuers catch sight of her brother, and
with loud cries make for him. There is now nothing
for it but an inglorious skirmish with women. Yet what
alternative? They come on with loud cries, the priests
behind, but the two friends stand firm.

A stout nun rushes on to seize the ladder; in an instant she is thrown back. A second follows her example, and shares her fate; the rest halt and parley. The priests are mute, leaving the task to better tongues than their own; and the brother looks sharp about him. His sister has disappeared, and is doubtless safe on the other side. In a few minutes some one may be sent round to intercept her; no time is to be lost. He whispers to his companion, and the two, with an Indian yell, rush upon the parti-coloured crowd. The Superior, in her fear, turns round, stumbles over and falls upon the other two dark-coloured bundles of bombazine; other sisters shoot off wildly into the darkness; the priests are nowhere visible; *now is the time.*

Up the rope-ladder go the two friends like old foretop men, and before the scared sisterhood have recovered from their alarm, the ladder is drawn over, and all traces of the fugitive have disappeared.

Such was the end of the adventure, which was never brought before the tribunals, as there were incidental facts relating to it which would not bear the light; and to this day, doubtless, the brother recounts and laughs heartily at his 'skirmish with the nuns.' His sister never regretted her liberty regained, and soon made her return impossible by obtaining a legal protector, in whose attentions, I hope, she speedily forgot her troubles.

In Britanny, the reason which fills convents is oftentimes poverty, and not religion. A man has a large family of daughters: what *is* he to do with them? Marriage is less easy in France than in England—i. e. marriage without fortune; the home *ménage* claims less time, as it is so small; trade is distasteful, besides requiring money: what *is* he to do with them? The

convent offers itself; if he can only get them there, they
are provided for life—*there is an end* of them. Thus
reasons paternal love, tinctured with prudence, and
embittered with many cares.

His daughters, young, enthusiastic perchance, and
ignorant, who think that convents are the portals of
Heaven, and nuns ministering spirits temporarily incarnate, seize gladly upon the idea, press it home upon him,
and if they do not subdue his innate, heartfelt, but
secret objections, at least weaken them, and give him
an excuse for putting them aside. So after a few struggles the matter is decided upon, and the convent gates
enclose another victim.

I have no wish to libel convents; but, without pin-
ning my faith upon 'Maria Monk,' or other similar
stories, I do not at all doubt that gross abuses and
crimes often prevail here. Of this no man who has
considered and read upon the subject can have much
hesitation of belief; and, appealing to all who know
human nature, I ask whether it is not what we should
naturally expect? Why should the confessional be most
purified where most uncontrolled? and why should
priests be precisely the most virtuous where there is the
least restraint and the most temptation? And how can
human passions and feelings be excluded by stone walls
however high, and gates however strong? But I will
not pursue the subject: it is too disagreeable to dwell
upon.

I have often thought how sad must be the disappointment to some who enter. Failure in worldly prospects,
affections blighted, high hopes destroyed, the ravages of
death, distrust of self, fear of being struck down in the
battle of life—these and similar motives may impel an
intellectual woman to seek relief in the seclusion of a

convent; but how must they feel when their eyes open to its real character, the trifling nature of its avocations, the galling petty restraints, the dull routine of childish duties, the limited scope for benevolence, the ample room for the meaner feelings, and all this, to say nothing of anything above alluded to.   Yet pride forbids return; therefore they submit to. the stunting process, and see their powers weaken visibly, and neglect and put by those pursuits which they once enjoyed as being now too heavy and difficult for their reduced faculties. They spin, they work, they embroider, they sew, they become skilful in confectionery and sweetmeats dear to the priesthood, they make those curious little toys of various kinds which we know so well as 'made by the nuns;' but many of them must be long ere they can do all these things with content — ere they can subdue the thought that women have other duties in this world besides those of such a poor, trifling, mechanical sort.   I do not believe that there is a convent wall in Britanny that does not enclose an amount of human suffering as great as is contained in a hospital.   Nor is that suffering lessened, but rather increased, by the fact that it is mental, and not physical.

And all this is held forth as woman's 'mission'!

The ceremony of taking the veil is pervaded with a hollow mockery which has always prevented me feeling any interest in it.   The prevailing tone *given to it* is that of joy.   The act is viewed by a wretched sophistry as the act *of marriage,* and the young girl is to look forward to her union with the sisterhood as to her union with a husband.   Her raptures are excited and dwelt upon, her transports of pleasure depicted as if it was a real marriage, but what emptiness is in it!

I remember noticing that the priest in his sermon

after one ceremony of this sort which I witnessed, spoke throughout of the act as a *matrimonial* one, and it did seem to me that he had a sneer on his lips, and must have had in his heart, in thus describing it. For is it not the very reverse—does not the whole system go, or is it not presumed to go, upon an opposition to marriage?— and is it not a mere hollow mockery to allude to the subject at all?

There is always an awaking from the dreams of enthusiasm, and cold and dreary must that awaking be within the walls of a convent. Then the kisses with which the novice is greeted are somewhat misplaced— rather those of Judas than those of a bridegroom. In one order, that of the Carmelites, which is severe and stern, and views the thing as it really is, a coffin is placed on the floor, and the novice lies down in it to show that she is thenceforth dead to the world *and buried also.*

And *yet* all is so sweetly painted, the convent life is *so* calm, *so* sinless, *so* even—no vain desires there, no troubles, no strifes, no jealousies; as if sin and trouble existed only without, and not within, and as if by excluding the material part of it we avoided it altogether. This idea would reverse the true principle. It says that bad thoughts proceed from bad acts, and not bad acts from bad thoughts—that the hand moves the head, not the head the hand; and that, consequently, where you *do* no evil you will *think* none. It gives an easy remedy for curing the defects of our nature, and that a *physical* one: take the patient and put him between four walls—keep him out of harm's way, and he is cured. Perhaps, if we could search the secrets of a convent, we should find that where imagination roves unchecked, and more freely because perform-

ance is impossible, more unnatural combinations are produced, and a more thorough corruption, than when the act
and thought are more nearly in relation with each other.

But one thing we *do* know, and that is that the minor
passions and feelings are fully developed in the convent
life. For want of great objects, they exercise themselves
on small ones; and if they have no other subjects to discuss, they discuss each other. The system of espionage
is in full vigour; women of high spirit feel themselves
surrounded by an irresistible net of small meshes,
through which they cannot escape, and which gradually
closes upon them; tale-bearing is encouraged, in order
that the character of each may be known; and all the
small annoyances and incidents of a school life are re-
produced to the sexagenarian, without the freshness and
power of resistance which was once able to turn them
into fun.

When we arrive at a certain age we have a feeling of
independence natural to age, and it must be galling
to have to submit to the treatment of children. But to
this all must submit who enter a convent, where the
Superior is as absolute as the most arbitrary pedagogue
who ever flourished ferule, and probably often as unreasonable.

I remember going to a convent, to see a ceremony
there, when the ladies of my party were accosted in
English by a nun. She was an English lady, and re-
cognising in our group the signs of English people, her
heart, I dare say, warmed towards us. She was a lady-
like, agreeable woman, evidently well brought up. In
time the Superior joined us, and we all walked together
over the convent, though we could not help noticing the
change from warmth to coolness which came over our
countrywoman from the time the Superior joined us.

We parted; but, feeling an interest in the nun, we went again, hoping to see her. We did see her it is true, but she neither looked nor advanced towards us during the two hours we were there, although the Superior and other nuns came to us, and had much conversation; and I have no doubt but that, from fear of contamination, and in remembrance of home feelings, stirred up, perhaps, by contact with her countrymen, the poor nun had been *forbidden* again to speak to us. This must be galling discipline to grown people, not made visible at their first entry into this terrestrial Paradise.

For my part I never pass a convent without pity for its inmates, and a wish that such institutions were all forbidden by law; and, despite of Miss Sellon and her oily words, I trust that we shall always have something better to do with our 'daughters of England' than to place them there.

A very fertile subject of conversation among Breton Catholics is Ireland, and the unjust and cruel way in which Romanists are *assumed* to be treated there. To an Englishman who is acquainted with the state of religious liberty in the two countries, any comparison between them on that head is simply absurd; but the general ignorance in Britanny being such as it is, many Bretons are firmly persuaded that Irish Roman Catholics are only just suffered to exist, and are tortured and harassed in every imaginable way short of murder and absolute extinction. Even as to England, they have a general notion that Romanism is persecuted and under various disabilities; but as to Ireland — *bah! c'est horrible!*

And yet truth obliges us to say that there is a perfect religious equality between Romanists and Protestants in Ireland. As citizens, the law and the practice regards all of them equally, and protects the civil and religious rights of each in exactly the same way.   It is not improbable that some of *the Protestants* of Ireland might rather object to this assertion, and contend that *they* did not meet with the regard and attention which Romanists receive.   For instance, I have now before me the report of a meeting of Protestants at Belfast, held Sept. 19, 1862, and attended by 70,000 persons — a very monster meeting — of which the stated object was 'to give public expression to their sentiments as to the systematic partiality and injustice practised *towards the Protestants* of the country in the administration of the laws;' and at this meeting various speakers, members of Parliament and others, express publicly their opinion that Romanism is not merely treated justly and equally, but is, in fact, preferred and favoured in Ireland; and they are highly indignant thereat.   Still I believe the fact to be, that the law is as equal as is possible between the two religions.

We may then safely say, in upholding the principles of religious liberty in Britanny, as we have done, that 'our hands are clean,' and that the Breton priesthood have no shadow of a right to reproach us with preaching abroad what we do not practise at home.

It is true that the Irish Romanists are in a state of perpetual agitation, and I believe ever will be, because general orders from Rome forbid them to be quiet until they have the dominant rule there, and towards this they seem now to direct their efforts.   At first, years ago, they agitated for certain extensions of liberty and for toleration; then they consented to Catholic emancipation, with 'securities' for the safety of the Established Church: then they threw the securities overboard and claimed equality with Protestants in all things; and

now they are agitating for the last step, namely, pre-
dominance, and 'Ireland for the Irish.'

This is Rome's game—to get the result little by
little, and make one advance the stepping-stone to
another.

Happily, however, for us, having now done for her all
which justice can require, we can oppose her further
encroachments with a firm foot and a united action.
For myself, I have never regretted the Catholic Emancipation Act, as I consider it to have been a great
political act of justice, and one of Peel's noblest public
measures; and it is with a clear conscience that its
supporters may now oppose the further demands of
Rome for increased privileges.

I should like to hear what the Breton priesthood
would say to a proposal for opening a *Protestant*
Maynooth college *in Britanny*, supported by the State.
I believe the bare mention of it would almost cause a
revolution in the country, and yet they count the *Irish*
Maynooth as nothing. I would not abolish Maynooth
by any means, but I think Parliament has a right, which
it should exercise—to inspect its management and
details, and to see that the public funds are not
employed in teaching sedition and immorality, and in
encouraging rebellion.

But the ignorance which prevails in Britanny generally, as to the state of religion in England, passes belief.
I have been asked whether we had religious services
there—whether Protestants prayed and believed in a God,
—for many think that Protestant and Pagan are synony-
mous terms. They look at England generally, and
Lord Palmerston in particular, as general disturbers
of the peace; and if now and then they contract
intimate relations with individual Englishmen, it is

with a saving clause of hatred of the nation and Government. I have had it said to me a hundred times, ' I
like *you* well enough, but I detest your country and its
Government.' In everything hostile to France they see
England as the chief agent, and if a plague of locusts
coming *from the East* were to cover Britanny, I verily
believe they would say that England sent them.

Under such circumstances, an English missionary
has need of wary walking to avoid pitfalls, and when he
does fall into one he has little chance of being helped
out of it, by a Breton at least. The good Samaritans of
Britanny are for the most part one-eyed, and have
therefore naturally a blind side, to turn towards what
they don't want to see.

There is no subject on which I have heard Romanists
dissert more complacently than the unity of the Church
of Rome, and the disunion of Protestants. They love
to speak of Rome as *the rock*, one and indivisible, and
of the innumerable sects into which Protestants are
divided, and which, according to what they say, carry
on a perpetual internecine war. It is their favourite
cheval de bataille for great occasions. They speak of
the English Church, the French Church, the American
Church, and all Protestant dissenters, as mutually
hostile—tearing Christ's body asunder, and yet never
finding the spirit in it.

Yet, in my humble opinion, these bodies or denomina-
tions of Christians do not differ in fundamental points.
A few exceptions are to be found, as is natural, in a body
of eighty millions of free men, who allow free examination and judgement in religious matters as a first
principle ; but in the main all agree in the essential
principles of Christianity, which, happily for the mass
of mankind, are few and simple.

On secondary points — points of form and detail, differences may be expected as naturally as we expect differences of size or complexion among men; and they do but prove the variety and freedom of the human mind, and justify on natural grounds the religious liberty which Protestantism holds so dear. Such differences seem to me to be in highly favourable contrast with the external unity of Romanism, a unity produced by violent and unnatural compression, and which will cease to exist when the pressure is removed; for no person can destroy or paralize human thought — that subtle essence which refuses to be bound, and which cannot be extinguished. It is like sea sand, which *by pressure* can be forced to assume certain forms, but, when the pressure is removed, resumes all its individuality, and becomes angular and distinct as before.

But as to the vaunted unity of Rome, possible though it may be, *it does not exist* in reality, much as it is paraded before us. By the last article of the Council of Trent each Romanist is made to declare ' that he receives and professes all things declared by the sacred canons and general councils;' this is the base — *the very modern* base — of this *ancient* doctrine of the unity of the Romish Church.

Now, at first sight, this looks like unity, but let us see how it *works*.

In the first place, learned doctors are not agreed as to what general councils are included here. Gibert, a Romanist author of great weight, admits the '*uncertainty* of the western Œcumenical Councils;' Moreri ' grants the disagreement of authors in their enumeration.' There are, in fact, *three parties* on the subject in the very bosom of this *united* church. One party reckons the general councils at 18. A second party counts 18, but includes and rejects some which the other party does not. A third party omits a part of those general councils which intervened between the 8th and 16th general councils. And even the whole of them are omitted by Clement, Abrahams, and Pole, and a part even by the Council of Constance. Bellarmine adds 8 to the above 18, and as to the Council of Pisa he neither rejects nor adopts it. And Pope Leo rejected the canons of the 2nd general council, and Pope Gregory the Great declared that the Romish Church held neither to the acts nor canons of the Byzantine Councils! *And this is Unity!*

With this 'confusion more confounded,' how is it *possible* to believe all things professed by the councils, when the validity of the councils themselves is still undecided, and is the subject of lively discussion from time to time? It is simply impossible.

Then, again, where is the 'unity' as to the exact position and power of the Pope? If there is unity, why do the Gallican and Ultra-Montane parties disagree upon this vital question, and carry on their 'war to the knife' about it?

Then, as to the infallibility of the Church, there are four different parties, who hold four different doctrines upon it. One places infallibility in the Roman Pontiff, another in a general council, another in a council held by a Pope, and another in the Church generally. Where is unity in all this chaos?—who can speak with authority in this Babel of opposing opinions? And yet forsooth there is *Unity*. 'We believe in the *Unity* of the Church.' All cry. Unity! Unity! as the bird of spring cries cuckoo! cuckoo! and thereupon all his congeners utter the same note in a way wonderful to hear.

And remember that these differences of opinion are on an essential point of doctrine, and occur in a church which professes to be united *par excellence,* and to allow no differences of opinion. Unity is the keystone of the main arch in the Great Roman Temple. What must become of the edifice when it is withdrawn ?

But one thing is almost certain, and that is, that in spite of all pression and compression—in spite of conclaves and councils, of popes and creeds—the more enlightened Romanists of the present day admit the defect in question, and would strive to remedy it. They see the inevitable decadence of their Church, unless she keeps pace with the progress of the age ; they see the state of those countries in which bigotry and the Romish system have had full sway, such as Spain and Italy and Rome itself, and with ardour they would reform that Church to which they are still attached. But alas! the difficulties are insuperable. '*Vestigia nulla retrorsum.*' Bowed down and bound by that heavy chain of Infallibility, change is destruction, and these choice spirits must ever follow the beaten path of their predecessors— see with shame and regret what they cannot alter, and die nominally within the pale of a Church one of whose leading dogmas they disbelieve and reject — the *pioneers,* and, alas! the victims, of religious progress, opposed by a so-called infallible system.

Yes! the Council of Trent set the seal to the destruction of the Romish Church, when it issued its so-called death-blow to Luther. Those learned doctors were, after all, but blind moles.

So that the evil and its cure come from the same source, though the latter comes involuntarily. As says *Gioberti,* the most eloquent and enlightened of modern Romanist writers, speaking of the causes of the decay

of the Romish system, which he deeply deplores —
'What is the cause of this state of things? It is because the Romish Church is behind the age in all
things, and the evil comes *from Rome.*' Mark these
words, 'the evil comes *from Rome*,' and that which *he*
calls the evil, *we* call the cure.

In all this are to be seen signs of the end.

A little incident occurred in the department of Finistère in Britanny, in the spring of this year (1862),
which shows the close watch kept upon Protestantism
in those parts.

As I have already stated, the Scriptures are distributed in Britanny by *colporteurs*, and of late the distribution has increased in a way to gladden the hearts
of those engaged in the work.

At the meeting of the Protestant Society at Morlaix,
in February 1862, this encouraging fact was stated by
one of the speakers, and his remarks were afterwards
inserted in the *Bulletin Évangélique*. This soon fell
under the notice of one of the many lynx-eyed priests
who abound in Britanny, and who immediately began
to pull some of those numerous but unseen wires which
connect the Romish Church with the State in France ;
and with good result, as will appear by the sequel.

The colporteur going on his usual avocations, was
stopped suddenly at Quimperlè by the *gendarmes*, and
conducted by them before the brigadier there, and also
before the *Sous-Préfet*. They ransacked his bag, and
examined his license and all his papers, but all were *en
règle* and no flaw was to be discovered there. So they
fell back on their power, and ordered him to cease distributing any more Bibles, 'by order of the Préfet,'
and sent his papers, &c., up to Quimper for further
examination.

The poor man was meanwhile to wait at Quimperlè, which he did during many days with great patience, and he might have waited till Doomsday, for Rome delights in a waiting game; but a friend advised him to see the *Préfet* himself, which he resolved to do, and went to Quimper for the purpose. But it is one thing to wish to see this great orb of the provincial system, and another to get actual sight of him. However, the colporteur stuck to his man like a leech, and made daily calls at the *Préfecture*, and representations were made by other parties on the subject, and the *Préfet* was made to understand that the Protestants of the country would not allow God's word to be Burked in this manner. So after divers goings and comings for upwards of a week, and much communication and consultation between the *Préfecture* and the bishop's palace and the Jesuit seminary at Quimper, and an occasional telegram from Paris from the *Ministre des Cultes*, the order was sent to the colporteur *to continue his work* if he chose. And thus the end of this opposition was to give greater freedom than before, and to cast discouragement on the enemies of the work.

This little incident proves three things — the active watchfulness of the priestly party in Britanny, their influence with the local authorities, and the present favourable disposition of the Imperial Government towards Protestantism.

Doubtless, on the fact of the increased circulation of the Scriptures reaching the ears of the priestly party, they immediately acted on the *Préfet* and other provincial powers with the usual exclamations, ' *Qual infamia! qual picardia!* ' &c. The *Préfet* and his counsellors at once gave way to the pressure, and stopped the work, and hoped the matter might end

there; but when Protestantism showed fight, and refused to be put down in such a summary way, it was
necessary to refer to the Government at Paris, and then
the increased liberality of feeling of the Government on
religious subjects came into play. It is probable the
Préfet was reprimanded for yielding so readily to the
priests, and he was left to reconcile matters with them
as he best could. As to the priests, they had to eat
their leek, *malgré bongré*, and could only console themselves by dreaming of the 'good time coming,' lately
foreshadowed by that thorough-paced old soldier of
Rome, the Archbishop of Toulouse, in his discourse on
the anniversary of the massacre of 4,000 Protestants in
that city in 1562, as to which see post page 222, *et seq.*

CHAPTER IX.

AS I have before said, and now repeat, let all wait
and hope. Already signs of returning day are
visible here and there, though as yet the light only
gilds the loftiest peaks; still there *is* light, and ere
long there is reason to believe that it will be more
generally diffused; and though it may be years before
the valleys are penetrated by it, yet we may be certain
that that happy time will eventually arrive.

As I have stated more than once in this work, I fully
believe that the Emperor sympathises in many points
with Protestants; and if his natural tendencies were
unrestrained, I am disposed to think that there would
be a more practical carrying out of the right at present
existing in the constitution merely as a phrase and a
theory, i. e. the right of Protestantism, as a separate
form of religion, to equal protection from the State.

I will add upon this point a fact which I do not think
has yet been given to the English public, but which I
believe is nevertheless strictly true. This fact, added
to others of the same kind, shows plainly, to my mind
at least, the real sentiments of the Emperor towards
French Protestants, and in my opinion they would act
more wisely were they to address themselves directly to

him for relief, instead of, as is often the case, abusing and suspecting him.

The circumstance occurred in the tour he took as Prince Président, and a short time before his election as Emperor.

In that tour he visited Nismes, on the 30th September, and after his arrival he had a reception, at which all the authorities, civil, military, and ecclesiastic, made their obeisance. Among them were the representatives of the Protestant churches in the department of the *Gard*, forming a deputation of eighty-three pastors, all in their gowns, and headed by the Rev. M. Tachard, President of the Consistory of Nismes, who was to present an address to the President on the general state of Protestantism in those parts.

The Jesuit party knew all this, and determined that the address should not be read if possible; and they are clever sappers and miners. At the moment M. Tachard approached the Prince, address in hand, an officer of the *Préfet* whispered in his ear, 'There is no time now for the address, nor should any be presented — pass on.' The time and place were not favourable for discussion — etiquette reigns in courts — and after a few rapid words of congratulation to the Prince on his arrival among them, the deputation filed on and passed away.

The Jesuit party was full of joy; their plans had succeeded, and they had put by the address cleverly; but their triumph was short, as we shall soon see.

The Prince, seeing the long file of pastors, looked surprised, then suddenly rising, he addressed himself to one of them who was in the act of passing, and asked him if he came from *Montauban*? From this question, it is probable that they had given the Prince to

believe that he had before him the Protestant representatives of the whole South of France, instead of, as
was the case, of one department only.   The pastor
addressed had his wits about him, and replied, 'No,
Prince; you have before you eighty-three pastors from
one single department, that of the *Gard*, representing
400,000 Protestants; and had the opportunity been
allowed them, they would have assured your Highness
that their fervent prayers and best wishes were offered
for you.'   'And who has prevented them?' said the
Prince.   'They told our President,' replied the pastor,
' that you were pressed for time, and he did not persist,
as he wished to consult your convenience.'   'I said nothing of the kind,' the Prince said; 'and I will see that we
meet again,' and so bowed them on, and they passed out.

In the evening, a grand banquet, at which all the
chief people were present, was given at the Hôtel de
Ville.   The Pastor President, M. Tachard, was far
away from the Prince, at the other end of the table.
The Prince was observed to look about, along the faces
before him, until his eyes rested on M. Tachard, and he
evidently recognised him.

After dinner, and when in the drawing-room, the
Prince approached him, drew him aside, and expressed
his regret at the misunderstanding of the morning.
The pastor replied, that happily the remedy was easy,
for he had his address in his pocket, and if the Prince
wished he would now present it to him.   The Prince
thanked him, took the address from his hand, and read
it with attention.   'He did not skip a word,' said the
pastor, who followed his eyes carefully.   At length the
Prince returned the address, and said, 'I sympathise
cordially with such sentiments.   I am in favour of
religious liberty, and I will maintain it.'   'Then,' said

the pastor, taking heart from the Prince's friendly manner, 'since you have so graciously allowed me this interview, allow me to add that I have confidential matters to communicate to you, and that I should regard it as a great favour to be honoured with an hour's audience to-morrow morning.' 'It will be difficult,' said Louis Napoleon; 'cannot you at once tell me what you want to say?' 'Not easily, Monseigneur, we might be overheard; besides, a long conversation at this moment might be wrongly interpreted.' 'Very well,' said the Prince, ' come to-morrow at eight o'clock;' and so terminated the interview, on which a thousand conjectures had already been hazarded by the lookers on, Jesuits and others.

However, according to the official programme, the whole of the morning was already occupied with one thing or other. Among the number was the laying the first stone of a Roman Catholic church. The Prince had the Préfet called before him. 'We must change the programme, Monsieur le Préfet: I shall not have time to lay the first stone of the church; the fact is, at that time I have an appointment with the *Président du Consistoire* of Nismes.'

The Préfet, who was devoted to the priest party (because it was the strongest), was in consternation. He remonstrated, and even begged the Prince to reflect, but in vain, and had to retire and change the programme, and put off the laying the first stone of the Romanist church until a later hour.

At eight o'clock, exactly, we may be sure, M. Tachard arrived, and was received by an aide-de-camp, who said gaily to him, 'The Prince is waiting for you;' and on the reception-door being opened, the Prince advanced to meet him, offered him a chair, and sat down by him.

During a full hour the Prince and the pastor remained in confidential conversation. The details of
what passed on this occasion will probably never be
known. The pastor said to one who inquired of him,
'No one but our Creator and ourselves will ever know
it completely.' He, however, communicated to one
friend, that, among other things, he said this to the
Prince: — 'The Protestants of the south were always
'the friends of the Emperor your uncle, for he was the
'friend of religious liberty; and they will be your friends,
'Monseigneur, if you also show yourself the friend of
'their liberty, and of their religious rights. The Pro-
'testants are easily satisfied on these points, but to
'deprive them of these would be like taking away from
'them what they consider their birthright.'

'Tell your friends,' replied the Prince, 'that they
'have nothing to fear from me in this respect; and if
'ever you are troubled or molested in the exercise of
'your religious rights, let me know, and address your-
'selves *directly* to me.'

This very remarkable interview and conversation is
worth recording, and it shows, I think, that the Emperor is friendly to Protestants and their principles, if
left to himself. But he has many and great difficulties
to contend with, and many great interests to reconcile;
and allowance should be made for him, if he does not
always act towards Protestantism as we should wish
him. He is in theory an absolute monarch, but he is
by no means able to do as he likes in all things; and
we should not overlook the difficulties of his position,
nor be so hasty in judging him as many people are.

In Britanny the friends of the cause are more cheerful, and see signs of advance in many things, small in
themselves, perhaps, but making together an appre-

ciable quantity. The department of Finistère, which, until within the last three or four years, was wholly closed and sealed up against the Gospel—for God's word in the *Breton* tongue had been during many years refused circulation there, — is opened in some degree, as the Bible is now allowed to be colported there, under certain conditions.

More liberty of speech and preaching has also been allowed to Protestants, and controversies have been tolerated which years back would have been summarily stopped.

Grants have been made by the administration towards a new chapel at Brest, to assist which, by donations, a collection has been set on foot, to which friends of the cause may most usefully contribute; and in general a more favourable, or at any rate a less unfavourable influence seems to prevail among the authorities, all of which is, of course, the result of orders from head-quarters, for nothing of that kind springs up naturally in France.

Then a Protestant minister, M. Vermeil, has been appointed at Rennes, and a chapel opened; and at Lorient there is a probability of a chapel being soon built. All these are visible signs of the progress of the Bible in Britanny.

When we look beneath the surface, also, there are various proofs that the leaven is working. Some of the little facts I have given, as to accidentally falling upon traces of a spontaneous vegetation of Protestantism here and there, are, I doubt not, types of a very large class, which more extended research would discover; so that, on the whole, and when we consider the naturally slow nature of the work, its friends have, I think, reason to thank God, and take courage.

I have always thought, and often said to friends in Britanny, that when the Emperor felt himself firm in the saddle he would give the priests a touch of the curb— enough, at least, to make them feel that they had their master behind them; and I believe that that touch is now being administered, and that the priests are chafed by it. Hitherto they have been on the sunny side of the hill, but it seems probable that they will soon feel some of that north wind which has blown so long and so blightingly on Protestants. But their in- fluence on the mass of the people is such that to oppose them requires forces of all kinds; and there is little doubt that if the priestly party were to exert all their power against the government, even Louis Napoleon would find his match. He is therefore obliged to act with the greatest caution.

As to his caring much for the religious value of either Romanism or Protestantism, I fear he does not think seriously about it, for he is not a religious man; but still, judging by the opinions expressed by him in his various printed works and elsewhere, I do believe that he has more sympathy with the latter than with the former. A man of his intelligence and liberality of mind cannot possibly, one would think, sympathise with the party that would, if it had the power, repress every effort of the human intellect that agreed not with the dogmas of their Church; and that would reduce the various intellectual forces to one dead level, to be judged of by celibate and often ignorant priests.

The interview and conversation with the President du Consistoire of Nismes, given previously by me in this work, is very interesting in this point of view, and confirms what I now say.

I am told, too, by Breton friends, that the Italian

question, as it is called, has reacted strongly in Britanny. The Pope and the Emperor are at variance, as is visible to all men, and the state of affairs is *tendu* to the highest degree; and Britanny being the very focus of the Papal power in France, the priests and the Legitimist party are in a hot and agitated state, and plot and talk treason, and act in such a way as to call for the anxious attention of the Government. The Emperor checks them, and looks around for friends, and *there* are the Protestants, loyal and tranquil, as they have always been; so he encourages them a little to keep them in good humour, and the effect of all this is to produce a certain warmth in the atmosphere which has not been felt for many years.

One of the consequences is, that the distribution of the Scriptures in the last year has been greatly increased, in fact, I think it is now equal to what it was in 1848; for it is a remarkable fact, and shows what the Bretons would do if left to themselves, that in the year of the Republic, when the priests and authorities dared not harass and bind up the people as before, the sale of the Scriptures was trebled as compared with the preceding twelve months.

All that Protestantism wants in Britanny is, a ' free stage and no favour ;' all that it asks for is, that practical equality of religious rights, which the French constitution *in theory* already affords.

If we look abroad into France generally, there are many signs showing that religion is in a state of effervescence and transition. Notwithstanding the sad fact that the men of France in general are (I regret to state my opinion, and yet it is but the opinion of Frenchmen themselves) of no real religious belief whatever—practical infidels in religion ; yet at this moment religious

questions are much more mooted than formerly, and
religious discussion is gradually becoming ' *à l'ordre du
jour.*' As an eminent French writer, M. St. Hilaire,
says : — ' Il y a toujours eu de la piété en France, et
cette piété a toujours fait fausse route.' There seems
a considerable probability that many Frenchmen will
no longer be content with the travesty of religion
which the priests perform for them, and that in this
age of free examination they will exert that freedom
which is denied to them in political matters, and will
examine *religion* and judge for themselves.

France has never been without religious instincts at
any period of her history—from Clovis to the Crusades,
from the Crusades to St. Bartholomew, from thence to
the Concordat, and from thence even to the Revolution,
when, having deposed the true God from his earthly
throne, they set up another—the goddess of reason—in
his place, and had their grand fêtes for the acknowledged
worship of *L'Être Suprême.* Perhaps she is now feeling
sated with having so long fed on that which satisfies not,
and her soul craves after nourishment more solid and
enduring—something more than pleasure and the mere
material well-being in this life ; and asks for something
to believe, and sighs for something beyond what she can
see and touch.

Romanism will never give this to her — *for it has it
not to give.* Besides which, France knows the system
too well already — has seen it· at work, and felt its
falseness and emptiness; and has a horror and contempt
for priestcraft.

France, too, sees what Romanism has done for other
nations — Spain and Italy for instance, and what Protestantism has done for England and America. These
are patent facts, which force themselves into view.

But if religious wants really exist which Romanism cannot satisfy—if the present system must be changed, there is only one change practicable, and that is towards a free examination of the Bible and its doctrines, and the adoption of a Protestant Christianity. *There* is a rock on which to build something stable; all else is but quicksand and mirage of the desert.

Great events are looming in the far horizon, and already visible, though only as little clouds. But progress is rapid in our days. Italy has made a giant's step towards civil liberty, and only waits to make another to acquire it fully. And shall religious liberty be left behind? When Rome has become the capital of Italy—an event now, I fully believe, near at hand, in spite of human combinations, however artfully contrived — where will be the Papacy?

And if Italy, throwing aside the chains of ages, should stand erect in the pride of freedom, and demand a free conscience in religion as in politics—should reassert her ancient dignity and preeminence, and boldly protest against Romanism—I think the shock would be spread as by electricity, and would overthrow the rotten scaffolding which supports Romanism in France, and breathe a new vitality into millions there whose hearts now seem as dead as the blanched bones in the valley seen of the Prophet.

Let no friends of the good cause then despair of its success in Britanny or in France, but let them pray, hope, and wait.

CHAPTER X.

ALAS! for the state of religious liberty in France! In the teeth of Article 5 of the Constitution, that 'each is to profess his religion with the same liberty, 'and obtain for his worship the same protection,' the Protestant does *not* profess his religion with the same liberty, nor is the protection given to his religion *equal* with that given to the Romanist.

Cases are continually occurring to show the truth of what I assert, and from time to time as they happened and were fresh in the mind, I have been in the habit of noting them down, and making remarks on them ; and such facts and remarks I will proceed to give to my readers, that they may judge for themselves whether equal protection is actually given, by the French law *and* its *practice*, to Romanism and to Protestantism, or not.

I only give a few cases, but I could have multiplied them tenfold if required, as unhappily there is a frequent supply of them ; but it would only fatigue my readers, and they can equally come to a judgement on the subject from a few clear cases as from many.

A very important and striking instance of the manner in which Protestantism is treated in France is afforded in the case of *Fresnoy le Grand*, in the department of the *Aisne*.

When men talk of toleration, and of equal religious rights being secured by laws, they often forget that to ensure the real execution of these laws there must be a sound state of public opinion among the people. We can no more produce liberality of feeling by Act of Parliament, than we can produce electricity: it is to substitute the cause for the effect. Practically to carry out and guarantee equal religious rights requires a high state of civilisation in a nation, and unless that condition exists, the possession of the *principle* is a mere mockery. The state of France is a proof of this. As we all know, the constitutions which have been showered down upon France so liberally during the last seventy years have all in words admitted the *principle* of the equality of religions ; and, as we all may know, such bare admissions have led to small results. The spirit of the people, despite all its real indifference and scepticism, remains Roman Catholic and exclusive, more so in a political, perhaps, than a religious sense : and to all intents and purposes Protestantism is persecuted and oppressed as much as she is in Italy or Austria, with the sole difference of a little more outward decency in the form. These remarks are so common, and are so frequently called forth by passing events, that we may as well stereotype them at once for future use, to save ink and paper ; but they furnish a powerful comment upon the spirit of Romanism. As in Tuscany, proselytism by Protestants was a crime, so in France it is a moral misdemeanor, which the authorities never fail to discountenance when it is brought before them.

Look, for instance, at the case of *Fresnoy le Grand.* For two years a Protestant service was regularly performed there by a minister delegated by the Consistory of St. Quentin. There being no chapel, the schoolhouse was used as the most convenient place for the worship, and all went on well until a decree was issued by the Préfet, stating that a numerous meeting having been held in the schoolroom at Fresnoy le Grand, and before the door of the school-room, 'with the *apparent object* 'of hearing religious reading and preaching, and such a 'meeting beiug likely to affect the public peace, it was 'necessary to forbid all religious meetings in the said 'commune, except in places set apart legally for wor-'ship.'

Just observe the quiet tyrannical insolence of this decree, 'with the *apparent* object,' &c., and 'affect the public peace,' &c., and the saving clause at the end, 'except in places set apart legally,' which seems so right and proper until the fact is known that the said school-room was *the only* place where worship *could* be celebrated, that there was *no other* 'legal' place; and that consequently when *it* was closed up, there remained *no means whatever* of Protestant worship for the people at Fresnoy.

Upon this decree appearing the President of the Consistory at St. Quentin informed the Préfet that a chapel was building at Fresnoy to receive the increasing congregation, and that the use of the schoolroom was merely provisional, and requesting that it might still be permitted for a short time, until the chapel was completed. But the worthy functionary was not so to be caught. He immediately changed his ground, and took an objection which would apply to schoolroom and chapel too; and in so doing we know not which to admire the most, the boldness or the skill of the Préfet. For it requires no slight courage to deny *a fact*. But Rome does not use this arrow with faltering hands.

It has often been her system, and boldness is often successful.

The objection of the Préfet was that there were *no Protestants* in the commune — nothing less! How surprised many of the Protestant inhabitants must have been to see one fine morning their very being destroyed by the Préfet. No Protestants in the commune! Well! an enquiry was made and duly proceeded with before the *Juge de Paix*, and it resulted that no less than forty-one heads of families, representing say nearly two hundred persons, professed themselves Protestants, and asked for the establishment of the Protestant worship at Fresnoy.

This enquiry was conducted in the following manner : It was carried on for eight days, the *Tamborier*, or crier, going round each morning to announce the commencement, and desiring all parties interested to attend ; and at same time a notice was posted requesting all who felt the want of a Protestant chapel at Fresnoy, *to sign their names* at the Mairie. Many of the poor people, though Protestants at heart, doubtless remained at home with some vague fear that in signing their names to such a declaration they might be signing their death warrant, or at least might expose themselves to trouble or persecution. Such a signature was equivalent to a profession of Protestantism, and in a Roman Catholic country, like France, the public profession of Protestantism, for the first time, is a step of serious import, certain to induce temporal loss. No better means, therefore, could have been devised for damping the zeal of the incipient converts, and diminishing the number of signatures.

Suppose, for instance, in a town in Protestant England, a movement in favour of Romanism was suspected,

and notably among the poor, and that a public notice
was given that on a certain day all persons wishing to
establish a Romanist chapel should attend at the Town-
hall and sign their names, in the presence of the
magistrates, the rector, the directors of the poor,
and the administrators of the different charities by
which the poor are in part supported — all such func-
tionaries being Protestant, and therefore naturally averse
from the movement.   Think you that many would
attend ? I trow not. Think you not, also, that various
influences would be brought to bear upon many, so as
induce them to stay away ?   Yea ! verily.

However in spite of all obstacles, moral and physical,
forty-one heads of families, representing some two hundred individuals, *did* appear, and signed their names
boldly and regardless of consequences; and the answers
of some of these men are worthy of record.   One is
asked, ' Since when were you Protestant ? '   ' Since
I learnt to know Him who died upon the cross for my
sins.' ' And your children ? ' ' I have five daughters
— they are also Protestants, and we read the Bible
together every day.'   Another is asked, ' Are you Protestant ? ' ' Not yet — because to become a Protestant
it is not sufficient to change nominally, but we must
also change our lives ; and this I hope soon to accomplish.'   All this has the ring of true metal.

How blind is man, and how, after all his puny efforts,
he does but work *for* God, even when thinking to work
against Him ; for the effect of this enquiry at Fresnoy
has been excellent.   All who have signed have, as it
were, thrown away the scabbard, and now stand committed publicly to the cause of Protestantism, and are
doubly occupied in strengthening themselves and their
brethren also.

The Préfet's desire for information was now gratified. He wanted to know if there were really Protestants in the commune — the enquiry showed that there were; and here is his cool unblushing letter to the President of the Consistory : —

'Laon, 22 Sept. 1852.

'Sir,—I have received with the documents accompanying it, your letter of the 12th inst., as to the exercise of the reformed religion at Fresnoy.

'I maintain in all points the terms of my dispatch of the 5th inst., and I shall not rescind the prohibition to hold religious meetings at Fresnoy, until I shall be *convinced* that there really exist *Protestants* in that place, and that you shall have addressed to me a petition signed by your coreligionists.

'Enclosed is the letter you have addressed to the *Ministre des Cultes*, and which I beg to decline forwarding to him. If you send it to him, I shall inform him of the motives of the decree which you attack.

Receive, &c.,
(Signed) ' DE BEAUMONT.'

In reply, the President forwarded to the Préfet a declaration, signed by upwards of forty heads of families at Fresnoy, and stated that as his enquiry was now so satisfactorily disposed of, he hoped there would be no further obstacles to the assembling together of the Protestants as formerly. And what objection could there be in reality, had the Préfet ever intended honestly? He wishes to know if there were really any Protestants at Fresnoy ; he finds as a fact, proved in the manner he had himself laid down, that there are certainly from one hundred and fifty to two hundred. There should properly, therefore, have been an end to the affair.

Doubtless the Préfet and his priestly friends were in a corner, but they were *not asleep* or to be caught. A bright thought, darting up at a white heat from below, penetrates him. 'Protestants perchance, but *soi-disant*; calling themselves so, paid to do it probably; but are they so in fact, are they *sincere and good* men? That is the question. I must have true men, men "in buckram," nothing else will do for me. My name is *Didymus*. I am not content with the outside; I can see farther into a stone wall than most men, I must look *within* these Protestants. I regard as nothing the present enquiry—the *Juge de Paix* was a blockhead; I will have another enquiry, and it shall (out of deference for the individuals concerned) be a *private* one.'

So enquiry No. 2 is commenced, though not with beat of drum as was the first. This is carried on with closed doors: no one knows how, for the parties concerned *were never summoned to attend.* The people were dispirited, there would be no end to these enquiries. Next they would enquire the color of their eyes — or if their physical walk was as upright as their moral, or if their noses were Roman or Grecian, or snub or cogitative, or what not?

However the enquiry was made, and most probably the priests furnished the information needed; though, as the proceedings were carried on secretly, it is impossible to say. Little matters it more or less who were the informants, for it is not now a question of fact but one of opinion, and opinions are diverse even as to the best men; as may be seen plainly when, not long ago, a worthy man in a London municipal council — a Mr. Beaton — expressed his opinion that the Duke of Wellington *deserved nothing* from his country.

This was the cleverness of the Préfet—he had first

joined issue upon a *fact*—i.e., whether or not there were Protestants at Fresnoy—and had been beaten. Now he takes warning, and joins issue upon an *opinion*—viz., whether they are sincere; and, with Romish priests and their allies for witnesses and jurymen, who can doubt the verdict? But let the great official speak for himself—in his letter to the President of the Protestant Consistory of St. Quentin, announcing his foregone conclusion:

'Laon, Oct. 12, 1852.

'Sir,—In consequence of my decision of the 1st 'August last, you addressed to me, on the 23rd Sep-'tember, a petition, signed by certain inhabitants of 'Fresnoy le Grand, *calling themselves* Protestants, 'desiring to be allowed to meet in a place assigned, in 'order to perform their devotions.

'The conversation which I had the honour of having 'with you some time since, would doubtless make 'you see how much I respected the great principle 'of religious liberty guaranteed by our laws! [What a face of *œs triplex* must this excellent creature have been endowed with, gravely to enunciate these good sentiments, and yet act as he was doing! How he must have slyly chuckled at the wretched glozing jugglery!]

'I should, therefore, have been altogether disposed 'to recall my decision, and authorise prayer meetings, '&c., at Fresnoy, if it had been *proved* to me that the 'individuals who claimed them were *real* Protestants, or 'that their desire to enter into the reformed Church was 'sincere, and agreed with the regularity of their lives, 'their morality, and their conduct.

'But the results of the enquiry which I have made '[the *secret* one] gives me the proofs that the persons

'in question are not animated by any religious senti-
'ments, and that they only attend the meetings as a
'means of agitation, as a way of arranging together
'in view of certain possible future circumstances.

'Among the signers of the petition there is, in fact,
'only one Protestant—as to the others, they declare for
'the most part that they are not Protestants, but at the
'same time they demand a place for religious worship;
'and those who call themselves members of the reformed
'Church declare that they shall leave their children and
'their wives to follow freely whatever religion they may
'prefer. [Pity but that the Préfet would have imitated
'their tolerant spirit.]

'Is it, therefore, to be allowed, Monsieur le Pasteur,
'to believe in such declarations—to trust in the sincerity
'and good faith of those who make them, when, above
'all, in examining into their morality, one is forced to
'acknowledge that those who call themselves, or who
'wish to become, your converts, are generally men
'without morality or conduct, whose reputation is bad
'in all points, who practise no religion, and who in times
'of peril are only remarkable by the radicalism of their
'political ideas and their democratic principles?'

A word upon this paragraph, so full of calumny and
insult.

Is it likely, think you, that the Consistory of St.
Quentin—a body of Protestants acting under responsibility—would have licensed a pastor to a congregation
so composed?—that they would have brought down such
a scandal upon their cause, as to embrace within their
circle only men 'without morality or conduct, whose
reputation is bad in all points?'

But they 'practise no religion,' says the Préfet.

Gently, if you please — they do not practise the *Romanist* religion — *hinc illæ lachrymæ* — but they *do* practise the reformed religion, to which end they wish for a convenient building. It is the very gist of the matter, the practising of the Protestant religion. We may, therefore, dismiss this charge also.

But, 'in times of peril they are only remarked by the radicalism of their political *ideas* and their democratic *principles.*' Well, at least, they have only *talked* — there have been no overt acts; ideas and principles break no bones, and in the present gagged state of France, when words are counted and reported, those who only talk may have the credit of sincerity if their talk be *against* the usurpation which presses down all things with its iron foot.

Protestantism is the religion of freedom, hence the hatred which is borne towards it by priests and despots; and it is quite natural that the same feeling of independent judgement which leads a man to change his religion, may make him canvass the immoral or arbitrary acts of those in power. A man made free by the truth, freed from the shackles of a false religion, is naturally led to endeavour, according to his power and opportunity, to loosen the chains of his suffering fellow men, and hence the exclamations and complaints of those whose living is gained, first by the forging of these same chains, and afterwards by rivetting and keeping them in good order.

And if, among the two hundred converts, were to be found some who had seen the error of their ways, and had reformed their lives — who, from being men of vice, had become thoughtful and virtuous — their former manner of life, so far from being a reproach, should have been a praise to them. It is not the righteous, but sinners, whom the Gospel calls to repentance.

M

But all this would be Greek to the Préfet. Conversion, with him, would mean a mere changing sides
by well-dressed people, as in a dance: or, to come
more home to himself, as in politics; for we may safely
aver that Monsieur *Le Vicomte Beaumont de Vassy,*
Préfet, &c., of the *Aisne,* was a staunch friend and
supporter of Louis Philippe five short years before the
date of his decree, and, in order to become a Napoleonic
Préfet, had changed his coat, and perhaps his waistcoat
also, and would, if necessary, have changed his skin if
it would have come off easily. *Such* conversions, he
would say, are laudable, are *à la mode*; but they are
luxuries, and *poor* sinners must remain as they are, and
not think of changing in anything.

But to return to the Préfetorial despatch, which now
adopts the paternal style and gives advice gratis, and all,
too, *so disinterested*—coming from a Romanist!

'Is it not wiser, sir — would not the interests of all
' religions, as well as those of society and of individuals,
' be better provided for, in leaving the persons in whom
'(with so praiseworthy a zeal) you have interested
' yourself, to return to the religion of their fathers,
' which they have often in their lives had the benefit
' of? I therefore have reason to believe, sir, that you
' will appreciate the motives which make me persist in
' my decision of the 1st August last. Receive, sir, the
' assurance of my distinguished consideration,' &c., &c.

Is not this a precious letter?—does it not merit pre-
servation in amber or other embalming process? 'T is
worth many pounds of Egyptian gum. With the Préfet,
proselytes, converts, men *disposed* to change their
religion, have no place; the world is either Catholic or
Protestant, and the intervening space must be passed
over in a hurry, at a skip, or not passed at all. Doubts

and fears, half-formed convictions, dread of the future, family troubles, distrust of individual judgement,—all the conflicting feelings which press upon and rend the heart of a person meditating a change of religion,—these are unknown to the unimaginative mind of the Préfet of the *Aisne*, and have none of his sympathies. With him we must 'gain remote conclusions at a jump,' or not gain them at all; we must acquire our new colour by a single stroke of the brush. And who can refrain smiling at the kind *naïve* suggestion he makes in conclusion, whether, *all things considered*, it would not be better to leave things as they were?

I believe that the charges he makes against the converts are as false as they are infamous and *ex parte*; and the chief result, up to the present time, has been that the poor people, in return for the scandal against them, have increased their aid to the chapel now building at Fresnoy; and so their zeal will be quickened, and not extinguished, by the temporary check. We shall soon see what pitfalls are in reserve for them when the chapel shall be ready; and, meanwhile, let us trust that One, who is above all, will send them a good deliverance.*

* Since writing the above, the chapel has been opened. Let us hope it may be allowed to remain open.

CHAPTER XI.

AT the moment when all this was passing at Fresnoy, equally great infractions of the principle of religious liberty were taking place in a neighbouring department—that of the *Aube*,—showing how Protestantism is everywhere beleaguered and oppressed.

In 'Britanny and the Bible,' page 72, I allude to *Estissac*, and the opening there, and I speak of the good promise for the future shown by the inhabitants of that town. But short-lived are human hopes! The Priests and Levites had doubtless their eyes upon Estissac at the very moment of my writing, and were devising plans to blight the harvest there at the time I was calculating its value in the sheaf.

Those who have read my previous work may remember that the inhabitants of Estissac had obtained the services of a Protestant minister delegated by the Consistory of *Meaux*, and that upwards of seven hundred were declared Protestants. A local Consistory had been appointed, a chapel and a school were in progress; and the flame kindled at Estissac, as a centre, was beginning to illumine other neighbouring places, when, on June 13, it was suddenly extinguished.

On that day, in the middle of Divine service, the Maire of Estissac and several gendarmes entered, and ordered the minister to descend from his pulpit, by virtue of an *arrêté* of the Préfet, authorising them to '*finir sur le champ cette précherie.*' In vain M. Recordon, the minister, remonstrated and begged permission, at any rate, to finish the service which was commenced; no heed was paid to the supplications either of him or of his congregation, but all were turned out of the room, and the doors were locked upon them.

Measures were immediately taken to remedy this flagrant abuse of power, and a deputation of influential Protestants waited upon the *Ministre des Cultes* at Paris, to lay the case before him and procure redress. He seemed disposed to blame the Préfet, and gave a certain degree of hope to the members who waited upon him. However, the process went on, and on the 17th of August the minister who had performed the service, the Rev. M. Recordon, was cited to appear before the Tribunal of Troyes, 'for having presided at a religious meeting at Estissac, without having obtained the authorisation of the Government.'

The Procureur Imperial supported the prosecution, by every species of abuse and insinuation. He stated that before M. Recordon came to Troyes there were no Protestants in the commune, that those who had since been converted had so acted from other than religious motives, and especially that they had acted from political ones; that, not being allowed to assemble in clubs, they attained the same object in the chapel meetings; that their Protestantism was only a cloak; that, in any case, and for whatever object, they had no right to meet at all, save by the previous authorisation of the

Government or its police, inasmuch as all meetings were, since the decree of March 25, 1852, placed on the same footing, and subjected to the authority of the police.

In vain the advocate of the pastor stated and proved, that the meetings were purely and simply religious, and that the public tranquillity had never been troubled ; that the Consistory had long ago formally notified to the authorities of the place their intention to hold these meetings, and had met with no refusal or difficulty during the preceding twelve months; that religious liberty was destroyed if placed henceforth under the care of the police.   In vain did he invoke the declarations of the Prince President on the subject of religious liberty, — but the decision was, probably, previously come to, and the eloquence of an archangel could not have changed it. Behold parts of the judgement — and henceforth let no one talk of religious liberty as existing in France.

‘ *Attendu* that the constitution under which we live, and the other constitutions which have governed France since 1789, have established in principle the *liberté des cultes*, but that the exercise of this liberty has always been subordinate to the measures of order and of police directed by law.

‘That if past legislation has been floating and uncertain on the subject, the decree of July 28, 1848, as to clubs, has profoundly modified the law in this regard, and that the articles of the code penal are applicable to all meetings, whatever be their object.

‘ *Attendu* that the terms of the decree of March 25, 1852, are general and absolute, and that where the law does not distinguish the judges cannot distinguish.

'Determined by these motives, the court declares
M. Recordon guilty, &c., and punishes him by a fine
and costs.'

We may, therefore, chant the requiem of religious
liberty in France. It only exists by the good pleasure
of the police—any one of whom can, like Cromwell,
turn the preacher out of the pulpit and the flock out of
the church, and lock the doors.

'*Finis coronat opus*'—this is the finishing touch.
For long time has the circle been diminishing, but
now it exists no more. First the Bible was prohibited, not openly and frankly, but by stealth—was
included indirectly in a law in which the word Bible
never occurred, and of which the application to the
Bible never was intended; then colportage was re-
strained and made difficult—the books must all be
stamped by a special stamp, or were liable to seizure;
then strangers were forbidden to preach in France;
and then, as the *coup de grâce*, religious meetings are
treated as political clubs, and are placed under the
direction of the police, and to be dispersed by the
undistinguishing baton of that epidemic functionary.

And yet France is '*la grande nation*,' highly civilised, highly enlightened, philosophic, and what not:
with a constitution guaranteeing *equal religious rights*
to each one of her thirty-six millions of population!
And Frenchmen of moderate opinions are so indifferent,
or so blind, or so cowardly, as to submit to this retro-
grade legislation and jurisprudence, without seeing that
they are becoming a very bye-word and laughing-stock to
the rest of Europe. Persecute and oppress, burn, slay,
torture, and destroy if you will, you are acting at least
openly and avowedly,—but this saying one thing and
doing another, this perpetually acted falsehood, broods

over us like a huge nightmare; and let Governors take heed lest the sufferer in his efforts to free himself from the burden which stifles and presses him down, overturn all around him in one common confusion.

Some pieces were produced at the trial showing how the French police poke and pry into everything. Ever since the meetings were commenced at Estissac these gentlemen seem to have been in high activity, and to have matured and deposited their daily egg in the shape of a report to the superior authorities; who in their turn display as much activity and alertness as henwives when eggs are dear.

For instance, M. Recordon little thought that he was honoured with such notices as the following, when he was quietly and earnestly devoting himself to his pastoral duties. They are extracted from a police report made to the Sous-Préfet on the subject, and the writer seems to enter fully into the enquiring spirit of his masters:—

'Sunday, the 15th June, a pastor of the reformed religion, M. Recordon, *made an irruption on the commune*, and developed his *subversive principles*, which were received enthusiastically by a populace not enlightened but fanatic. The brigade of gendarmes was placed in readiness. The judicial authorities had their eyes open, [this must have been borrowed from the poet's description of Justice as ' never sleeping,'] and any crimes would have been immediately punished. [No doubt — but there *were* none.] It was chiefly before a lot of lads, with great pomp — scarfs displayed—one national guardsman as a *piquet d'honneur* —that they installed the Protestant pastor, and a sermon was dealt out with emphasis. It has since been printed, and it is curious to read the mistakes, and the lies, historical and others, which swarm in it from one end to the other.'

Many passages follow of a like tenour, and then comes a little paragraph showing how the police look after *politics* also, and keep an eye always to the main chance ; for if the republic comes again they know where *they* will be sent to.

' There were only forty-two votes against the Government candidate at Estissac. Therefore we may conclude that the number of the agitators diminishes, and that Estissac asks for nothing better than to return to the way of order. But to arrive at that end it is necessary *wholly to destroy the dissenters.*'

What a pity this man was, as it were, thrown away at paltry Estissac — at Madrid he would have been first *familiar* in the Inquisition. But good masters make good servants, and those above him kept him well to his work, we may rely upon it. And so the report goes on, all being of the same tissue, to the last word.

It is cheering to find that the Protestants at Estissac were not cast down by these difficulties. On the contrary, they redoubled their efforts. The chapel is progressing rapidly, and the poor men work at it voluntarily and gratis, so great is their zeal in the cause. They all express their determination to remain firm and to persevere in their profession of Protestantism, and give whatever money they can spare to the building fund. The other day there was a *fête des Bonnetiers*, or capmakers, and, as is usual, a collection was made among the persons in that trade for the purpose of a dance, &c., in the evening. When the money was brought in, amounting to upwards of twenty francs, an old man got up and said, ' My friends what is the use of spending this money in cakes and

nonsense, when the chapel is in want of it. *I* vote we
give it to the chapel, what say *you* ? ' And young and
old with one accord agreed with him, and the money was
handed over accordingly. This is a fact worth a thousand
arguments, and may be placed against the got-up report
of the police that there were no real Protestants, but
only a few lads, &c., attracted by novelty and love of fun.

But it is well to give the authorities rope enough —
and they will hang themselves. In a short time the
temple will be built, and, *if allowed* to be opened, we
shall see it filled by a numerous congregation ; and in
proportion will be the failure and defeat of those who
have backed their cause by such falsehood. They will
be forced to admit either that their agents were wrongly
informed or incapable, or else that the endeavours
made to deprive Estissac of a Protestant worship, have
only served to increase the Protestant body there in
a most remarkable manner. Let us, therefore, wait
patiently, and all will yet be well.

At Trouville, near to Havre, occurred a further
instance of the intolerance and partiality of the authorities towards poor Protestantism. I almost fear to
tire my readers, and were I to record all the instances
of oppression to Protestants I should certainly tire
them sufficiently, but I do wish to show them the way
in which the principle of religious liberty, *guaranteed
by the constitution*, is systematically violated in France,
and to prepare them for those times in which Romanism,
again become rampant as it was three hundred years
since, shall undertake a fresh crusade against Protestantism. All tends towards that consummation as
naturally as a stone falls to the earth, and we may
yet see, in an age philosophic and enlightened as we

deem it, wars undertaken and carried on from religious zeal, and in which the fierceness of national rivalities will be outdone by the excesses of a ferocity sanctioned from the altar. Who that has heard of the excesses of the French revolution of 1790, and since then of the revolutions of our own day—of the wholesale butchery of Naples and in Italy — who will dare to say that human nature has got rid of and left behind the evil passions which formerly disfigured her ?

And to be forewarned should be to be forearmed!

It appears that Trouville was becoming a watering place, much frequented, and upwards of one hundred and fifty Protestants, chiefly persons of a certain social position, having met there during the summer, a desire was expressed to have a place of worship. A Protestant resident there accordingly commenced a chapel, which was to have been opened in September. Suddenly, however, (for these things are not notified beforehand to the parties interested, in a way consistent with a civilised or *civil* jurisprudence,) a decree was issued by the Maire of Trouville forbidding all worship in the new chapel. This, of course, caused great consternation and discussion, as the preparations were rapidly going on. The decree, having been posted up on the chapel door, was rendered illegible by the heavy rain, and the intended pastor of the new chapel applied to the Maire for a fresh copy, which was politely refused, as were all explanations, for there is safety in silence.

However, the chapel being completed, the congregation determined to open it for worship if possible ; and accordingly, the day being fixed, a week's notice of it was given to the Maire.

The Maire replied that he had decided to prevent it, and that in case of any meeting for the purpose, he

would disperse it—if necessary, by force, under Articles
2 and 29 of the Penal Code. It was therefore useless
to persist in addressing the Maire, and steps were taken
to represent the matter to the Préfet of Calvados, in
which department Trouville is situated.

The Préfet was charmingly polite—I should say
dangerously so, for there is always something suspicious
in such treatment—'latet anguis in herbâ,' and declared
that, as far as he was concerned, he would not for the
world prevent the Protestants of Trouville from following
their religious opinions as they chose; only that it was impossible that he could allow the service in the chapel
already built, because the builder and proprietor had been
pointed out to the police as a man of dangerous character.

The deputation in vain produced certificates of the
good life and manners of the individual in question;
the Préfet continued firm. But in what did his bad
character consist? Let it be stated—although really
immaterial, let it be stated. And, accordingly, the
cat was quietly let out, and it seemed that the worthy
M. Grelley, the proprietor of the chapel, had been
selling Bibles and New Testaments! This was the
gravamen, and the minds of the deputation were much
relieved on hearing it. But, though their hearts rose,
their hopes fell; for, in truth, it had been better for
their cause that M. Grelley had been a burglar.

In vain they argued the matter; the Préfet, with an
attractive blandness, repeated that he was very sorry,
exceedingly sorry; that anywhere else they were at full
liberty, but that in the chapel built by M. Grelley should
no worship take place; and they were bowed out. This
is a cruel mockery, is it not? 'Anywhere else you
please, but not there;' that is to say, you build a house
and spend all your money in doing so, and then are

smilingly told that you must not live *there*, though you are quite welcome to build another—to be met, perhaps, by the same objection as to the second habitation, if you are wealthy and resolute enough to build a second.

The Consistory of Caen, after having in vain attempted to get the polite Préfet to change this decree of the Medes and Persians, finally determined to commence another edifice—the Protestants of Trouville meanwhile losing their time, and M. Grelley losing his money. In the interim, religious services are held in a private room in the Rue St. Honore, as best they can.

This is the way in which Protestantism is played with, as cats play with mice, to amuse the leisure and gratify the whims of dainty Romanist officials. Is it wonderful that Englishmen detest the tribe? With us, we have the pleasure of service in return for our money, or at least we have the inward relief and outward pleasure of a healthy grumbling, a copious discharge of spleen on the head of the offender in a letter to the *Times* or the board of directors; but in France you must bottle and cork down your wrath, regardless of internal injury thereby. Oh! John, John! you little know, when you dilate to Mrs. Bull upon the insolence and tyranny of English Jacks-in-office, what are the freaks of the said Jacks across the channel. Would to Heaven you had the rule and ordering of them for a year or two, and I will engage that under your rough towelling they would soon be as polished as are Master John, junior's, cheeks on Saturday night!

And this is the state in which religious liberty—we will not say exists, but lingers and is starved in France! To what causes is this retrogression owing? Mere indifference, a general feeling of scepticism, would, we should imagine, end in a general contempt and a general

permission of all kinds of worship—there must, therefore, be other causes than these.

One cause, undoubtedly, is the increased vigor of late
displayed by Romanism, not in consequence of any
renewal of zeal generally on the part of its professors,
but in consequence of the good fellowship existing until
lately between it and the present Government.   Louis
Napoleon, despite all the boasting and fanfaronade of
his sycophants, has had much ado to get into and keep
his seat, and has had to bid high and on all sides for
support.   And who so powerful as the priesthood ?   At
their bidding thrones rise and fall, if not so quickly, yet
as surely as of old; and their hold upon a large portion
of the ignorant and unenlightened peasantry of France
is as firm as ever.   Not that I feel any doubt that Louis
Napoleon will not soon endeavour to get rid of them,
but meanwhile they must be kept in hope and good
temper.   Hence the treatment of Protestantism by men
in high places, to some of whom it is most agreeable so
to act.   For they are all Romanists nominally; and, like
those who ' compound for sins they are inclined to by
damning what they have no mind to,' these men make
up for their neglect of outward observances by thump-
ing on the backs of plain John and Martin.   This pays
off a grudge, and quits the score to the priest at the
same time.

Then all Frenchmen in office have a mortal fear of
and antipathy to independence of any kind, and Protestantism is and has ever been of a sturdy disposition—
another reason for punishing its professors when occasion
serves. And all these causes, and others, bring about the
fact that religious liberty in France seems of late
years to have endured one long death struggle.

Certain it is that, in a Catholic country, the ground

won in the cause must always be kept by force; if its
possessors sleep, the enemy comes upon them immediately, for liberty is death to the spirit of Romanism—
there is a mortal feud between them, ever existing, and
impossible to be reconciled. Therefore, in such a state,
the aspect of things will be perpetually changing as one
or other gains the ascendant, and there will not be a
steady progress, rising gradually from one height to
another, until the summit is gained.

There are principles of which the conquest is very
difficult, owing to the nature of the human mind; and
religious liberty is one of them. We think we have
gained it—it is accepted, invoked even by those who
opposed it, a reconciliation is effected, peace is signed,—
it passes into the institutions of the nation and forms
part of its laws. The strife ceases, the victors lay down
their arms, some become slothful, others die and disappear, thinking that the goal has been reached and won.
Vain hope! Events progress, ideas alter, circumstances
change. The vanquished take courage, raise their heads
at first furtively and in secret, by degrees with courage,
and reappear boldly on the scene—the strife recom-
mences, and the former victors, surprised and dis-
armed, for a while hang their heads in despondency.

Such has happened in France with the principle of
religious liberty. The constitution of 1848 seemed to
assure for ever the triumph of this sacred principle.
Even Catholic writers enrolled themselves as its de-
fenders, and wrote eloquently on its side; to hear them
you might imagine that Rome was the great parent of
liberty. Since then we might imagine that half a century had rolled back upon us, so much have ideas and
institutions changed. Where is now the eloquence expended by Catholics so short a time back? Alas! with the

change they have changed too, with that unprincipled
facility with which Rome knows so well to turn about
with the wind. That which legislation granted, legislation withdraws. The preventive system takes the place
of liberality, and the ancient strife begins with a new
ardour. The Catholic press becomes as intolerant as it
was timid. It now defends what it once attacked, and
attacks what it once defended, with an *aplomb* and
assurance astonishing even to the initiated. It despises
logic and argument, and writes with the insolence and
the inconclusiveness of successful tyranny. It argues, or
rather asserts, that it is just and right that the Romanists
should be free in England, and the Protestants oppressed
in Italy—that Victoria violates every principle of right
in forbidding religious processions in the streets of London; and that the Duke of Tuscany does his duty in
imprisoning the *Madiai* for reading the Bible. It
boldly speaks of fire and faggot, of crusades and inqui-
sitions, of heretics and martyrs, and shows clearly to all
who choose to see, that if Romanism again reigns, she
will rule, as before, with a bloody rule, and will leave no
other alternative to Protestantism than recantation or
martyrdom. These signs are open, to be read by all;
and let all read them and take warning in time.

One human hope remains for Protestants, and that
is that Napoleon III., who is so devotedly attached to
Napoleon I., and who endeavours in all things to follow
out his principles, may remember the course he held as
to religious liberty. I always think with pleasure of the
excellent reply Napoleon I. made to the Protestant deputation from Geneva, and it is worthy of record here:—

'I see with pleasure here assembled the pastors of the
'reformed churches of France, and I take this oppor-
'tunity of testifying how well I am satisfied with all I

' have heard of the fidelity and good conduct of Pro-
' testant pastors and their flocks. I wish all to know
' that it is my intention to maintain religious liberty.
' The empire of the law finishes where that of conscience
' begins; neither law nor prince can do ought against
' this liberty. Such are my principles and those of the
' nation; and should any of my race who may succeed
' me forget the oath which I have taken; and, deceived
' by the inspiration of a false conscience, violate it, I
' devote him to public censure, and I authorise you to
' give him the name of *Nero.*'

May Napoleon III. never merit this name of Nero;
but should he merit it, we do but follow the great
Napoleon's commands in giving it to him. Let him
beware, lest the Shade of his uncle baptise him with that
name of doom. It would be worse than the poisoned
shirt of Nessus, and would enfold his memory for ever.

As I am on this subject, I will give other specimens
of the manner in which Protestantism has been treated
in France in our day. It will remind us of the
state of things in the time of Cromwell, as described
in Scott's 'Woodstock,' when the churches were invaded either by the stern Puritans to turn out the
Royalist preacher, or by the roystering Cavaliers, to
turn out the 'crop-eared Roundheads;' and ere long,
perhaps, it may remind us of the scenes in 'Old Mor-
tality,' for French Protestants *may* again be obliged to
worship God among the rocks or in the desert, with
sentinels to announce the approach of the troopers..

Not that Napoleon III. would under any circumstances allow this; but were the Legitimists, i.e. the
branche aînée of the 'beloved Bourbons,' to return to
power, I should certainly look out for it, as a very
probable result. As it is, it is rather from subordinate

than high authorities that such acts proceed; and they,
with encroaching ecclesiastics ever at their back, are
the constant enemies Protestants have to contend with.

At St. Michel, in the department of the Basses Alpes,
a M. Verum was accustomed to preach and perform religious service for the few Protestants of the commune.
On Sunday morning, Feb. 22, just before the hour of
service, he was ordered to attend at the *Mairie.* There
he found the *maire,* who said to him, ' It is time to
put an end to this schism in the commune, and I will
not allow any more meetings,' and then read to him
the order of the general officer commanding in the
district. This order was dated the 17th of the month,
but the *maire,* to enhance his triumph and give it all
possible *éclat,* had kept it in his pocket until the 22nd,
the Sunday; when he sent for him just before the
service, in manner already mentioned, and then ex-
ploded upon him as a bomb-shell in a magazine, which
would doubtless make him of sweet savour in the
nostrils of the priesthood. The order of the General is
short and pithy. No reasoning—for the sword is a
cutting and not a reasoning instrument — all is sharp-
edged, and with a point. As follows: — ' Seeing that
' the presence of Mr. Verum in St. Michel is inconvenient
' for public order and tranquillity, and that he is not a
' resident there, we order him to be expelled from the
' department of the Basses Alpes.'

In vain M. Verum showed that he was and had been
for years resident at St. Michel, and to prove it produced his receipts for householders' rates and taxes
there, his elector's card, and other papers; in vain he
showed that the meetings were simply meetings for
religious worship; the General was as hard and inflexible
as his sword—his word was as the law of the Medes and

Persians. At length, irritated by the persistence of 'this stupid M. Verum,' who being innocent, and having means to prove it, would not take a denial, or keep his mouth shut, he actually ordered him to prison, whither the worthy man was immediately taken and kept for weeks, the exasperated hero having meanwhile cooled down, and (there being many other fish to fry at that time) having probably forgotten him. He was afterwards delivered over to a military commission, and removed to another prison 500 miles away, and I never could find out what then became of him ; and all this abominable cruelty and injustice was committed simply because M. Verum was faithfully preaching the Gospel at St. Michel, and was so unpolite and ill-bred as to persist in staying there after he had been told to 'go away.'

I will give yet another case illustrative of the mild way in which military rule settles difficulties, i.e. crushes them by its iron-shod foot. I am wrong in saying 'settles' difficulties; happily that result will come in spite of all efforts to prevent it; meanwhile doubts are resolved by the sabre, or blown into the air by the cannon, in a summary way.

In the department of the *Yonne,* is a commune, or parish, called by the singular name of St. Maurice *des riches hommes,* or ' of the rich men.' In this commune, according to the census of the year, there was a Protestant population of 233 persons, and as a natural consequence, a Protestant school was established there. Now this school was an unpleasant thorn in the sides of the ever-watchful priests, who love not education; and besides, the education given was so superior to that afforded in the Romanist schools, as to be a standing reflection and reproof on them. By hook or by crook,

therefore, the school must be suppressed. But how? there's the rub. Yet to a clever mind the 'how' speedily follows when the 'why' has been settled; and as the department of the Yonne was under military *régime* at that time, the only thing requisite was to gain the ear of the officer in command. This was soon done, and apparently well done, and speedily appeared the following 'order of the day':—'The Lieutenant-
' Colonel of the 1st Regiment of Lancers, commanding
' in the Yonne, Considering that the commune of St.
' Maurice des Riches Hommes contains *no Protestants*,
' and that a school of any given form of religion is only
' allowed in order to supply the wants of the professors
' of that form of religion, and that, consequently, such a
' school is in this case useless — considering that the
' establishment of a Protestant school at St. Maurice des
' Riches Hommes has been brought about simply with
' the intention of stirring up disunion in families by the
' different systems offered for the education of children
' —and considering that it is urgent to remedy this state
' of things—*We decree*, that the school in question be
' immediately closed. Signed, *A. de Cheffontaine,*
' Colonel 1st Lancers.'

This is a fine specimen of Rome's manner — her *modus operandi.* 'T is a 'real native.' 'Get money— *honestly if you can—but get money.*' The school of this St. Maurice of the Rich Men is a hard bit, difficult to cut up according to rule, and tough to digest. Its management is excellent, its books unexceptionable, its teachers irreproachable, it has n't a smack or whiff of Socialism about it. We need not attack it on those points, for we shan't have a leg to stand upon. But, say the priests (we may imagine), 'So much the worse for us; there it stands staring us out of counte-

nance, shaming us by its better system, and driving us
mad with vexation; and there it shall not stand much
longer, please the Pope and *Nôtre Dame*, if the wit of
man can move it.' Yet 'how?' that's the question.
At length a quiet-looking priest may be supposed to
rise and ask, 'Are you certain, *as a fact*, that there *are*
Protestants at St. Maurice?' 'Certain!' replies another, 'I wish I was n't; there are unhappily only too
many of them.' 'But how do you *know* that? Is it
that other people tell you so, for personally you probably *know* none of them? Now hearsay is no proof;
and for myself I can most conscientiously say, speaking
according to my own knowledge, and according to law,
that there are *no Protestants* at St. Michel.' Well,
some laugh and think it a joke; some think it nonsense, and trifling with valuable time; until an elderly
priest rises. 'My friends, our brother Theophile is
quite right, and his view is the one to act upon, and
let us only get the Colonel-Commandant to adopt it,
and down will go the Protestant school.' *Ah— h—h!*
breathe out some, and others whisper, and then talk
aloud: and the end is, that a representation is made to
the Colonel, who knows no more of the locality than
the man in the moon, and out comes the 'order of the
day,' and away vanishes into thin air the Protestant
scholastic establishment at St. Maurice of the Rich Men
—*for a season.*

Altogether it is the most flagrant instance (out of a
large number), of overbearing tyranny and disregard for
truth I have yet met with. The *naïf* and very simple
Colonel must have had a strange idea of Protestants,
must he not, when he stated that *their only object* in
opening their school was to 'stir up disunion in families?' Sad and bad fellows must be these followers of

Luther and Calvin, not to be content with stirring up
family discord by ordinary means, *but to set up a school
to do it.* 'T is such a cumbrous way of doing things!
Like going from Bristol to London *viâ* Edinburgh, or
leaving your card on a friend's drawing-room table by
means of the chimney instead of the hall-door. But
Rome was always given to devious and crooked paths.

I will not waste more words on this most arbitrary
and unblushing act, and so leave it to my readers.

French Protestants seem to me to have lost much of
the nerve and vigour they once had. In 1520, with small
numbers, they controlled princes and ministers, and
confronted the most powerful monarch of the time
without shrinking. In France, in 1862, there are upwards of 2,000,000 Protestants, and yet, from want
of union and combination, from apathy, fear, or indifference, or something, they lie down quietly before the
Government, and give but few signs of life or vigorous
resistance. Like Shakspeare's Jew, 'when pinched
they feel, when pricked they bleed, as other men,' but
they suffer in silence, instead of remonstrating manfully,
and complaining openly and boldly. In the present
state of parties in France, it seems to me that their
force might be so applied as to be of great value, and
so as almost to *compel* the attention of the Government
to their wants; but these advantages are lost for want
of union and organisation. And therefore it happens,
that upwards of 2,000,000 of men, comprising a
great portion of the intellect, riches, and power of the
country, are grievously neglected; persecuted by the
reigning Church, and barely acknowledged by the State.
Here and there a solitary newspaper, little read, and
emanating from isolated individuals, lifts up its feeble
voice and cries in the desert; or a dwarfed periodical

struggles into existence, supplying to its readers a few religious stories, and a small trifle in the way of news; but the Protestant press generally, speaks as through a muzzle, with a muffled, half-audible voice, instead of proclaiming to Europe, as with a trumpet-sound, the state in which religious liberty now lies bleeding and torn; and discussing boldly, and in a manner suited to the age, the various questions affecting their common interests.

O'Connell, when he represented the Roman Catholics of England and Ireland, made a much better use of his position than this; and after a series of bold contests with the law, succeeded in forcing upon an unwilling people, and an opposing King and legislature, the great act of Catholic Emancipation, the first roots of which were laid in a soil and climate as inauspicious as has ever existed towards Protestantism in France; and he did this by combination, boldness, perseverance, and a firm reliance on the justice of his cause.

A strong proof of the want of organisation among French Protestants may be found in the almost total absence of Protestants in the legislative bodies. This has long been the case. After the revolution of 1848, there were only two or three Protestant members at most, and these — *M. Coquerel,* for instance — very poor representatives of the Protestantism of France. The Senate, it is true, is nominated by the Government, but by proper efforts it is probable that more Protestants might have appeared there. A short time ago, among the 150 members of the Senate, there was just *one* Protestant and no more, and yet, according to comparative number of population, there should have been ten. And in the Corps Legislatif, elected under universal suffrage, there were among the 260 members only three or four Protestants instead of, say twenty-five. Thus Protestantism, as a party, is almost wholly unrepresented in the French Legislature, and it is not therefore so astonishing to see her badly treated by the law. As far as the making of laws is concerned, the opponents of Protestantism have the field almost wholly to themselves, for the opposition of such a ghost of a minority would be a farce. Better, indeed, to be wholly left out of Parliament than be mocked with such a shadow of representation as this, which gives you the name and denies you the substance.

But it only adds to the list of proofs of the infantine state of France in political *practical* knowledge. As a people, they have little idea of improving the constitution by constitutional means.

In England, if a law is generally obnoxious, the means of attacking it are not long wanting. But we attack it constitutionally. We do not set the world in arms because bachelors must still pay the double tax on hair-powder, or because the duty on nutmegs is unrepealed, but we go to work, quietly and surely, at the fountain head. *We grumble,* first singly, and then in chorus; unite, speak, discuss, and petition. We fill the public papers with reports of meetings and speeches which would make Pym blush and 'orator' Hunt go mad with envy; and the said meetings being noisy but determined, and the speeches being logical, but well seasoned with facts and figures, the public mind at last rubs its eyes and wakes up, gets well hold of the subject, and grows animated and lively. By and by petitions pour into Parliament; casual motions by eccentric members of the independent class are made and come to grief; are renewed, and fare better; the project grows into shape and form; until finally some rising or falling minister, in want of a good stalking-horse, adopts and mounts the long-debated measure, rides it triumphantly, by its help upsets and turns out his less far-seeing opponent; and finally the once bespattered and wriggling embryo becomes the full-grown and venerated law of the land. And this is all as it should be.

But in France they adopt another course. They talk and grumble everlastingly, but in private; and all public complaint is stopped by the remark, that the matter in question is part of the existing public law, and must not be attacked, for 't is dangerous to attack *any* law. So the nuisance goes on, and all the festering and the anguish too, and, the ill-humours wanting a vent, all goes on and nothing goes off; and so a heap of similar abuses and nuisances is accumulated, each standing in each other's way, and blocking up the only safe road of retreat, until fermentation commences and increases rapidly, and one fine morning the world is awoke by the cry of 'Fire!' and lo, another revolution in Paris! But a poor proof all this, methinks, of the wisdom and good sense of *La Grande Nation*, as France loves to call itself.

And if we may judge by recent events, experience has not taught the French people much in this respect; for it seems to me that they are again on the high road to events identical in principle with those they have so severely blamed when under the influence of repentance and matutinal headache. The perpetual motion of philosophers would seem to be morally realised in our own days, in the perpetual change of French public opinion. There is no known form of government which has not been successively execrated, sought for, adopted, welcomed, abused, and thrown aside in France during the last seventy years; no principle of morality which has not been successively upheld as the best and

scouted as the worst; and scarcely a Frenchman who
has passed his tenth lustrum who has not testified by
his repeated changes of opinion to the unsoundness of
his own political judgement.

I myself know personally scores of men who previous
to the *coup d'état* were decided opponents, *on principle*,
as they would say, to anyone who should be so rash as to
attempt to revive monarchy in any shape ; but who,
now it has succeeded, are as decidedly in favour of
Napoleon III. One gentleman in particular, before the
coup d'état, was positively savage in his denunciation
of anyone who should attempt any such violation of
the constitution, but especially loud against Louis Napoleon, on the ground that he was a *Corsican* and not
a Frenchman. He said France would rise as one man
against him if he dared attempt it; and he, for one,
would oppose him to the death. Well, the *Corsican*
made his attempt, and not by mild means either, and
made a clean sweep of law and gospel when they tried
to stop him on his way. Soon afterwards I saw my
friend, and found he had become an ardent Bonapartist;
and I rather maliciously said to him, that I supposed
France would with one voice protest against the usurpation of a *stranger.* ' A stranger, *mon cher* ! how so?'
' Why you know Napoleon is a *Corsican*, and not a
Frenchman.' ' Oh! but are you not aware that Corsica
is now part of France, having been incorporated since
1793?' &c. &c.; and my friend had apparently no
greater recollection of his previous expressions and
sentiments than if he had uttered them in a past state
of existence.

This sort of thing offers an enormous premium to
usurpation, and so usurpers have become *an institution*
in France.

CHAPTER XII.

INTOLERANCE TOWARDS PROTESTANTISM IN FRANCE — BURIAL IN
'DOG'S CORNER' OF CEMETERY — FUMIGATION OF GROUND AFTER
PROTESTANT BURIAL — CUGAUD — ESTISSAC AGAIN — CASE IN THE
VAR — PROTESTANTISM ALWAYS 'IMMORALLY' PROPAGATED —
ROMANIST PROCESSIONS — AT MORLAIX — INCREASING OF LATE,
THOUGH ILLEGAL.

THE intolerance of tolerant France certainly passes
all belief, and may serve to convince us more
firmly of the impossibility of a *Roman Catholic* republic. It is a political contradiction. We laugh at
our sires for their search after centaurs and mermaids,
but the junction of Romanism with liberty would be a
far greater *lusus naturæ* than that of a man with a
horse or a woman with a fish. Constitution-mongers
and manufacturers may grind and regrind, insert, erase,
and discuss with becoming gravity; but despite their
learned but practically absurd notions, the human
machine pursues its way. A Roman Catholic republic
will never work, we may be certain. How can it? Equal
civil and religious rights and popery and exclusive salvation! *given* to reconcile these — *q. e. d.* — a hard nut
for logicians to crack. If you doubt it, look at France
from 1848 to 1852. In theory, and according to the
legal constitution, all religions were to be on the same
level — in practice — and according to law *de facto,*
Romanism alone existed, and Protestantism was nowhere.

You can hardly take up a paper without seeing proofs
of this. For instance, look at what passed at Cugaud,
in La Vendee. A Protestant gentleman having died

there, his friends wished him to be buried by a Protestant minister, and applied to Mons. Vaurigaud, the pasteur of Nantes, for the purpose. He went over, and applied to the *maire* of the place, and he, after having concerted with the priest, gave permission for the interment. But where and how? In the corner of the cemetery allotted for executed *criminals* and *suicides*, and with the condition that the pastor should not accompany the procession; in other words, that the corpse was to be trundled into a hole like a dog. But further, it was stipulated—most singular stipulation!—that the procession, even after the above conditions were agreed to, should not enter by the gate, the usual entrance, but *by a breach*, expressly made for that object, in the cemetery *wall*; and so come into the fold, not as of the flock, but avowedly as 'thieves and robbers,' having by their own apparent avowal no *right* there. And all this, remember, in the teeth of the law, which declares the cemetery common property, equally open to all; for the law of France, though it denies the right of the poor man to support during life, freely admits his right to burial.

Doubtless, you will say this poor corpse, when living, was a bitter opponent of the priests and their practices, and therefore it was that their anger pursued it even when dead. But no! he was, on the contrary, a great benefactor to the commune; had been maire for five or six years; had received the Bishop of Luçon and several priests at his table; and, above all, had actually given certain decorations to the Romanist Church at Cugaud; *but* he was a *Protestant*, and therefore a *leper*!

The family very properly refused this degrading mockery of decent sepulture, and had the body preserved until the issue of the affair. They then applied to the *ministre des cultes* on the subject, and he

promptly ordered the maire to arrange so that the
burial might take place 'honourably.' Accordingly,
Messrs. *Maire* and *Vicaire* had to swallow the pill, and the
interment was performed with propriety and in peace.
But our friends were not even yet 'out of the wood.'

Hardly had the grave closed over the body, when on
all sides arose threats and outcries. The maire was
menaced with death; the property of the deceased was
obliged to be watched night and day, lest it should be
burnt; such was the excited state of men's spirits, that
sixty infantry and several extra *piquets* of gendarmes
were stationed in the commune, and numerous arrests
were made. The commune was partly excommunicated,
as in the days of old; the ecclesiastical authorities
forbade the grand mass to be said there, or any further
burials to take place in the cemetery; the place had
been profaned, and was therefore tabooed and under ban.

Great was the heat, and dire the fear, and interest was
brought to bear upon the Government, to have the
defunct Jonah—source of all the trouble—dug up
again. And, strange and shameful to say, the application succeeded, and an order to that effect *was actually
obtained*, under date July 9! The préfet, however,
who knew the circumstances, delayed the execution
of this new order, and furnished fresh information,
which effectually prevented the exhumation being performed; and the poor unconscious clay, which had been
the innocent cause of so much strife, was at last
permitted to repose in peace.

But I will give another proof of the intolerance of
Romanism in Britanny, and of the poor spite wreaked
on a corpse. It is extracted from a newspaper,
'L'Espérance,' of Nantes, and dated June 1855:—

'Great sensation was caused in this place (Guerande, near Nantes) by the report that a lady who was attached to the Protestant faith was about to be interred in the Catholic cemetery. A grave, it appears, was dug for her in the reserved part of the cemetery, *which is not consecrated,* but the Protestant minister objected to it. After waiting five days, the minister, who came from Nantes (M. Vaurigaud), came to bury the deceased, but to the great scandal of the faithful he caused the body to be interred in the Catholic part of the cemetery. Complaints were made to the authorities, but nothing being done murmurs arose. At length the exhumation was ordered, and the piety of the faithful received full satisfaction, and the body was removed to Nantes. *But reparation was necessary.* On Sunday last, accordingly, after celebration of mass, a letter from our beloved bishop was read from the pulpit. This letter, *which breathes charity and moderation,* like everything else which proceeds from the pious prelate, ordered *a new consecration* of the cemetery. After vespers, a large crowd left the church and proceeded towards the burial-ground. *Each person was happy,* for the rights of the Church were at last recognised, and the tombs of ancestors were respected.'

Surely this must have happened in Turkey, in the time of Sultan Mahmoud, when the Christians were saluted with spittle, and their common name was 'giaour,' or 'dog.' At present the Turks are far too civilised and tolerant even *to think* of such an act of barbarism. And this is the treatment given by one Christian people to other Christians — for, be it remembered, Romanists allow to Protestants that title, as in truth they are obliged to do; for what but a belief *in Christ* is the very essence and cause of the name?

There is something profoundly afflicting in the sentiments breathed in the above extract: let us hope they are shared by but few Romanists.   What! is the daily and oftentimes friendly intercourse 'twixt Romanist and Protestant but a mere hypocrisy? Is the expressed good will, sympathy, and friendship, all outward show, used merely to cheat during life the being we despise and spurn *in death*? Is there such an odious contamination in the dead body of a Protestant, that its mere presence in a Roman Catholic cemetery infects it as with the plague, so that 'reparation' and 'a new consecration' is necessary?   Forbid it religion, forbid it friendship, forbid it every enlightened and Christian Romanist!

When this shameful act was occurring, the Crimean war was in full rage, and the allied French and English armies were beleaguering Sebastopol.   Think you that our brave allies, fighting side by side with our own gallant soldiers, and respecting them as brave men mutually respect each other, pouring out their hearts' blood for them when needed, and receiving the sacrifice of our blood in return — think you that they, esteeming their friendship an honour in life, would have deemed it a profanation to be near to them in death, requiring 'reparation' and 'a new consecration'?   I am sure that the question would only require to be stated, in order to receive from those brave men one universal and indignant denial.

And this case is not an isolated one, for about the same time a similar one occurred at Chelles, in the department of the *Oise*, and there the Protestant family was made to pay 60 fr. for the expenses of taking up the body *and reburying it* in the dog's corner.

These facts will show what is the spirit of Romanism

in Britanny and France, despite of all paper law. The Protestants have all legal rights equally with Romanists. Oh, certainly! *if they can get them*! but the judges are hard of hearing on one side the head, and Protestantism is unfortunately always placed *on that side*, and must speak loud to be heard; and as some men are timid and weak in the chest, their just demands are passed over.

For these cases are not chance and singular ones. They abound. Here is another, at Estissac. A Protestant having died there, the Rev. M. Recordon of Troyes went over to bury him, having previously communicated with the préfet and obtained from him a verbal permission to do so. Arrived at Estissac, he waited on the *maire*, who told him that the municipal council was at the moment occupied in debating the matter, and when the decision was come to, it should be communicated to M. Recordon. Owing, however, either to the toughness of the subject-matter, or the slow mental digestion of the municipals, nothing was settled down to five o'clock, and the maire, in ill humour visited the obtuseness of his brethren on the Protestant minister, and said he would wait no longer, but would bury the corpse *himself*. In vain M. Recordon claimed his rights as pastor to read the service, and required the maire to give his reasons in writing. *M. le Maire* would attend neither to one thing nor the other; and, assisted by his *adjoint* and the police, and disregarding the tears and entreaties of the poor widow and friends, raised the corpse, and bundled it into the ground as one might do with a dead dog or cat.

I do say that such acts as these are a disgrace and a reproach to any country, but in one which professes equal favour for all religions, they are *infamous*.

If the authorities proclaimed to all men that Protestants should cease in France, that there should be no place for them living or dead, we might understand the practice; but this intolerant cowardly *double dealing* is at once disgraceful and disgusting.

For myself, I cannot say that it would greatly trouble me to know beforehand that I was not to lie in consecrated ground, but others are of a different opinion, and hold strongly to such an interment. Let such hesitate before coming to France, for against their will they may find themselves in bad company as regards their 'mortal coil.' Little matters it to me where the ' vile body' finds its last resting-place, and makes its first acquaintance with the worm. The 'effacing fingers' of decay will equally destroy its beauty and reduce it to loathsomeness, whether it lie in the deep, in the quiet village churchyard embosomed in trees and under a tombstone strewed with flowers, or alone whitening on the mountain. As a matter of feeling, I might wish to take my final repose in company with those who loved me, in hopes that we might together rise at the blast of the trump that wakes the dead, and be reunited not again to part. But little recks it of the body. The soul and its destination is the only thing needful; and if that be secured, we may leave the rest unregarded, as the joyous butterfly thinks no more of the case which covered it when a chrysalis.

In the South of France is a large department with a small name, called the *Var*, which has lately had an unenviable notoriety. The three letters *V a r* contain a great deal of meaning, equally with *b a d* and *m a d.* It was in the Department of the Var that occurred that celebrated curiosity in modern jurisprudence, where Ducloux, the Paris publisher, was tried and condemned without knowing it, the court sitting with closed doors (see *Britanny and the Bible*, p. 38).

To what can this extreme ultra-bigotry be owing? Marseilles and Toulon are, the one close to, and the other actually within this department, and one would imagine that the usual liberality and largeness of view of the dwellres in seaport towns would have corrected the evil, even if the purifying and healthy sea-breezes had failed in the *deodorising* work.

But whatever be the cause, the *Var* has recently eclipsed even itself, and let us henceforth think nothing of condemning with closed doors and in the absence of the accused — of being hung up behind our backs, as an Irishman would say—for such are mere harmless eccentricities — only the freaks of Madame Justice—done after dinner, and in her cups perhaps.

But here are the facts. In 1842, the affluence of invalids, travellers, and others, having assembled at Cannes a large number of Protestants, a place of worship was opened, and continued open for some time undisturbed by the authorities. After a while, certain of the Romanist inhabitants of the town began to frequent the *réunions*, and the priests became alarmed, and their influence at that period being great, they, by means best known to themselves, procured an order from M. Duchâtel, then Minister of the Interior, to expel from France a M. Charbonney, who had conducted the service. This being done in an excessively arbitrary manner, *à la mode des prêtres*, and M. Charbonney being in general esteem, a petition was signed by sixty-nine of the chief men of the town *all Roman Catholics*, praying for his reinstallation; and this was sent to M. Duchâtel; but no attention was paid to it.

After the departure of M. Charbonney, a M. Boucher,

a minister of the Gospel, was delegated by the Consistory to officiate as minister at Cannes, but the maire refused to acknowledge him ; and when he attempted to celebrate Divine service, the maire sent the police and gendarmes, who expelled him and the congregation from the chapel. This gross outrage, however, was set right, and the préfet, seeing that the authorities had exceeded their powers, ordered the opening of the place of worship, which was done in 1847, and the number of hearers was from sixty to eighty.

Sometime afterwards, the Protestant inhabitants being still on the increase, a request was made to the local authorities to allow a school to be opened for Protestant girls. This caused great excitement among the priests ; and the Committee of the Academic Council, which decides such matters, being secretly convened, and without notice having been given (as should legally have been done) to M. Boucher; the legal delegate of the Consistory, decided that the school should not be opened ; giving as the reason, ' that there were *no Protestants* at Cannes.' This certainly is refreshingly cool—no special pleading, or explaining away — but a straightforward taking of the bull by the horns — and despite the sixty or eighty Protestants attending service in their place of worship, and despite the place of worship itself, they gravely *shut their eyes*, and say, ' *We see no Protestants* at Cannes.'

On the same principles we may shut our eyes and say there is no sun. But as notwithstanding our shut eyes *there* the sun *is*, lighting and warming everybody, so this enviable *aplomb* in ignoring a notoriety, could not long stand its ground ; and after an appeal to the higher authorities, the eyes of the worthy committee were miraculously opened, and they admitted

that there *were* Protestants at Cannes really existing
' in the body.'

Accordingly the *girls'* school was duly opened. But
soon, (as the equal law of nature gives to anxious ma-
ternity boys and girls in about equal proportions,) it
became necessary to provide for teaching the young
male idea also, and an application was made to the
authorities for permission to open a *boys'* school; but
this singular committee, which first shut its eyes and
then said that nothing external existed, now refused to
give any school at all to the boys, although it had
granted one for the girls previously.

A strange curiosity must this committee have been—
one would like to have seen it—doubtless it must have
been a quaint specimen—perhaps a relic of the Crusades,
— and, influenced by hatred of the infidel Turks who
admit men to Paradise, but keep women out, this
eccentric committee would reverse the rule and exclude
boys, while it took in girls. Singular department this
of the Var; good, one would imagine, for antiquarians
and geologists seeking for antediluvian specimens, but
recommendable, at least, for its preference of the softer
sex. Let us therefore be kind, and *so* remember it.

This obtuse committee being thus encased and impracticable, appeal was made to the Academic Council of
the Department, who gave judgment on the matter, and
not only did so, but were so considerate as to deliver
judgment in written characters, and as ' *litera scripta
manet*,' we are able to present our readers with a legal
curiosity, equal in its way to the ' living skeleton.'

Le voici, ' Room for the *Var*,' if not for the ' *Bar!* '

' *Considering* that from the record of this matter it
' appears that the means employed up to this time for
' propagating the Protestant religion in this country

' *have been and are always immoral*; that *conscience*
' *disapproves* them; that in the town of Cannes all
' attempts, such as gifts of money and obscene books,
' the turning aside of poor children under six years old,
' forced visits to death-beds, have presented, and still
' present, a special character of immorality; that in spite
' of all efforts, not one family belonging to the country
' has been prevailed upon to follow the Protestant re-
' ligion; that the number, hardly perceptible, which *do*
' follow it are strangers, and that this number is dimi-
' nished and reduced to almost nothing; that the whole
' population of Cannes exclaims against the establish-
' ment of the projected school, and *especially the sous-*
' *préfet*, in the name of morality, and the public peace;
' for these and other reasons the Council decides that
' the boys' school at Cannes shall not be opened.'

A wondrous decision — a second Daniel come to judgment! And this document is signed by a rector, as
President of the Academic Council, three priests, the
public prosecutor, and six other persons, *all Romanists*
of course.

It is enough to make a man laugh to think of the
admirable gravity of the sentences, that Protestantism
has been ever, and is still, spread by *immoral* means,
of which the conscience (*subauditâ* '*Catholicâ*') disapproves!!

When we read and reflect upon this case, it is evident that the materials for a religious war still exist,
and indeed many think that the next war between France
and England will be of this character, for France is
perhaps more Catholic, and England certainly more
Protestant, in other words, the two nations are more
antagonistic on the subject of religion, than in the last
war. In that case, the horrors of the great battle of

Armageddon may be realised; but may God grant that it be not in *our* time!

It is needless to refute the charges of *conversion* by distributing *obscene* books, &c. &c. &c. Such charges carry their own refutation with them; so let us return this Var curiosity carefully to its case, lock it up, label it as ' *Very rare*,' and pass on.

But justice towards Protestants is singularly difficult, even in the smallest matters, despite all theoretical equality of religions and other ' paper stuff,' as Carlyle calls it. Here, for example, is an instance which occurred, in September 1861, which I extract from the *Opinion Nationale*, an independent French journal.

A certain worthy man, named Loubat, formerly maire of Sevres, left 300fr. to be given annually in prizes to the best pupils in the Sevres school. Of this some 50fr. was to be given in the girls' section to the child who was judged most deserving *by the other children*.

The choice of the children, eighty in number, fell upon Henriette Foras, but, alas! she was a Protestant.

Now M. Loubat had made no distinction as to Protestant or Catholic, and only two years before, the brother of Henriette, who was also a Protestant, had gained a similar honour in the boys' school. M. Hebert, however, the vicar, who presided, declared that Henriette should not have the prize, because she was a Protestant, and, after some hesitation, the lay-members present gave way and ordered a second choice.

But at the second choice, still the lot fell to Henriette, yet, in spite of that, the vicar gave the prize to another pupil. However, some Protestant ladies made a collection of 100fr. to give to the child as a recompense for the loss of the prize, but even then the president refused to give it in the name of *Protestant* ladies—he would not sully his lips with the word—and therefore gave it as coming from some *benevolent* ladies. Can anything be imagined so ridiculous and unfair as this paltry matter? And yet forsooth, ' *il y a égalité des cultes en France.*' Oh certainly ! *equal injustice* for all who are not Romanists.

At a time when a country, for instance France, is in a state of transition, it is interesting to mark the degrees in the process. It is a favourite dogma with many that Romanism may be safely left alone; that brought into contact with the spirit of the age, it will fade and expire, as barbarism before the advance of civilisation.

This doctrine is philosophic, and of easy practice ; it says, *laissez faire, and do nothing yourself*; perhaps, too, in the end it *may* be true, for it deals only in the future tense, and has time indefinite to work in; but to judge by what passes under our eyes, there has been until lately a certain progress of Romanism, showing something faulty in the principle of the *laissez faire* doctrine, or else something out of order in the ropes and pulleys.

All the world knows that, in 1792, Romanism seemed destroyed in France ; its priests hunted like wild beasts of the forest, tortured and torn in pieces; its temples burned, overthrown, and profaned; its possessions confiscated, and its very name rooted out; and that, since that period, it has never (save for one brief period) been recognised as the State religion ; and yet, at present, we find it endued with a very marvellous vitality, extending itself far and wide, above ground and below it, and bidding fair shortly to regain a good part of its lost territory. Such a system must not be despised if we would hope to overcome it, and we may rely upon

it, that it has its roots deep down among the very foundations of our nature, and that to eradicate it we must
very thoroughly change that nature. *Laissez faire* is
not the remedy for *this* disease, and mild palliatives will
be about as effectual as poultices would be to remove
the humps from a dromedary's back.

Look, for example, at the late question about religious processions. By a law of 1802 it was enacted
that 'no religious ceremony shall take place *out* of the
edifices appropriated for Catholic worship, in the towns
where there are temples belonging to other forms of
worship.' The object of this law was purely civil. It
cared neither for Catholic nor Protestant, and was supremely indifferent to both; but was framed to prevent
such scandalous disturbances of the public peace as would
probably arise in case of the meeting of public party
processions. It said 'fight dog, fight bear, *in the proper
'place*, but you shall not fight in the public streets.'

In towns, therefore, possessing a Protestant chapel,
with a minister paid by the State, Roman Catholic
processions were forbidden, and we may imagine the
suppressed anger of 'flams and arch-flams' as Carlyle
calls them, thereupon. Nice news for *them*, to hear of
the probability of a Protestant minister being allotted
to their town, and all their exhibition of finery thereby
put an end to! So the law was submitted to — *in a
way* — not without grumblings infinite — and secret
councils without number. Symptoms, however, soon
appeared, showing an intention to evade or deplace
the law, and at Lille, the Government in a very
cowardly manner has yielded to the priests, and another link has been added to the chain continually forging
for Protestantism.

Lille is the seat of a Protestant Consistory, and has

several places of Protestant worship, nor has it had a grand religious procession since the law previously cited. The year 1852 being a propitious one, and the horoscope of *St. Louis* having been duly taken and found favourable by adding the word *Napoleon*, special orders are understood to have been given by the Jesuitical heads to celebrate the festival of the *Bon Dieu* on an unusual scale of splendour, so as to dispirit the Protestants and elevate the hearts of the faithful in France.

At Lille, therefore, it was announced that the procession would be revived. The Protestants did what they could to oppose it, and the maire of Lille, in order to prevent a probable breach of the peace in the town, formally forbade it. Upon this the priestly party applied to the préfet, and prevailed upon him to revoke the decree of the maire, which he did; and again the question was opened; to be closed again, however, by an order from the *Ministre des Cultes* confirming the judgment of the maire.

It was, however, apparently a mere matter of tossing up, 'heads or tails,' and therefore, to secure another toss, the Romanists at once commenced getting up the steam to an alarming height. They stated that the preparations had been all made; that the people were full of devotion, and much excited; that Government influence would greatly suffer at Lille if things were not allowed to go on as they wished; in fine, they raised such a hubbub, that by a telegraphic despatch from Paris it was announced that, as the end of the strife, the 'procession was to go;' and it accordingly went in great pomp and with great *éclat*, as a revival, a return from the dead, to the glorification of every Catholic heart, and the abasement and annoyance of every Protestant. And as if to inflict a kick on the dead lion, and show Protestants what they . had taken by their motion, the garrison at Lille were ordered to form part of the religious ceremony, contrary to the rule which allows the presence of military only at *political* fêtes.

For be it remembered, that a great point of religious scruple is involved here. The army is composed of Protestants as well as Romanists, and yet all are ordered *to go on their knees* at the passage of the consecrated wafer. But can a Protestant conscientiously do this? I do not by any means say that it is a sin in itself, but if the party thinks it one, it *is* sin *to him.* Some might consider it (*a soldier,* for instance) like the case of Naaman, when he went with his master into the house of Rimmon; and as Naaman was allowed to bow down without sin, so it might be here, but all might not view it in the same light, and to such it would be an act of grievous oppression.

And all this is done in *liberal France,* in this nineteenth century, professing to allow *equality* to all religions! Why, even in Russia, where the army is composed, among others, of Mahometans and pagans, even *their* scruples are respected, and no one is forced to take part in any other religious ceremony than that of his own religion. And yet in enlightened and philosophic France, governed by a Napoleon Buonaparte, Protestants shall be *obliged*, under pain of death, to bow before the golden image. It is Nebuchadnezzar and the plain of Shinar revived: let France beware lest the Writing on the Wall follow! And so the procession went on grandly at Lille, and the Protestants had to submit as they best could; *and they did so*, as they almost always do.

At Paris it is observed that the processions are

more splendid and prominent than they had been for
years.   There the law *is* in force, and consequently no
religious processions appear in the streets ; but of late it
is remarked that they have encroached a little.   At the
Madeleine, for instance, instead of promenading round
the inside of the church, with banners, images, &c., they
promenade round the *outside colonnade.*   At Nôtre
Dame de Loretto *an altar* was fitted up on the *outside,*
and some few houses were ornamented, and hung with
drapery; and at St. Thomas's church the procession
fairly *entered the street* and marched to the Artillery
Museum, where the altar was erected.

Everywhere in the provinces unusual ardour was displayed, as if to warm and illuminate the hearts of the
multitude with the light of the good days coming.   At
Morlaix, in Britanny, the exhibition was sumptuous.
Many priests were there who came from far, and I was
so struck by the evident newness of some of the banners
and crosses, that I could not forbear asking the reason,
and smiling at the reply.

It seems that on a previous year, on the anniversary
of the *Fête Dieu,* the heavens were unpropitious and the
rain poured in torrents.   A deputation waited on the
curé who had the direction of affairs, requesting him to
shorten the line of the procession as much as possible, so as
to spare the ladies and their fine clothes, to say nothing
of the wooden saints and angels in best bib and tucker.
But as ill luck would have it, that stout ecclesiastic was
determined to pass in front of the Protestant chapel in
the town, in order, as he said, ' to beard the heretics,'
therefore the deputation's request was refused ; and the
said chapel was at the very end of the town.

So the procession started, and soon became a long
and lugubrious string of umbrellas — banners flapped

heavily, and then stuck to the pole—ladies' thin muslins grew transparent, and their forms became delineated with classic correctness, not to say indecency — paint was washed off, and looked streaky and muddy—all were cross and sulky, anathematising the curé who thus dragged them through the mire for an ill-natured motive, and it was universally agreed that a less devotional procession, one less abounding in Christian graces, virtues, *and purity*, had never been witnessed. But that was not all : the flags, decorations, garments, and drapery had all been 'got up' expressly for the occasion, and were all spoiled, to the tune of upwards of 100*l.*! nor was it until the following year that the losses could be repaired ; at which period the general wish to produce something striking had showed itself in a renewal and regilding of the exhibition stock. It is to be hoped that the zeal of the curé will not again spoil all as before, or at least that he will previously consult the barometer, and call a council of old ladies or rheumatic washerwomen on the subject; or at any rate expend a small sum from the *Treasury of the Saints*, in purchasing one of the Barometers exhibited at the International, and patented for distinguishing ' wet ' from ' wind.'

CHAPTER XIII.

A NOTHER of those cases has recently occurred in France which are enough to wear out the patience and spirit of any people — especially of a people living under 'an equality of religious rights,' as guaranteed by the precious ' code.'

It is really hard on the reader to have so many similar cases brought before him, and this shall be *the last*. I could give a score of others with ease; but I will be merciful, and will only give this ' positively last' one more.

Perhaps I may be asked, Why give *any* more? But I wish to drive the subject home, so that my readers may have a definite idea and settled conviction of the way in which their fellow-Protestants are treated in France, a country separated from us only by an hour's distance; and that they may feel for their difficulties, and sympathise with and help them whenever an opportunity offers.

In truth many Englishmen seem to think that in this nineteenth century Rome has become a dove instead of a raven, and that it must be quite a privilege to live in enlightened France, where one of the fundamental

articles of the 'Charter' is 'equal religious rights,' and
where there is no state religion. I therefore wish to
disabuse their minds of such mistakes, which are just
the opposite of the truth, and to give them some *facts*
which they may consider and judge for themselves, as it
becomes wise men to do.

Fifteen years ago a singular event happened in the
Department of the Haute Vienne in France. A whole
'commune,' of 600 inhabitants, breaking away from the
Holy (*Roman*) Catholic Church, applied to the Consistory
of Paris to send them a Protestant pastor. The request
was granted. In a short time the neighbouring com-
munes of Chateau Ponsac, Rançon, Balledent, and Thiat
followed the example; and even at Limoges, the chief
town of the province, a chapel was built and a pastor
appointed, and a continual increase of converts followed.
This was under the reign of Louis Philippe.

Then came the Revolution of 1848; and in due time
followed the Empire and the increase of power of the
Romanist party—for, as has been said, the first effect of
the Empire was to breathe fresh vigour into the Romish
Church in France, and to give to it double its usual
pretensions and arrogance; and in about two years
afterwards, all the chapels of which mention has been
made, in the district of Bellac, were suddenly shut up
by order of the *préfet.*

The poor Protestants, troubled but not dismayed,
used every effort to procure the reopening of their
chapels, but without success. They then held religious
worship on Sundays in the houses of different inhabitants,
and for this they were dragged to the bar of criminal
justice, and punished with heavy fines for holding meetings in unlicensed places; although it was admitted that
their meetings were merely for religious objects.

Still they bravely renewed their attempts to reopen

their chapels; and failing again, they again met for worship in a house, and were again punished as before, They were defended by M. Edmond de ˙Pressensè, the Protestant minister of Paris, in an admirable speech, which he concluded by these words: 'So long as our friends stand thus in vain before their closed churches, and are punished for praying to God — so long as the churches of the Haute Vienne are thus harassed, religious liberty is but an empty name in France, and conscience is violated in its inmost part.'

Still they persevered; and at length, in 1856, during the Crimean War, they gained access to the Emperor, and by a special order *from him* the chapels were all re-opened, and have since remained so.

And here let me make a remark. When the Emperor was in Britanny in 1857, a deputation of the Protestants of the south of Britanny waited on him to congratulate him, and recalled to him the words of his uncle: 'The empire of the law ends where that of con-science commences'— noble words, worthy of a great man! The Emperor and the President of the Consistory (equivalent to our bishop) had a friendly conversation, apart from all the others, and the Emperor finished by saying: 'If you have complaints to make, send them direct to me, and not through the *Ministre des Cultes*' —and yet, strange to say, they have never since, so far as I am aware, made use of the privilege! This con-firms what I have before said as to the personal feel-ings of Louis Napoleon towards Protestants.

Well! the chapels were reopened; and so far so good. But after chapels come schools, as a natural consequence; and as this was a new thing, all the difficulties had to be surmounted over again. Was it not enough to dispirit the most determined and persevering? At length schools were opened at Bellac, after every possible hindrance had been thrown in the way. But even yet we are far from being 'out of the wood.' By a decision of the Academic Council, composed of four Roman Catholics and *one* Protestant (most impartial tribunal!) they were again ordered to be closed, *in the interests of morality;* and since then, in spite of every effort, they have remained closed, and are closed at this moment.

In 'the interests of morality' to shut up *schools!* No comment is needed here, methinks.

But what are the parents to do with their children? Are they to grow up like little brutes, without education of any kind? So they engaged a person to give '*leçons à domicile,*' that is, to go from one house to another and teach the children in each, allowing no others to come in. But even *here,* was too much education for Rome. Spies were employed, and an accusation was brought against the teacher; and I think that this '*acte d'accusation*' must be a *bijou* among even French legal, or rather illegal, curiosities, and merits a place in the rarities at the Louvre, along with the arquebuss with which Charles IX. picked off flying Protestants across the Seine, at that great *battue* of Protestants on St. Bartholomew's day, of which history speaks somewhat warmly.

Jusnel, the teacher, is found guilty of keeping a school, by going to the house of one *Bouland* and giving a lesson to his son, aged seven years, and the tribunal gravely condemns him to a fine and costs, and that *his school* (*which he never kept,* for it was in another man's house) should be instantly closed!

But still the people were not beaten. They appealed to the High Court of Paris against this absurd and illegal decision—for it is admitted that giving lessons *at the house* is *not* keeping a school—and their appeal was allowed, and finally they triumphed, and great was their joy, and the valleys of the Haute Vienne resounded with cries of exultation and gratitude.

But Rome is not beaten yet; her quiver has yet another arrow. Delays occurred, difficulties were raised, and finally, when two teachers presented themselves ready to recommence the work, the préfet, urged by the clerical authorities, again stopped them 'for the sake of public morals;' and as the préfet is scarcely ever disavowed by the Government, the matter is thus—finally and to conclude—*settled*—until the next, and let us hope, speedy, act in the politico-religious farce.

Ah! acts like these are the true causes of revolutions; for they make even moderate men pray for them!

Meanwhile, let us sympathise with and express our sympathy for the poor suffering people of Bellac.

And here I will close my list of instances in which the principles of religious liberty are grievously and flagrantly violated in France; and I appeal to the feelings of every enlightened and just man, whether the case is not one that cries loudly for relief; especially in a country—*mark this!*—where the fifth clause of the fundamental charter of the constitution *guarantees equal religious rights to all its citizens?*

And who is the moving agent of it all? whose is the spirit that inspires these odious persecutions? 'T is *Rome —unchanged and unchangeable —* Rome, who would repeat all the cruel and oppressive acts which history records on her pages, if she had only the power.

But I am uncharitable, say some. The state of modern enlightenment, the march of intellect, the spirit of the age, &c. &c. &c., all render it impossible for Rome ever to be again what she has been. She has become philosophic rather than practical—deals in dogmas

P

rather than acts — and burns only on paper, and not in
auto-da-fés.   Does she? — then what shall we   say
to the recent *mandement* of the Archbishop of Toulouse,
a dignitary of large calibre even among Romish Tritons?

This enlightened and most Christian prelate has just
issued (April 1862) a *mandement* for the celebration of
the *glorious* anniversary of the *massacre* of 4,000 Protestants at Toulouse in 1562!

A public procession was to take place, and high masses
to be said, and preachers were to exhort their flocks in a
suitable manner.   In this way, as the Archbishop mildly
expresses himself, the ' chain of the past ' was to be kept
up — until (we suppose) another blood-red link is forged.

But we should thank the gentle Archbishop for directing our attention to the ' chain of the past.'   It is a
letter which has two addresses, and its effect will be as
much felt by Protestants as by Romanists.   We may say
with Shakspeare, ' I thank thee, Jew, for teaching me
that word;' and it will act as a timely stimulant to
dozing and soporific persons, whose nature disposes them
to a too easy deposit of flesh.   This ' chain of the past '
has eaten too deeply into the Protestant body to be easily
forgotten.   Stir it ever so lightly, and it will still give
pain.

And its effect has been happy on the French Government also, for by an article in the *Moniteur*, the Government says — ' The celebration of a jubilee on the 23rd
May next (1862), which has been prescribed by the
Archbishop of Toulouse, is nothing else than the comme-
moration of a grievous and bloody episode of our ancient
religious discords;' and then goes on to interdict and
forbid the procession, &c., and so good comes out of
evil; and this is another proof that the Emperor is
disposed to put a bit into the mouth of the priesthood,

and not allow them to prance and caracole and trample upon the people at their will.

And with this instance, which arrives *tres apropos,* both as to the proof of the ancient spirit of Rome still animating her, and as to the disposition of the Emperor to put a check on the exhibition of that spirit, I will close this part of my subject for the present. As I have before said, I could increase it tenfold, but I should only fatigue my readers and myself, and I wish to avoid both one and the other.

How elastic is the Romish system *in practice,* and how cleverly does it adapt itself to circumstances! There is almost as great a difference between the system as applied in Britanny or any other intensely Roman Catholic country, and as applied in England ; as there is between the latter and Protestantism itself. And yet the veritable unchangeable *spirit* of Rome is such as we find it in Britanny; and if we do not find it in England also, it is because it *dare* not show itself there.

In England we have seen Romanists in league and solemn pact with the ultra-Liberal or Radical party—as at the time of the ' *Lichfield House compact,*' dis-coursing eloquently on the liberty of conscience, the rights of citizens, and, I doubt not, in many cases up-holding the five points of the ' Charter,' and fraternising with Dissenters at the time (happily now almost gone by) when Dissenters had many real civil and religious grievances to complain of; in fact, making political capital out of all or any circumstances which in the least degree advanced their own cause ; and coolly kicking away the ladder they had mounted up by, as soon as it was no longer useful to them.

In England they are obliged to use the *pattes de*

velours only, and to keep their claws concealed; yet there they are, ready for use, if the good times of old would only return.   But England - has felt the claws too deeply to endure them again; she has only to look at the scars of the wounds they have inflicted on her, to strengthen and confirm her determination not to run the fearful risk a second time.

Now and then a devoted but imprudent son of the Church breaks out and speaks his mind, recalls us to a sense of what the system really is, and prevents us lapsing into a false security, and does us good service without intending it; as Sir George Bowyer has just done in the debate on Italy (see Hansard, April 14, 1862), and we owe him thanks for it; but, generally speaking, the party is well generaled, and acts on the principle of being all things to all men, and keeping its ancient principles in the background.

But let us ever remember that Rome *is unchanged and unchangeable.*

An infallible power, as Rome pretends to be, *can never alter* its principles, or retire from a position it has once taken up.   It cannot retreat, for retreat is ruin.

In the year 1859, judgement was given by the Court of Cassation in Paris, which is the Supreme Court of Appeal in France, on the question whether casually giving a book or tract was 'distributing' within the terms of the law forbidding such an act.

This law was passed in 1849, when Socialism prevailed in France, and when books of the most infamous and subversive nature were circulated through the country, and was never intended to apply to the circulation of moral and religious books, and especially the Bible.   But, by what I think was a very culpable

neglect and inattention on the part of the Protestant
Members of the Assembly, the attention of the Legislature was not sufficiently directed to the point; and as
it was not the interest of the Romanist members to
object (indeed it is highly probable that the far-sighted
among them foresaw the powerful use which might in
due time be made of it), the project passed and became law, and its very inconvenient and restrictive
effect was soon apparent.

The words used are 'distributor of any book,' &c.
Now the Bible being a book, was of course, included;
but I always desired to have had the point expressly
decided, as forbidding circulation *of the Bible* by law is
such a flagrant act in this our day, that it seemed to me
very improbable that the French Government would
have insisted upon it. This opinion I often expressed,
but it met with but little support; and things went on,
and it was assumed, on almost all hands, that the
Bible *was* included under the law, and therefore forbidden to be distributed save under a special licence.

The second question then was, what was meant by
'distribution,' i.e., whether it referred to the mere giving
a copy or two of any book by A or B, or whether it
only meant giving books *generally* by a person employed, or *making it his business*, to do so.

This question in due time came before the courts,
and after sundry decisions by inferior judges, was brought
finally before the High Court of Cassation in Paris, the
supreme court in all cases.

The case was, that the defendant (a Protestant) had
given *one single tract* to a little boy, but had admitted
that during the previous *three or four years* he had
given three or four more such tracts to other people.

The day was looked forward to with much interest,

and the Protestant notabilities from many parts of France were there. It was extremely difficult to procure access to the court, but by the kindness of a Protestant minister in Paris I procured admission, and heard the decision.

The discussion no sooner commenced than I felt certain how it was going to end, for there was a very evident *animus* against the Protestant side. M. Jules Delaborde was the Protestant advocate, and argued the matter extremely well and boldly—for France, at least —but I thought he took lower ground than would have been taken by an English advocate; still, as I have before said, allowance must be made for opposition, and the deadening weight of ill-disposed authorities, and for a different way of viewing things. In spite, however, of all his efforts, Romanist views and interests prevailed, and in a very short time the matter was settled, and a decision given by the court *against* the Protestant.

And yet meanwhile Romanists of all kinds, Jesuits, *sœurs* of every colour, black, white, and grey, charitable and religious societies, zealous individuals, and, in fact, all Romanists who liked, were circulating and 'distributing' floods of tracts, abusing and calumniating Protestantism in every possible way, and the Government never interfered with *them.*

I have now before me three different tracts which were placed in my hands at that very period, as being distributed by agents of the Society of St. Francis de Sales in Paris, and I dare say there were a score of others. Most of them are full of abuse of Protestantism, accusing them of buying over converts, and of practising all kinds of vice, and loading them with calumny.

One of these little tracts is entitled 'La Bonne Année,' and merits to be called the flower of the flock. It accuses Protestants of being drunkards, thieves, fornicators, liars, adulterers ; and says that a Protestant is in case of need authorised to appeal *to the devil* as '*le grand coup.*' And while all this was going on in almost every part of France with impunity, a poor Protestant is solemnly condemned by the High Court of Cassation, with its full court of judges in all their paraphernalia, for having given away *a single copy* of a tract to a small boy ; and a Protestant religious journal is menaced with prosecution for using the word '*errors*' in respect of Romanism !

And yet, *croyez moi*, the constitution gives *equal religious rights to all its citizens ! !*

CHAPTER XIV.

IDEAS OF ROMANISTS AS TO PROTESTANTISM — THEIR IGNORANCE
OF THE BIBLE — CALUMNIES AGAINST PROTESTANTS — NO REPLY
TO THEM PRACTICABLE — INDULGENCES A PROFITABLE SYSTEM —
ENGLISH RESIDENTS — WORSHIP IN ENGLISH — ANECDOTE —
GOOD EFFECTS OF PERSEVERANCE — ROMANISM A SYSTEM OF
JUSTIFICATION BY WORKS — FRENCH CHILDREN AND THEIR
BRINGING UP.

THE ignorance of the great body of even enlightened Romanists about the principles and practice of Protestants is, as I have already stated, considerable. In England there are few educated Protestants but who know the general doctrines of Romanism with tolerable accuracy; not merely such as prejudice and bigotry lend to it, but such as are actually held, and as they are expounded by its chief authorities. Controversy has cleared up and placed all these points before us as they actually exist, and there is such an interest felt on the subject, that the press teems with works of all kinds relating to it, which are eagerly perused, so that it is not improbable that as great a proportionate number of Protestants are well informed on the subject as of Romanists. Here and there you find a priest who has read extensively, and here and there a layman; but taking even the educated classes of Romanists, I do not think them well informed upon religious matters generally.

Nor should this be matter of surprise, when we consider that almost every valuable book of liberal views which has been written is to be found in the *Index Expurgatorius*, and that, as a rule, the priests discountenance religious enquiry, for fear it should go too far. We all know the story of the man who was about forming a library, and asked the opinion of a friend as to the selection of good sound works, and his friend advised him to select from the *Index Expurgatorius*. In addition to this is the principle of the authority of the Church, under which the non-enquiring spirit is not merely sheltered, but encouraged. The believer is saved the trouble and risk of investigation, by believing all which the Church believes; and the Church takes on herself the responsibility of believing for him.

These principles naturally allow free scope for the indolence and apathy on serious matters natural to a great part of mankind, and hence the ignorance in question is what might be expected. Nor should we so much object to the practice of taking the responsibility, *provided* that the *punishment* was thus capable of transfer also; but knowing, as we do, that everyone 'shall bear his own burden,' that our faculties are given us for *our own* guidance, and that hereafter we shall be responsible for the use of those faculties; we may well object to the doctrines thus held, and to the practical effect of them upon great bodies of people.

In arguing with a Romanist, one great authority to which a Protestant naturally appeals—the Bible—is, if not rejected, yet little regarded, and thus it is difficult to arrive at a common ground; and the deference to authority is so great, that a question is often considered settled by a reference to any writer of name.

Independent judgement, examining for instance the authority cited, and showing that it is itself valueless or open to objection, is thought irreverent, and received with little favour. Like muscles unused to exercise, which are unequal to sustained exertion, and are exhausted by a single effort, such disputants are satisfied with quoting an authority, but have not sufficient strength or courage to examine and discuss it.

One common notion about Protestantism which I have frequently heard stated, and which is extensively held by Romanists, is that it is a religion of *convenience*. This is certainly a strange idea to entertain of a religion which regards the thoughts and the heart chiefly, and in which the monitor being within, and therefore always with us, will naturally be more strict than any other; provided, of course, that the profession of religion is sincere.

Some time since I procured a modern French Romanist book on this subject, entitled, ' What are we to think of the religion which permits every one to do as he likes?' This work contains the grossest and most calumnious misstatements as to Protestantism, representing it as a mere cloak under which vicious men take refuge, in order to sin with impunity. There are several books of the same character, but I will cite a few extracts from this one, which will give an idea as to the rest. Let me also add, that this book was given as a prize in a Romanist school *supported by public money*, and under the direction of the Academic Council of the Department, who must be presumed to have been cognisant of the fact.

The book starts with this principle — ' Protestants interpret the Bible to suit their convenience, and therefore they may conscientiously do what they like '— and proceeds thus to enlarge upon it. ' Good works, such as acts of repentance, of sobriety, temperance, justice, modesty, chastity, and pity, are mortal sins, and in no way serve to gain heaven. More than that, it is a received doctrine that good works hazard rather than help salvation, that it is sufficient to believe in Jesus Christ, and that no sin, *past, present, or future*, is hurtful to him who believes. Thus, only believe firmly, and you need not trouble yourself about thefts, fornications, or murders.' ' For instance, sobriety is not a virtue, and the principal thing which Protestant missionaries teach to the poor savages whom they evangelise is drunkenness.' What an impudent calumny is this! and permitted to pass unnoticed by the Government, let me observe, in a country which does not allow Protestants to use the word *errors* in reference to Romanism.

It then states that all crimes can be justified *by the Bible*, and adds — ' So, you rob your father, you do wrong to your master, your conscience pricks you. But if you are a Protestant, and a little clever, remember that the Israelites stole the treasures of the Egyptians, and you read in Genesis that Jacob robbed Laban of his golden images. You are therefore quite *en règle*; your conscience, as that of an honest man, can say nothing against an act which with a little address you can justify, and even sanctify, *from the Bible.*'

It then tells two little stories to enliven the subject. ' A certain Timothy of Cambridge, with whom a sum of money had been deposited, denied that there was any claim upon him, and defended himself by these words of St. Paul, " O Timothy, *gardez le depôt*." " Keep that which is committed to thee." The apostle meant to say, keep the faith; the Protestant interpreter understood it, " Keep the money." ' Again — ' Another having stolen his host's cloak, excused himself by the apostolic command, " Bear each other's burdens." ' The gravity with which the author quotes these ancient and irreligious Joe Millers as facts, in a religious discussion, is edifying. How surprised would ' Joe ' be to find himself elevated to the witness box in an ecclesiastical court!

It then quotes Luther as expressly sanctioning fornication and adultery, and also the keeping of mistresses, in terms which I will not introduce here. Charity then comes in question: — ' Charity goes on the doctrine of works, and good works are abhorred by Protestants, as "a burden which prevents us reaching heaven," according to Luther. And besides, if faith is enough, of what use is charity? Protestantism only tolerates charity towards women, and those young and pretty; as for charity towards your neighbour, if he is of the masculine gender, there is no question about it.'

Then follows the passage with reference to sins practised by Protestants: — ' They easily accommodate their doctrine with the Bible. You remember the favourite principle of Luther, Calvin, &c., that God allows himself *to lie* occasionally, by way of joke. (*How awful this blasphemy!*) Therefore a Protestant, who knows Luther and Calvin by heart, considers as lies and jokes those passages which make against him. If, however, the text is too serious to be taken as a joke, the Protestant masters have other resources. 1st. If it is only a word or a line which embarrasses them, they suppress it. Thus, in the sixth verse of the Epistle of St. Paul to Philemon, mention is made of good works; but as Luther feared good works more than the devil, *who used to visit him under the form of a blue fly,* he cut out this word in his translation of the Bible. 2ndly. They suppress a chapter or an entire book, when they find there doctrines or points of morality undoubtedly Catholic. For instance, the Epistle of St. James', which shows the insufficiency of faith without works; the Second Book of Maccabees, which speaks of prayers for the dead and of purgatory, have been suppressed without appeal, one by Luther and the other by Calvin. 3rdly. If there is a means of leaving out the word, chapter, or book, of altering the sense, or of adding words which are not there, Protestants are not behind hand; they know that the common people, who know neither Hebrew, Greek, nor Latin, will not dig out their rogueries, and will take as the word of God whatever shall be presented as such. For instance, where the Bible says " Faith justifies," Luther translates " Faith *alone* justifies." Where the Bible says " This is my body," Zwingle translates " This is *the sign* of my body." 4thly. Where there is no way of mutilating, cutting out, or changing the text of the Bible, a Protestant is authorised to appeal from the Bible *to the devil* — this is the great stroke — *c'est le grand coup*.' I have given this passage entire; it will show Protestants what some Catholics think of them.

A person then remarks (to go on with the book) — ' Luther, Calvin, and the ministers in general who give to their flocks these falsified Bibles, *do they wish* to deceive the people? Why not,' answers the writer, ' when they admit that God can deceive and lie. It is their wish to be perfect *as their Father in heaven is perfect.*' ' Protestants are not obliged to listen to their ministers. The minister says what he believes, and each hearer believes what he likes, without ceasing to be a Protestant. The duty of a Protestant minister, *à la rigueur*, consists in opening and shutting the church. Their pretended evangelical ministry is the mere trade of *a door-keeper.*'

The concluding passage is as follows: — ' The Catholic religion proposes to its children to fly from vice and practise virtue, after certain rules which are always the same. From the time when we depart from these rules proposed by the Church, we become bad Catholics, and we are condemned by the Catholic religion; we therefore cannot accuse *it* of authorising vice. But the Protestant religion, permitting to each one to make his own rule of conduct, it is certain that each will draw up a rule favourable to his passions; therefore a man may be vicious, and at the same time a good Protestant. You will understand now how the Catholic religion is not responsible for the vices of her children, since she opposes them, and how the Protestant religion *is* responsible for the vices of *her* children, since she authorises them.'

How far this book contains the truth I leave to my readers to judge. I only ask them, what they think of a Government *professing toleration*, which permits the circulation of such trash, and forbids the circulation of the Bible and good books; and refuses to allow a Protestant to say to a Catholic that he is ' in error '? See what was done with respect to the little *Bulletin*, p. 11, for only using this *very mild* word.

But some may say, why not reply to such foul libels, why not place the author in the pillory of public opinion? I will tell you why; because the reply would probably not be *allowed* to be published. Governments of the paternal form do not like quarrels between their children, and uphold the rights of the first-born ; and, therefore, if Peter calls Martin bad names, or even beats him, Martin must say nothing in return. Peter is the eldest son, and the peace of the family is best preserved, and collisions avoided, by letting *him* do as he likes. When, therefore, such books are circulated and read, and no contradiction or counter-statement appears, do not let us

wonder at the strange ideas that Roman Catholics have
of us, and, above all, do not let us wonder that they
consider our religion as one of convenience.

Only the other day, on two Breton women going to the
house of a Protestant minister, whom I know, to hear his
explanation of the Scriptures, the Catholic *curé* charged
them with going there for immoral purposes, stating that
it was notorious that the minister kept *a bad house!*
And I myself know that the opinion that Protestantism
is a religion of convenience is generally prevalent in
Britanny, and I have myself heard it so stated frequently.
For when they see that we go not to early mass, that we
cross not, that we fast not, that we count no beads, and
set up no images, that we confess not; they, who do little
else, are at a loss to imagine what we *can* do; and not
being able to fill up the void, conclude that we do nothing.

And yet were we to bandy terms, we might fairly say
that the religion of convenience is that *which allows you*
to buy *dispensations* and *indulgences* for money. A
plain man, for instance, thinks that a sin is a sin; but
Roman Catholics divide sins into classes. There are sins
mortal and sins venial, or, to call them more properly,
sins *venal*, as pardon of them is to be *bought*. Unless
the money is paid, the sin remains, a thing puzzling to
an unlettered Christian man.

To be sure these venial, *or venal* sins, are chiefly sins
of the invention of the Church; and, as the Church
gains by the invention, we may suppose that she has
been fertile in inventing. They constitute *her treasury,*
and therefore she has a direct interest in coining them;
and of such 'coins of vantage' she has a good stock.
If you eat meat on fast days you will certainly be
damned; but for a small sum you can procure a *dispensation*, and eat till you are stuffed. You must not marry

your cousin, or you go at once to a place not to be named, but pay his Holiness a fee and marry her with pleasure. A saved soul should go at once to Paradise, but unless you can pay for a mass it is stopped by purgatory on the way.

But *indulgences* go farther than this.

Here is the form : — ' I, by the authority of our Lord ' Jesus Christ, and that of his blessed apostles Peter and ' Paul, and of the most Holy Pope, do absolve thee first ' from all ecclesiastical censures, in whatever manner ' they have been incurred, and then from all thy sins, ' transgressions, and excesses, *how enormous soever* they ' may be, even from such as are reserved for the cog- ' nisance of the Holy See; and as far as the keys of the ' Holy Church extend, I remit to you all punishment ' which you deserve in purgatory on their account ; and ' I restore you to the holy sacraments of the Church, to ' the unity of the faithful, and to that innocence and ' purity which you possessed at baptism, so that when ' you die the gates of punishment shall be shut, and the ' gates of the paradise of delight shall be opened, and if ' you shall not die at present, *this grace shall remain in* ' *full force* when you are at the point of death. In the ' name of the Father, and of the Son, and of the Holy ' Ghost.'

This was the form of indulgence sold by Tetzel, which stirred the soul of Luther, and we shall say *not without cause*; and these forms are still made use of. But hear Tetzel's *explanations* on the subject: — ' Come, and I ' will give you letters, all properly sealed, by which even ' the sins which you *intend to commit* may be pardoned. • I would not change my privileges for those of St. Peter, ' for I have saved more souls by my indulgences than he ' by his sermons.' And hear him as to the efficacy of

his papers: — 'There is no sin so great that an indul-
' gence cannot remit, and even if anyone (which is im-
' possible doubtless,) *had offered violence to the blessed*
' *Virgin Mary, the Mother of God*, let him pay, *let him*
' *only pay well*, and all will be forgiven him.'   'And
' for a quarter of a florin, too, all this happiness.'   And
he concludes — 'At the very instant that the money
' rattles at the bottom of the chest, the soul flies straight
' to heaven.'—*D'Aubignès Reformation*, vol. i. p. 242.

To encourage business and save time, there was a
regular tariff.   Polygamy was charged six ducats, sa-
crilege and perjury nine ducats, murder eight ducats,
witchcraft two ducats, infanticide half a ducat, parricide
or fratricide one ducat.   Thus for twenty-six ducats and
a half, or about seven pounds, you might buy a license
to commit a great variety of sins *here*, and be free from
the punishment of them *hereafter!*   Who would not
purchase safety on such terms?   And yet we must on no
account call this a religion of *convenience!*

But the doctrine of indulgences is old, perhaps, and
not now in use.   What if it is?   The chain of infallibility connects all acts of the Romish Church, however
remote; there is no age *there* in the ordinary sense,
thanks to him who invented the doctrine of infallibility.

But it is *not* old.   In 1825, Leo, then Pope, granted
a plenary indulgence to all sinners who were content to
pay for it ; and it is notorious that particular indulgences
are of frequent occurrence.   General ones have grown
into disuse as comprehending too much, and being
therefore too cheap to make money by.   It is no difference in principle, but simply that the Church finds
the trade by *retail* more profitable than that in *gross.*
At present, you must purchase each pardon separately,
instead of (as before) all together; that is all the

difference. If, therefore, there is a religion of convenience, we should say it was that one in which the
system of dispensations and indulgences prevails.
' Those best can paint it who have felt it most.'

It is to be regretted that English Protestants resident
in Catholic countries, and especially in France, do not
show forth the *practical* nature of their religion better
than they often do. Example is better than precept,
and the sight of one religious family, regular in their
religious duties, and of good life and conversation,
would be more effective than a dozen treatises. But
many of our countrymen who reside in France are care-
less of these things, i.e. I do not think there is the
same average religious standard among them as among
residents in England. Then Protestant worship is
only celebrated in a few places, and scarcely ever in
English, and the effect of the want of a Sunday assembling together is speedily seen. Added to this,
temptations to gaiety and immorality abound, and the
cheapness of spirituous liquors operates strongly, and
these causes combine to lower the standard of morality
and conduct among many of our countrymen who reside
in France, and to prevent them exhibiting to the world
that example which would be so valuable.

The importance of public religious worship it is impossible to overrate, but there are few places, save
in large towns, where there are opportunities for it.
The few English missionaries, supported by different
societies, who are scattered here and there throughout
the country, may not always be *disposed* to give to their
countrymen the benefit of an English service, as, to a
certain extent, it may be an infringement on the peculiar
duties of their mission; but wherever this service can

be given, it should be. True, that most of the English residents in France speak French, and, strictly speaking, can *understand* a service in French ; but it is a *mechanical* matter — it reaches the ear rather than touches the heart — at any rate, the difficulty of understanding precisely what is uttered, either intercepts a large portion, or else clouds and reduces to generalities that which, to be effectual, must be practical and particular.

I know of one case where the minister, Mr. Jenkins of Morlaix, kindly complied with the wishes of his congregation, and gave them a service in their mother-tongue, and I can speak of the good effects of it. The attendance was regular and devout, and it was touching to see so many assembled, far from their native land, and without regard to denominational differences, for the common object of religious worship. Let us hope that the example may be more widely followed.

For *our countrymen* have a peculiar claim upon the ministrations of every English pastor, no matter for what object he is sent to France; and even if he has urgent and peculiar duties greatly occupying his time and attention, it is his *duty*, and should be his pleasure, although it may be a sacrifice of time and trouble, to organise a service for their spiritual welfare. A soul is, in theory, equally valuable, to whatever nation or colour the body may belong, but when it is of the same country as ourselves, that heart is cold which does not feel an additional glow towards it, and an increased interest in its well-being; and we should despair of those, and doubt their patriotism as well as their Christian spirit, who required to have this duty forcibly and frequently impressed upon them. Of course, if other duties of importance actually intervene, nothing can be said ; but so long as it is merely a matter

of increased exertion only; so long, in truth, as it is
possible, there can be no doubt, I think, as to what is
the plain *duty* of the Minister in such a case.

Let no one despise the day of small things in evangelisation.   Every flourishing church has had its commencement: time was, if we go back far enough, when
even Great Britain could count her Christians by units.

The other day I heard an interesting anecdote on
this subject, connected with a district in *The Charente*
in the south of France, which I will relate.   The
narrator was then colporting or hawking tracts and
Bibles at Amand, a small town there, and with little
success.   Testaments were in no demand — tracts of a
general nature less so — and the good man felt dis-
heartened.

However, he procured some of *Roussel's* admirable
controversial tracts, a sort of little work in which that
eminent French preacher excels, and tried *them*.   By
degrees the mountain began to move, signs of internal
agitation appeared, and the demand rapidly increased.

One market day he went as usual to the market
place, opened his pack, arranged his books on the stall,
and waited for customers.   By and by a priest passed,
and stopped to look at the books.   'What have you
got there?'   'Tracts and Bibles.' ''Bibles! ah, bad
books! bad books!' 'But what is this?' said he, taking
up one of Roussel's tracts.   He read and re-read, —
mused, and at length grew into a furious passion, and
abused Protestantism and all connected with it roundly.
His tones being loud attracted the passers-by: one
dropped in and then another, the circle increased, until
upwards of 200 were grouped around the little book-
stall, listening attentively to the dialogue.   The colporteur was a man well fitted for his calling, instructed,

calm, and good-humoured, and he soon had the field to himself; for the priest, lost in passion, abandoned it and fled away.

From that moment great interest was excited, the stall was speedily cleared of its stock, and the seed sown broadcast on the fallow ground. The morning afterwards, my friend was leaving the town, when he met with a *garde-de-chasse* with his brazen insignia on his arm. ' Are you the book-hawker?' said he; and on the colporteur answering in the affirmative, he was desired to follow him, which he did — not without inquietude, for be it remembered these devoted men march among pitfalls at all times, and are exposed to continual perils. Arrived at a park-gate, he entered and was conducted to the house of the proprietor, whom he found playing with his children. He was introduced. 'Have you your books with you?' 'I have.' 'Turn them out and let me see them.' He did so, and the gentleman, taking pen and paper, wrote down their titles, &c., one by one, until the whole stock was exhausted. 'Have you others?' 'Yes, at my inn.' ' Fetch them all.'

He returned, and mused on the occurrence in fear. What could this man want so many of his books for, taking them down in this dark abrupt manner? did he intend a prosecution? He had better not return to him;— so whispered prudence; but another and better spirit gave him confidence, and he returned with the remainder of his stock to the strange man.

Again were they duly written down, until the last was finished. 'And have you more?' 'No, I have not; but may I ask what you want with so many?' ' I want them for myself, my family, and my friends,' cried the other. ' I have taken the titles and the price,

and here is the total amount,' said he, eagerly, as though
fearing that the colpórteur should retake his precious
parcel; and handed him the full money.   The colporteur was astonished and could but thank God and take
courage, and go on with a glad heart.

The strange purchaser was an influential person who
feared compromising himself, and adopted this mysteri-
ous and roundabout way of getting the books; but soon
spreading them among his friends and neighbours, the
demand was more active than ever.   Fresh stocks were
applied for and distributed, reading caused reflection,
and reflection conviction, until a large body of Protestants in principle, if not in name, was formed.

An application was then made to Paris for a minister,
and one was sent — *Roussel* himself.   A temporary
chapel was formed out of a large barn, and was fitted
up, and there, on the spot where two years previously a
Testament was placed with difficulty, was assembled a
meeting of *a thousand* auditors.

Since then all has settled down into steady and
successful action — a regular minister and a regular
congregation are installed together, and other churches
have been founded in the neighbourhood.

And therefore let us not despise a small beginning,
when such results as these may flow from it.   As said
my friend, all was dark and gloomy as the camp of the
Philistines; but when the tracts were introduced he
thought of Samson and the lighted furze tied to the
foxes, for on all sides and in all quarters was spread
light to the righteous and confusion to the opponents of
the Truth.

Luther said well, when he exclaimed that ' Justification *by faith* was the keystone *of the Reformation*.'

For so it was and is; and equally true it is, that ' Justification *by works* was, and is, the keystone of *Romanism.*

The system of Romanism is essentially a material one, *of works*, into which faith as a necessary element counts for little. The important part, as to the church and the individual, is the external part, and as to the rest, the internal part, it is left chiefly to itself.

But how marvellously is all this adapted to human nature! Take the great bulk of mankind, and how incapable are they of judging of, or appreciating or comprehending things unseen : how slight and evanescent are the effects of such things upon their minds! But it is precisely to the bulk of mankind that Romanism addresses herself, leaving aside, as ciphers, the few crotchety exceptional individuals who endeavour to look farther than their fellows.

Look at the doctrine of Penance, for instance. What can be more *material* ? You commit a sin and wish to avoid being punished for it in a future state, and the means used are *to do* penance *here* — not to repent, amend, and believe—but to *do* penance, or, in default, pay the *fees.* Very *material this*, in *every* sense.

You have amassed a fortune, say by unlawful traffic, or by overreaching your neighbours, and as you have enough and to spare, and begin to grow old, you think it is as well to compound for your sins with some of your useless and surplus money. By all means, says the priest; it is a good thought, a pious thought, put into your head by the Virgin herself, and you shall gratify Heaven and *yourself* by practising it. Give so much to me for masses, and so much for charity, and so much to such and such a work, and your soul shall be whitewashed and made clean and pure for ever.

You distrust your power to resist temptation, and

are visited by momentary compunction for past transgressions; what a relief to purchase an indulgence,
which, for *a consideration,* acquits you for the past and
guarantees you for the future.

You touch a relic and are sanctified for forty days, or
buy one with a warranty, and are made holy for life.
You make vows in sickness to amend, and perform them
by a pilgrimage and a payment.

All this looks like a system *of works, of acts,* in which
the shell seems to usurp the place of the kernel, and in
which faith or belief seems properly to have small
place — to be non-essential.

It is true that the Scripture says that ' Faith without
works is dead;' and it is necessarily so, because, in fact,
it is not faith at all in the sense intended.   The faith
intended is that living principle, that ' evidence of
things unseen,' which as naturally produces works as life
produces thought and motion.   Faith without works
can therefore do nothing for us; but according to the
Romish system works without faith are important means
for reaching heaven.   According to that system a man
may work out his own salvation by his own efforts, and
without either fear or trembling, provided he is rich
and powerful.

Look at confession, for instance.   If, oppressed by
the weight of your sins, you feel disposed to look up to
heaven for pardon, this act of the heart will not avail
you, unless you openly confess to your priest and receive
his absolution; and yet the first feeling was heart-felt
and heart-cleansing, in comparison with the second,
which is simply *material* and external.

Again, what are the weekly fasts of Wednesday and ·
Friday but material means, steps in the ladder framed
by Rome to reach heaven *direct from earth,* without

heed to the precept that to do so man must be 'born again.'

The Romish system seems to say that human nature is not irretrievably vitiated by the fall, but only lowered, and that it can uplift itself to its former level by certain prescribed means. Romish doctors state that the saints and holy men of old, having raised themselves up to the requisite height long before their deaths, had consequently a superabundance of good works, a *surplus of sanctity;* and this having been bequeathed to the church as general legatee, she holds it in her coffers, to be doled out according to the needs *and means* of the petitioners; and thus shortens the pangs of purgatory for them. In all this faith enters not, belief enters not — it is simply a system of works; and therefore Luther well characterised the doctrine of justification by faith when he called it the keystone of the reformation.

One reason for the restlessness and impatience of control of the French *man,* I am much disposed to think, is to be found in the treatment and bringing up of the French *child.* All will acknowledge that habits are formed by degrees, and when once formed constitute the character; but how few apply this maxim in practice.

The child is father to the man, and possesses within his small body the germs of those future virtues and vices which he will exhibit on the world's stage; and if we wish to produce a good specimen of the genus *homo,* we must cultivate him when in the bud. As far as I have seen and heard, the French apply the doctrine of *laissez aller* to their children with small qualification. The young Gauls, even when but callow fledgelings, do much as they please. If independence be the charm of life, then should France be a child's paradise; but instead of bliss and peace, there is, I verily believe, a double allowance of those unpleasant varieties of domestic life which arise from cross and wayward children.

All this is quite natural, simply because children do not know what they *really* want, and therefore in the enjoyment of their desires they are sure to be disappointed. For myself, having a practical conviction (arising from the possession of a tolerable number of young cherubs of not more than average naughtiness) that children are great nuisances unless kept in good order, I am in an earthly purgatory when in company with infantile France. Being obliged ' to let I dare not wait upon I would,' I have often been forced to make myself scarce, lest I should *malgré moi* uncover a breach in good manners or elsewhere ; for it is annoying to see their wilfulness. And the parents generally look on, complain, and do nothing. They freely admit the evil in theory — I have heard it admitted a score of times — and (being liberal philosophers) *as freely* admit it in *practice.*

I feel certain that this is a root of great mischief, and I firmly believe that many of the defects in the French character spring from it. For, consider a moment. How is it likely that a child of wandering uncontrolled habits should settle into a man of fixed character ? He may *possibly* become such, but it must be an accident, not in consequence, but in spite of, his bringing up. As well expect a nomadic Arab to develope into a tailor— hatching on his shop-board. To have obedience to the laws of the realm from the man, we must have obedience to the laws of the house from the child; for the realm is but an aggregate of houses.

I see little in France answering to that careful maternal training which prevails in England, and which insensibly forms the character when it is tender and plastic. How many of us owe all that we have and are, to a *mother's care?* Who but she repressed our selfishness, tamed our rising passions, excited emulation, stimulated devotion; and all imperceptibly, by that gentle, soothing, but firm influence, grateful and fertilising as the dew of the morning? Who but she could have borne with our petulance, our ill tempers and our rudeness, suffering much with patience and repressing with tenderness in the hope of bright days to come? And who but she, thus acquainted with every hidden spring in our character, could in after-life so effectually have comforted, softened, and strengthened us?

Sacred and blest be thy memory, oh, my Mother! The little good I may have done, belongs to thee; the frequent evil I have committed has been in departing from thy precepts. Oftentimes thy memory steals upon me as a strain of music, lifting up my heart and hallowing it; or gushes upon me at eventide, as refreshing water from a fountain. When heated by the world's conflicts, or harassed by its cares, I look back as through a verdant vista upon *thee,* and my spirit regains its elasticity, and my mind its calm; and may the constant remembrance of thee here, be the foretaste and pledge of our reunion hereafter!

When, heated by the world's turmoil, to home's green shade we haste,
As to the blest oasis in Libya's burning waste,
There, cooling in its genial air, we soon forget our pain,
And return, our courage strengthened, to meet the foe again.

Instead of a mother's training, the youthful Frenchman is trained by his *bonne* or nurse, and this training is rather physical than moral. A shake when naughty, a sugar-plum when good, are the extremes of the system of awards and punishments betwixt which the child vaguely oscillates without guide or compass, and thus he rather *grows* than is *brought* up. He goes where he likes and eats what he likes and does what he likes, always supposing the *bonne* is thereto disposed by the caprice of the moment; and he soon imbibes, doubtless, a very natural aversion from control of any kind.

At school the discipline is very slight — let us say rather that there is no *corporeal* discipline at all; and how can a school be managed without it? I am not of the opinion of the old Doctor who thought that classics could only be taught *a posteriori*; but that line of argument is often essential, and is tried with success where the *a priori* has failed; nor do I believe that any family or school can be managed without it. Mild remedies are good for mild disorders, but milk poultices will not set a broken leg.

When, therefore, at 16, the young Frenchman emerges upon the world, is it *very* astonishing that he should have a very fixed idea of the great value of *No.* 1, and a very rooted dislike to the principle of subordination, as applied to himself? It would be very astonishing if it were otherwise. Carry on these principles a few steps farther, and we arrive at the Frenchman of mature age, impatient of authority, holding all kinds of political doctrines by turns, and nothing long, and (judging by events) always ready for a change, and disposed towards it.

Napoleon the Great was well aware of this disposition. He says (*Las Cases*, vol. i. p. 268), 'The French nation is naturally fickle, and given to change. The men are like children, and know not what are their real wants; they must be amused and governed in order to be happy.'

Some time ago it was rather the fashion in England to affect 'the familiar' with parents; the father was called 'Governor,' the mother 'Old Lady;' in fact, outwardly, Master Jack and Tom seemed on the way of becoming the heads of the establishment. But *old John* did not at all like it, however popular it was with young Jack; and one fine morning, something having put him out more than usual, he grasped his cane, sallied out, and put to flight the whole accumulation of the 'free and easy' with a good stick; nor has it since appeared, except below stairs, where it is to be hoped it will rest.

· Respect to parents, and obedience to their wishes, are at the base of the social fabric; nor can any society hang well together in which these duties are neglected or carelessly observed. The French children *love* their parents well enough, I do not doubt, but that is not sufficient; it is doing no more than the brutes do. We must *respect* them and do their requests from duty as well as love, or we cannot be said properly to observe the commandment, which says '*Honour* thy father and mother.'

When I first came to the country, our French nurse went out to walk with the children, and soon returned. 'Why are you returned so soon?' 'Oh, Madame! Master Samuel would not go any farther, but said he would return home.' 'But what has that to do with it?' said my wife; 'you are to take them out so far and back again *whether they like it or not*, and if they are disobedient to you, tell me, and I will punish them.' The girl opened her eyes very wide, but we never found them coming home before their time afterwards.

Another consequence of this want of system is, that the French child is remarkably precocious. Even with

us in England, we find our children are quite early
enough,—that they become men quite as soon as they
are fit for the duties of men, often indeed before; but
we are behind France in that respect. There we find
children of twelve and fourteen with the manners and
habits of grown people. Few remain at school after
sixteen, and so come upon life, we should say, before
they are ready for it. Boys of fifteen, swagger, smoke,
and strut quite easily and man-like, and girls of the
same tender age have the manners and bearing of
women. Take up any history of any one of the various
French revolutions, and you will find that the *gamins*,
or *lads* of Paris, and the Polytechnic *schoolboys* have
been important actors in it. The *Garde Mobile* included in its ranks many children under fourteen;
and some of them had even won their decoration at
the cannon's mouth, when at the same age in England
they would only have got a good whipping and have
been sent to bed. But then a French revolution is
always, more or less, a kind of 'lark' to some of the
actors, however tragical it may be, and always is, to the
others.

CHAPTER XV.

HOW extraordinary is French ignorance of England
and her affairs — i. e. extraordinary, speaking
generally; for to speak specially it is easily explained.
Not one Frenchman travels in England for fifty Englishmen who travel in France, and the same principle
holds as to knowledge of the respective languages.

If an Englishman goes to France, he probably knows
certain rudiments of the French language to begin with,
unless he has been brought up in a very rude manner;
and, to do him justice, he never hides his light under a
bushel. He boggles, stammers, flounders out of one
difficulty into another, refers to his constant friend the
dictionary, which he carries in his pocket, and finds the
wrong word, during the livelong day, without fatigue
or shame; but he seldom blushes from a false modesty,
or cares what others think of him. With an excrucia-
ting self-possession he delivers himself of errors which
would drive *Levizac* or *Hamel* downright mad, or
politely and with a smile addresses what he means as
compliments to the ladies, which are either unintelligible
or had better remain so; but he goes on right ahead,

as he follows the fox or meets the foe, and ends by finding himself a tolerable Frenchman.

Not so the Gaul. Not one in a hundred knows English at all, and that one seldom or never speaks it; contrary to his usual practice, he carefully hides *his* candle, either from fear that it will not burn, or that it will burn too fast and go out; but there he sits, more voluble naturally than any other created biped, yet in fact mute as a mouse.

The same with literature. Few Englishmen of moderate education but who have read works on France, by Frenchmen, and in the French language; whereas not many Frenchmen have done more than read their own light, skipping, false, newspaper sketches of England, or else caricatures of travel there, *drawn* rather than written by their inventive fellow-country-men, *residing the while in Paris*. The practical effect of this is obvious and natural, that Frenchmen know much less of England than Englishmen of France.

Then look at them as tourists. The true *John Bull*, whether young, old, or middle-aged, regards a tour as a serious matter. In general he accumulates as much baggage as would be necessary to take him to the North Pole, together with all imaginable and unimaginable conveniences for performing *un*necessary things, and sets out on his travels. With spectacle on nose, an umbrella under his arm, a guidebook in one pocket, a dictionary in another, and a sandwich-box in the crown of his travelling-cap (manufactured at the ' *Golden Trunk*,' or some other noted place, ' expressly for travellers '), he plods gravely on, poking himself into the premises and face of everybody; asking explanations, boring with questions, constantly suspecting imposition, and yet, after all, paying twice as liberally as any other person, ' for they are a poor set, sir;' yet returning to his home with a vast heap of digestible and other materials.

Who ever saw a Frenchman act so? But *he* is a poor tourist. In a foreign country he generally goes no-where but to public places, and not always there; stays at his inn; travels on wheels; asks few questions, for fear he should be thought odd; eschews the country as *sauvage*; and then returns to his friends saying that there is nothing to see, because he has seen nothing; that the *cafés* are odious; and the sky made of wet brown paper.

Two French friends of mine went to the Exhibition in 1851. When they came back, I asked them what they thought of London? 'A great city, but nothing in it.' 'How so?' said I. 'Did you go to such and such a place?' I asked. 'No,' said they. 'Nor to St. Paul's?' 'No.' 'Nor to Windsor?' 'No.' And, in fact, they had 'done' nothing but the Crystal Palace, and had driven about in cabs for fear of being lost, and had naturally seen next to nothing. Another complained bitterly of the diet, and declared to an admiring audience that there was nothing to be had in London but raw meat and rhubarb tart. He declared he had dined on nothing else. But I asked, 'Did not you order your dinner, or see the bill of fare?' 'Oh no! I ordered a bit of meat and tart, or something, and up came this raw meat and rhubarb;' in other words, *a beefsteak and a spring tart*, each dainties in their way. Another complained horribly of the expense—it was *affreux, effrayant*, &c.; but I found he had been at a Burling-ton Street hotel, and had drunk claret every day, though, as he said, he had had only a bottle of *vin ordinaire* (i. e., claret at ten shillings a bottle), a *petit diner*, and a desert—in other words, as expensive an order as he

R

could well have given, and which would figure in the
bill for at least a sovereign.

One frequent subject of misapprehension with them
is our public meetings; and the occasional disturbances
which take place from strikes of workmen and other
causes also puzzle them terribly. They are generally
in extremes, and see no medium between a street row
and a revolution. A local quarrel is an *emeute*; a
political meeting, with its spoken fustian, is *rebellion
organisée*. The other day I called on a friend, who is
always prophesying the downfall of England. 'Have
you seen the papers?' he asked. I had not seen them.
'Then you have some news to hear. There is a very
serious outbreak in Ireland. Ah! my friend, you will
find I am right; if you *will* go on harbouring these
democrats, these vagabond refugees, you must pay
dearly for it, and this is the first fruits.' I felt uneasy,
and enquired for particulars, but got meagre answers,
save that it was at Cork, that the military had been
called out, and many people killed and wounded. On
my return home I found the paper, and eagerly
devoured the 'latest intelligence,' and discovered that
the incipient rebellion and engagement which had
so disturbed my prophetic friend was nothing but a row
with the paupers *in Cork workhouse!*

The same with our public meetings. They never can
understand them, for they have nothing analogous by
which they can judge. Public meetings in France
are illegal, consequently when they do take place, and
as they are a breach of the law, they take place under
high pressure, and generally end by an explosion.
High words are followed by hard deeds; but not so in
England. There the public meetings are the safety
valves of the political engine; and when steam is gene-

rated to an alarming degree, instead of bursting the boilers, it escapes, with noise it is true—*plenty of that*—but without danger, by that admirable invention the public meeting. An Englishman's right to grumble at his government is inalienable and invaluable, for it at the same time improves the doctor and relieves the patient: and after weeks of painful thought and gestation, in which the throes have been alarming to witness, the birth is effected by a convulsion which seems to shake everything; and after which worthy John Bull goes to rest in peace, draws his night cap over his face, snores, and wakes up in the morning with a countenance as shining and tranquil as Aurora's!

Speaking of French ignorance, an amusing specimen of extreme *naïveté*, not to say nonsense, was exhibited to me this morning. A French gentleman, who prided himself on his knowledge of English affairs, and had just pronounced after several trials the names of Shakespeare and Byron, so that at last I began to understand him with tolerable correctness, commenced talking of the Duke of Wellington. 'A great man, a far seeing man that,' he said; 'I was always struck by a little anecdote of his long-sightedness which I believe is undoubtedly true.' 'Pray, favour me with it,' I asked. 'At the battle of Waterloo he ordered a charge of your heavy cavalry, and suspecting that the men might not relish our cuirassiers so well at close quarters as at a distance, he gave previous orders for the curb-chains *to be removed* from the bridles, so that once launched, the men should be carried to the attack whether they liked it or not.' 'But, my dear sir, that would be sheer folly; how could they ever get *back* again, or manage their horses? the Duke never ordered such an absurdity.' 'Absurdity or not, the thing was done; you need only

R 2

read Lamartine and Valaubelle (*where it is really re-corded*); besides, it is a recognised fact.' The re-cognised fact is, that our cavalry horses were always a little too *bloodish,* and often got the better of their riders; and in the charge in question, they charged so home that had their return not been well covered, they would all have been cut to pieces; and as it was, they left poor Ponsonby and half their numbers on the field. Instead of taking away their curb-chains, it would have been more to the purpose to say that the Duke had ordered the use of an additional one.

But those who wish to read the account of the battle of Waterloo ' with variations on the original air,' should read Lamartine's *History of the Restoration,* vol. ii. Poets should not write history; their imagination runs away with their pen — *they* lack the curb-chain we have been telling about. And Lamartine *paints* perpetually — pictures beautiful, highly coloured, embracing all which can attract you, *except* the truth. He describes the ' palisadoed entrenchments' of Hougomont and the British lines, with eloquence — alas! for the ink thrown away—as all the world *should* know that there was nothing of the kind. He speaks of the dragoons being made drunk with brandy before they were got up to the charging point; need I say that this is as true as the other? He describes the dispersion of the first English line when Picton was killed—when the fact is, that it was the French who were dispersed with the loss of two eagles and 2,000 prisoners; and enlarges on the final advance of the English army in five large columns, when all the world knows the Duke disliked columns and advanced in line.

But the great tableau, wanting nothing but correct-ness to make it perfect, is at the 405th page. He

describes Wellington as driven to desperation by his
fearful losses and the absence of Blucher, also says that
eleven of his generals lay dead around him, and that
seven horses having been killed under him, he mounts
the *eighth*, and gallops from brigade to brigade, &c. &c.
This beats Falstaff's men in buckram — 'ay, in buckram suits'—as there were only *nine* generals in the whole
allied army at Waterloo; and as to mounting *eight*
horses, the Duke's favourite charger, 'Copenhagen,'
alone carried him from the beginning to the end of the
day. It is cruel thus to break the illusion.

The world may remember that some time back, in consequence of some rather cutting remarks in the 'Times'
on the manner in which the French Government interfered and tampered with the suffrage, the 'Moniteur'
contained a very studied and carefully drawn up article
on the unlimited character of the suffrage in France,
and the limited nature of it in England; and went
on with general observations on various points in the
English constitution, couched in an apparently disinterested, but really very offensive, tone.

I could but envy the writer of that article in one
respect—his admirable countenance and self-possession.
He must have written with the gravity of a judge
passing sentence; not a muscle of his face could have
moved; there could not have been even a ripple to
disturb the calmness of his mind; and yet all the time
he must have known that he was penning sentences
which he and nine-tenths of the French world knew
had scarcely an atom of truth or reality about them.
That man would have made, if he was not one already,
a great comic actor, extreme gravity being the finest
setting for wit. If the thought has never before
struck him, let me recommend it to his notice, for I am

sure his fortune lies that way. I have heard of religious hypocrites who acted so well as to deceive themselves into occasional belief that they were really pious; and I think this grave scribe, when he penned his solemn sentences, must for the moment have imagined that he was uttering realities and not shams. Because a more complete sham than the so-called free suffrage in France never existed.

The article in the 'Moniteur' described the election of Louis Napoleon as the *freely expressed, universal will of a great nation.* If out of the six component members of this paragraph we suppress four, and then alter the fifth, we shall be nearer the truth; but this is to make rather a great deduction.

'Freely expressed!' Why, never was demonstration so coddled and cooked up before ; never did any government so get up and direct the popular current into its own channel. The only merit of the thing was its barefacedness. The préfets boldly said, 'You good people do n't know what is best for you ; listen to me ;' and downwards to the pettiest official, all held the same language, and universal France pricked up its ears. Petitions to the legislature, in favour of the empire, were circulated in every government establishment, and woe to the independent man who declined signing. Everyone was 'free,' but it was 'to give up his place.' Do just as you please, no compulsion or menace of any kind; but if you do n't vote on our side, you will be turned out of doors.

I knew one young man, who was a public-road surveyor, and who had conscientious scruples, and could not make up his mind to sign in favour of the Emperor, but yet, for family reasons, he feared refusing. He delayed and delayed, still hoping they would pass

him by, but he reckoned without his hosts; his name
had been counted, and must be given in. His superior
officer came to him one morning: 'Have you signed
the petition? it is going away to-day, and I heard the
chef say that if your name was not placed there, he
should be obliged, in spite of himself, to dismiss you.'
In vain the young man urged his well-known republican
opinions. 'Pooh! pooh! my dear fellow, do not make
yourself so fearfully virtuous. What are half those who
sign but the same as yourself? What am I, for instance?
Why do you set yourself above us all?' The young
man still hesitated, but he thought of his wife and
family, all dependent upon him for support, and with
a shudder he gulped down the bitter draught and signed.
This is opinion 'freely expressed.'

And who, under such circumstances, dared get up a
counter petition? Certainly not Frenchmen. To the
honour of the nation, however, be it recorded, that *one
solitary individual* did present a petition against the
Empire, and I only regret that his name has escaped
me. It deserves an enduring record, and 't is pity no
one has preserved it for history.

'The great body voted *oui*; one man protested, and
the rest *abstained*;' yes! that is the fashionable word
now; 'abstained'—held themselves aloof. A convenient
safe policy too, chiefly connected with *No.* 1; you may
turn it many ways by means of ciphers, like that useful
primary element of arithmetic. It may be illness,
unavoidable circumstances, or that indefinite word 'in-
disposition,' which make you abstain, *Quien sabe?*
while to your own party you dilate gloriously upon the
self-denying act. A most cowardly, unmanly, negative
policy, leading to nothing and doing nothing, unworthy
of the name of act, for *ex nihilo nihil fit.* A great

question demands solution, you feel strongly upon it, and speak strongly too; but when it comes to the vote, you stay away—*you abstain.* Your absence, you say, speaks volumes; shows how indignant you are; is a moral protest. Suppose *all* did so, how would anything ever be settled? Could you better serve your opponents? for *them*, the more of such protests the better. It is a mean course, unworthy of a man, though suitable in a 'thing,' and generally consistent with selfish interests and fears; but it is doubtless often *convenient.*

In the municipal elections the same repression of the popular voice was practised. Every *ruse* was resorted to, which ingenuity could devise to prevent an anti-imperial candidate succeeding. In a little Bourg near here, when the chances were in favour of a legitimist member, they burnt the poll books; in another they gave a wrong return. In one town, not far off, where on a first scrutiny the opposition list carried the day, the *sous préfet* annulled the return and appointed a fresh day of election; meanwhile, issuing an address which, for bombast, might have been copied from Hudibras. But everywhere were practised the same tricks and strategems, from the election of a *garde champètre* up to the election of the Emperor himself, and then the 'Moniteur' comes in with a grave face, speaks of the majesty of the '*universal will freely expressed,*' and the French nation with equal gravity, inhales and adopts the phrase.

The other day I met with a forcible illustration of one great cause of Louis Napoleon's success, I mean the bitterness of party spirit in France. For here lay his best hope. It was less his strength than their divisions, and weakness. We occasionally find individuals who will encounter certain ruin in order to gratify their spite, and when party spirit runs high, this spirit comes out strongly. No one can imagine the hatred with which many Legitimists regard the Orleanists. In order to defeat them they would adopt any means, they would see the country given up to anarchy, their feelings against them are so intensely bitter. To a certain extent we may explain this. At the revolution of July 1830, when Charles X. was forced to fly and was replaced by Louis Philippe, the aristocracy of France again received a heavy blow. They saw themselves again reduced to comparative obscurity, again the subjects of obloquy and suspicion. Many emigrated, others retired to their country seats; the hopes of all were dashed rudely aside. To the young aspirants for fame in the army or the state, who already courted the promotion and honours which their rank made almost certain, the disappointment must have been severe when these avenues were suddenly and violently closed in their faces. And at that period, too, there seemed a certain regard for oaths and principles, which we seldom see now. Thousands refused courtly favour and preferment at the price of an oath of allegiance to the new King, and withdrew sullenly from the scene, to brood over their misfortunes and grow sour in stagnation at home.

Such was the case with my friend the *Vicomte de R——e.* He had been in the *Garde Royale* of Charles X., had witnessed the treason of some and the cowardice of others, and when the monarch fled, had, in a frenzy of passion, broken his sword rather than swear fidelity to the usurper, and had then gloomily retreated to the country, his career stopped, and a long perspective of honours and preferment clouded apparently for ever. And he has ever since remained staunch to his

principles and his hatred, and has nursed it well and
kept it warm.   Talking with him last week about the
Empire and the weakness of his party, he said : 'Anything rather than the Orleans dynasty.   I prefer Napoleon, bad as he is, a thousand times.   I know that the
adoption of him is a burning shame for France ; I know
that we strengthen the foundations of a third dynasty,
and so augment our own future opponents, and involve
the country's future in greater dangers than ever.   I
know that it is a death-blow to the cause of Legitimacy,
but let all these things come sooner than the Orleanist
princes, all of whom I would *kill* to-morrow if I had
the opportunity.'   He was deeply excited, and looked
like one who had the will to do the deed he spoke of;
and he was, I firmly believe, the type of thousands of
others, who, in their blind unreasoning folly and bigotry,
have thus opened the gate to the re-establishment of a
new dynasty in order to gratify their hate towards an
old one.   It was useless discussing the matter ; such he
was, *and such his party are*, and owing to such has the
new dynasty triumphed over the liberties of France.

No one can know the blessings of a free government
unless he has lived under an arbitrary one.   To hear
Englishmen complain of their government, and of its
oppressive acts, what a grave farce it is !   Englishmen
can have no shadow of an idea of tyranny save by
reading the present state of other governments, or the
past doings of their own ; and the perusal of a thousand
books does not strike so forcibly upon the mind as the
actual experience of one solitary fact.

For instance, suppose that a wealthy tradesman, of
whig politics, enjoying himself with his family and
friends in his snug villa at Brompton or Hampstead,
was suddenly and without warning pounced upon by the

police in the middle of the night, dragged from the warm side of his weeping and dishevelled rib, consigned to the local lock-up house, and only removed from thence to be packed into a convict ship, and sent to Norfolk Island, and this without trial, judge, or jury; and all for having shouted ' Pam for ever! down with the Tories! ' What would Cheapside and Oxford Street say to this, think you? ·

Or suppose that a sedentary tailor in Liverpool, whose profession, as is said, almost invariably makes him ferocious as a tiger in talk, but mild as a lamb in act, is violently removed from his shopboard; and without respect to trowsers half completed and coats not yet ' set up,' is ordered to remove forthwith to Southampton, and there pick up what shreds, patches, and cabbage he can, and reconstruct therewith his tattered connections; think you, that instead of a petition from the ' three tailors of Tooley Street ' on behalf of the people of England, we should not have a demand from the people of England on behalf of the transplanted tailor?

Or what would the men of the 10th hussars say, if they were to learn that their colonel had been arrested in the night, and was then on his way to the hulks, for having, the evening before, at the mess, when heated with wine, cried ' Long live Johnny Russell! ' or ' Over the left with Judas Disraeli! '

But these facts have happened hundreds, if not thousands, of times in France during *the last few years*, and especially during the *régime* which succeeded the *coup d'état*; and the three instances that I have named are within my *personal* knowledge, along with many others; and yet people looked on, shook their heads, and shrugged perhaps, but did nothing more.

Were I a Frenchman, I think I should adopt some

plan like that of the monomaniac, who thought himself
always dying, and made his doctor certify his existence
every morning, that he might have some visible proof
of life to reason from. At any rate, I should feel
additionally thankful when each returning sun found
me still lying peaceably in my bed.

During the last few years there are hundreds of
families in France dismembered by the mere illegal
sic volo sic jubeo decree of arbitrary power, whose
fathers, brothers, and sons are languishing in the
marshes of Cayenne, or broiling beneath the hot sun of
Lambessa, and all for *upholding the law.* Then there
are numbers who are *internès,* i. e. sent from their
usual residence to some distant place in France, usually
as distant as possible, in order that they may be wholly
cut off from their friends; and in their new abode
ordered here and there by the police, whose very foot-
ball they are, and obliged to pick up a living as they
can. I have seen several of these poor *internès,* and it
made me sad to look at them. In England, their very
appearance would produce a rebellion — here people
stare, shrug, sigh, and pass on. And to talk of 'public
spirit,' of 'public opinion,' of the 'will of the nation,'
after such sights and things as these! Talleyrand's
mot, that 'language was given to conceal thought,' may
fitly apply to such a misapplication of words.

Let Englishmen look as sharp after officials as
they please; let them frown at the tax-gatherer, but
pay him; let them ransack Hansard for the votes and
speeches of their members; let them attend reform
meetings with fierce looks, and shout till they are
hoarse — but let them be grateful for their birthright,
and thank God that they *are* Englishmen! I never
had this feeling till I came into foreign parts, and

especially into France, and ever since I have had it so strongly that at times it *will* break out; and as travelling is cheap and agreeable now-a-days, I recommend a journey abroad to all those who are discontented at home, and, unless the disease be constitutional and *very* chronic, I will answer for a perfect cure at the first dressing.

I think it is Gibbon who says, that flatterers surround an emperor as naturally as parasites entwine the oak. Under the Empire there has always been a goodly crew of these sycophants, ever polishing their periods and out-bidding each other in adulation; but up to the present time we must award the prize to M. le Baron Chapuys Montlaville, préfet of the Haute Garonne; '*palmam qui meruit, ferat.*' Henceforth, let it be known that, in the manufacture of 'fustian,' we must give place to a Frenchman, and let canny Yorkshire hide its head for evermore.

For instance, what *material* could Huddersfield or Bradford produce, equal in quality to the following? It is a proclamation to the inhabitants of the department, on the subject of the vote for the Empire; and we may bear in mind, in reading it, that the writer *had been* a staunch Orleanist under Louis Philippe, and subsequently a hot Republican, and would probably have been an equally staunch Legitimist under Charles X. had he lived at that period. It is not everyone who can dance the political '*double-shuffle*' cleverly. *Nemo repente est turpissimus.* Your clumsy man of principle cannot do it at all, no matter how long he is taught, and even your slippery waiter upon fortune makes a bungle of it at first, until frequent occasions perfect him; but here in France *ou on fait la danse toujours*, and men may have constant practice, the adroitness and completeness with which this *tour de*

force is performed passes belief, and there are *stars* among
the performers in the political *ballet* equal in their line
to Taglioni or Cerito. But a clear stage for Baron Montlaville — here he comes ; ladies, prepare your bouquets.

    ' Inhabitants of the Haute Garonne,

    ' The time arrives.   France after a half century has
' at last found a base and an equilibrium.   Europe, the
' world, ruled in their turn by the profound wisdom of
' the prince whom God has placed at the head of the
' ideas and men of the time, enter without anxiety,
' with security, into those great highways of progress,
' opened formerly by our fathers.

    ' In those future ages of which he now assumes the
' direction, Louis Napoleon will not be called merely
' the Saviour of society.   His understanding of those
' questions which govern the well-being of man, of the
' necessities of Europe, his love of the classes which
' work and suffer, his genius for practical affairs which
' organise the ideas of work by inspiration, will confer
' on him the title of Benefactor of his epoch.

    ' The change he has brought about is one of those, of
' which worthily to give the results to posterity, would
' demand the pen of a Tacitus or a Bossuet.

    ' It is not only an empire which rises, a throne which
' is founded.   It is *an epoch* which is born to us, and
' which, impregnated with the genius of two Napoleons,
' to whom, together, will be given the title of The Great,
' developes itself to poor humanity, and takes possession
' of it for present and future generations.

    ' It is this wisdom, the essential attribute of his
' genius, which, after having conquered Rome, has sub-
' jected Europe to its imperial destiny.

    ' This is what causes the fact that 35,000,000 of
' men (?), bowing humbly before him, confer on him the

' imperial crown, and give to his descendants the care of
' rendering happy our children, and of directing and
' enriching the ages which are yet to come.

' And this is the reason why the people of the Haute
' Garonne will come *en masse* to the voting places, to
' take part in this magnificent enthronement, and to
' leave to their families the remembrance of the glory
' which belongs to it.'

Talk of Tacitus and Bossuet! why, what could *they*
produce equal to this? It would be impossible, were
they to use their pens to the stump. Let us at once
confess the Baron inimitable; let us admit that up to
this present writing he has out-leaped all others; that
he has performed this delicate *pas seul* in a way unknown before. Now, however, comes the most wonderful feat of all, ' Alps on Alps arise;' the Baron shall
out-do himself, like the man who, after swallowing hot
pokers and eating live cats, announced that he would
jump down his own throat in the sight of the audience.
Not content with the proclamation, he makes a decree;
and as he bids so high for immortality and *promotion*,
let us serve it up 'to follow' the proclamation, and
we may venture to herald and foretaste it to our readers
as a real *bonne bouche.*

' We, Préfet of the Department of the Haute Garonne,
' Officer of the University and of the Legion of Honour,
' Commander of the Papal Order of St. Gregory the
' Great, and of the Orders of St. Maurice and St.
' Lazarus' (*this Harlequin Tacitus does not appear to
have capered for nothing*),—

' Considering, that it is important to transmit to
' posterity by imperishable monuments those acts of
' God which are about to be accomplished in France

' through the people on the 21st and 22nd November,
' in the year of grace 1852.

' Considering that with the nations of antiquity it
' was the custom to engrave on bronze and marble
' memorable facts interesting to history.

' Considering that the re-establishment of the French
' Empire is a fact destined to exercise a most powerful
' influence on the fortunes of the country and on society
' universally.

' *We decree*, that the result of the voting in the
' Haute Garonne shall be engraved on *bronze* and
' marble tables, which shall be placed in the Mairie of
' each commune of the Department, with the addition
' of the number of votes in such commune, and that
' each table shall bear the date of the 1st day of the
' reign of His Majesty the Emperor Napoleon III.

' CHAPUYS MONTLAVILLE.'

There is one manifest omission here, which we beg to
fill up by way of supplement, for we are certain it must
have altogether escaped the nimble Baron, viz. that as
his stock *of bronze* must have been enormous to have
enabled him to manufacture these notable documents,
he should generously offer to supply the metal himself
at a small profit ; or should this hint not be acceptable,
we would respectfully suggest, that considering the
average duration of dynasties in France, and the taste
of the people for light materials, it would be better to
send the order for the ' tables' to a pastry cook, and
have them made *in sugar candy*.

But who shall describe the baseness, the abject flat-
tery of these men, with their stereotyped praises, their
sickening adulation?   As says Victor Hugo:—' Those
eternal préfets, those eternal maires, those eternal
magistrates, those eternal sheriffs, those eternal compli-

menters of the rising sun or of the illumination lamp,
who the day after success crowd round the Con-
queror, round his Majesty Napoleon the Great, round
his Majesty Louis XVIII., round his Majesty Alexander I., round his Majesty Charles X., round his
Majesty Louis Philippe, round *Citizen* Lamartine,
round *Citizen* Cavaignac, round *Monseigneur* the Prince
President, and round Napoleon III., kneeling, smiling,
overflowing, bearing upon salvers the keys of their
towns, and on their faces the keys of their consciences!
But 'tis an old story, *imbeciles* have always made a part
of all institutions, and are almost an institution of
themselves.' This rings good and true, and finds a full
echo in France.

It would seem that the Senate, though it has suffered everything, and thanked and glorified the inflictor,
has of late been amusing itself with an afterpiece of
independence, in order to keep up the play and divert
the audience. The Emperor, as is known, has recently
proposed to modify the constitution so as to give to
himself additional powers over the finances; and it
seems that, in doing this, he claims a greater power
than was exercised even in the days of the early Bourbons. This stirred the tranquillity of the Senate, who
reminded him that he had always professed to hold to
the principles of 1789, but that he was now departing
from them. Perhaps some of the excellent and innocent senators began to dream of Parliamentary opposition, eloquent speeches, clubs and coteries, and so forth,
but if so, they must have been rudely awoke. When
their remonstrances were presented to Louis Napoleon,
instead of a lengthened and reasoned reply, an answer
motivé, as they express it, all he said was, ' So the
Senate wants a conflict?' and without more ado, away

s

scudded all the legislators, with their hearts in their
mouths, and their big wigs under their arms, like
rabbits at the bark of a terrier, and uttered not another
word.   ,

By such arms, and with such tools, government must
be, one would think, an easy process, despite of the
most ponderous and voluminous report of M. Troplong
on the subject; which, though profound, was like its
author, and decidedly *trop long.*

CHAPTER XVI.

CAN anyone tell me the exact value of an oath, over and above that of a simple asseveration? There must be something mystical in it, and one might think *material*, something of the *opus operatum* kind. The name of the Roman oath, or *sacramentum*, has been transferred to a religious rite, and in the transfer of name it would seem as if the old substance, the binding part, had disappeared from civil affairs.

When my question is resolved, I then will put the further question, What is the value of a French oath as compared with the simple asseveration of an honest Englishman? If it be less valuable, there was a good deal of mockery going on in the good year of '52; if it be more valuable, the French Government need fear nothing, at least during the present generation of men. Time will show; but such a general swearing, such a new phase in the system of oaths, was never before exhibited.

If an oath be supposed to act as a hammer on the head of truth, then is that cardinal virtue driven deep into the social fabric, and society may be said to be nailed well together, supposing always that the afore-

said head be not destroyed in the process, and truth
thenceforth dead and extinct. Cowper says, ' Oaths
terminate, as Paul observes, all strife;' and adds,
'Some men, then, surely have a peaceful life.' Let
Napoleon, therefore, nap at his ease, he will never be
disturbed, for all France has sworn it; but still I feel,
with Horace, ' Credat Judæus Apella—non ego.'

In 1849 oaths were abolished in France—perhaps
because men were so habitually truthful as to render
them unnecessary—perhaps because experience had
shown them to be worthless—and no one swore allegiance and fidelity to the Republic *save the President*;
and he not only swore this oath at the beginning of his
office, but recalled it to memory fifty times afterwards,
as though he wished to strengthen his virtue on the
principle of the man who whistled in the dark to keep
up his courage. This oath being the only one taken,
stood out in bold relief, and it was sworn with all due
solemnities, military and religious. Tell me now, gentle
reader, what is the *present marketable value* of this
oath, once thought so very valuable? Its value, weighed
honestly and fairly, without using apothecary's weight
and its scientific ' scruples,' is *nil* and cannot be quoted.

In 1852, however, and ever since, the system has
·been reversed, and whereas beforetime nobody swore
but the Emperor, now everybody swears *except* the
Emperor; and let us hope that this time the oaths will
be better kept, for their name is ' Legion.'

All have sworn, from the General-in-chief to the
private in the ranks, from the Prime Minister down to
the paid day-labourer who works on a public road as a
' cantonnier.' Every person employed and paid directly
or indirectly by the state, by the department, or by the
commune, officers on half-pay, municipals, road-sur-

veyors, custom-house officers on duty and off, *gardes champêtres*, members of commissions, people keeping tobacco shops, and holding grants of government privileges, in fine, *everybody*, has sworn a solemn oath. Of what? of allegiance? of fealty to the government? No! an oath of fidelity *to the Emperor Louis Napoleon.* A very *personal* oath truly, and looking at the past very numerous personal oaths of allegiance taken in France, and 'when taken to be well shaken,' I should hesitate before predicting everlasting duration as the probable fate of this oath now before us, and can but ask, ' *Cui bono ?* '

One morning I met a friend, a Legitimist. ' What news this morning?' said I. 'Nothing new, except that I have been taking the oath of allegiance to Louis Napoleon.' ' What! you, a *Legitimist,* how can *you* possibly swear fidelity to him?' '*Ma foi!* for that matter I detest the man, but what to do is the question, and if I refused I should lose my appointment.' ' Lose it then, but keep your honour at least, like your own king, Henry V.' 'Ah! my friend, I see you think an oath something serious, but just reflect on this fact, that I have myself taken the oath of allegiance *to seven different* governments in France, embracing every shade of political principle, and it would be absurd to boggle about the *eighth*; after all, it is but a matter of form.' So that there is little real security for the future peace of the country in all this swearing. 'Tis like supporting an aqueduct with bolsters!

The drama, however, goes on, and the sun beholds the most multitudinous oath-taking on which he ever shone, and each separate oath being nothing but so much pie-crust, who can calculate the breakage!

For all swear this oath of fidelity *to the Emperor,*

whatever may be their politics—Legitimists, Orleanists, Republicans or Reds, all swear — *sooner than lose their places*; and from the same principle of self-pre-servation, all will, in case of need, break their oaths *in order to keep their places;* and if some few exceptions have appeared, '*rari nantes in gurgite vasto,*' they do but prove the rule as I state it.

Three observations only need be made here; the first, that such a national swearing is a sign of, and certain to increase, the national immorality; the second, that the universality of the act will only hasten its violation and legalise the breach; and the third, that Louis Napoleon must be struck with a more than regal blind-ness not to see that instead of thus surrounding his throne with defences, he is but fencing it about with cobwebs.

For evidently, those who have once, twice, thrice, broken their oaths, will do it again. To quote a French writer, a good witness upon this point: —   .

'A man arrives, one fine morning. What man? Is he an adventurer or a prince? Which, *or both?* The man has his hands full of money, of bank-notes, of rail-road securities, of places and pensions, of decorations and sinecures; the man presents himself before the func-tionaries and says, " Functionaries, betray your trust." And all the functionaries *do* betray it.   What! *all?* Yes, *all,* without one exception. He then calls upon the generals, and says, " Generals, massacre the people." And all the generals do it. He then turns to the irremovable judges, and says, " Gentlemen, I am going to break through the constitution, to commit perjury, to dissolve the sovereign assembly, to arrest the in-violable members, to plunder the public treasury, to sequester and confiscate all I please, to banish those

who displease me, to transport, shoot, and bayonet all I
please without summons, to execute without trial—in
a word, *Behold the laws! I trample them under my
feet.*"

' " *But we see nothing,*" say the magistrates.

' " You are a parcel of insolents," says the man ; "*you
see it plain enough,* but it is my will that you assist me.
You Judges! you shall this day wish me joy, I who am
force and crime, and to-morrow you shall condemn
and pass judgement upon all who have resisted me,
though they have honour, right, and law on their side."

' These irremovable judges kiss his boot, take cogni-
sance of the troublesome state of things, and also take—
the oath of fidelity !

' Then he perceives poked up in a corner the paid
clergy, crossed, banded, and mitred, and he says to
them, " So *you* are there, my Lord Archbishop! come
here and give me your blessing, and bless all I am going
to do." And the archbishop immediately chants his
Magnificat.'

Severe writing this, yet it is that of a Frenchman
against his own country. It is by Victor Hugo, and we
may be sure that nothing but an imperious sense of
truth wrung these sentences from him. And to what,
therefore, does this universal oath-taking lead, but to
universal perjury?

When the high magistrates of France went to swear
allegiance, a curious scene is said to have occurred.
As if to show his contempt of the creatures who thus,
with smiling faces, adapted themselves to every turn of
the wheel, they were kept waiting for a long time in an
ante-room without chairs or other conveniences for
sitting down. At last the door of the audience chamber
opens, and they are ushered into the presence of the

Dictator. He received them with coolness, not to say contempt, and while they were swearing, talked to his staff and officers without noticing them. When all was over, he allowed them to depart without salutation, and they retired with all the humility of men who felt that they had been used as tools, and were now receiving their merited reward. The ·following dialogue is said to have taken place between some of them. 'An unpleasant thing this, but it was necessary to take the oath.' 'Yes,' said a second ; 'and I fancy it will be necessary to keep it :' said a third, 'Certainly, but only in the same way in which the master of this house has kept *his own*.' How disagreeable these *tu quoques*!

But before pitying these men, let us remember the scene that took place in the High Court of Cassation in Paris, in December, 1851 ; or let us suppose it was the High Court of the Exchequer Chamber in London.

The court is assembled in full number. The judges in scarlet, black, and ermine, look thoughtful and solemn : an unusual stillness pervades all men and things —it is the precursor of a tempest. All is severe, classical, austere; you might think it was the Roman senate waiting the approach of the Gauls. But yet, pleadings go on as usual — the law is in vigour — justice is being administered.

Suddenly heavy footsteps are heard, as of men marching in order, and accompanied with the clang of arms. The door opens; all eyes turn towards it, and through it file steadily a company of infantry, headed by their officer and a commissary of police. What! soldiers in the sanctuary of justice! retire, miserable men, or you are doomed! Does Providence sleep? will not heaven blast them with its bolts? But *lo*! they advance ; and arrived at the bar, *halt*!

shoulder arms! and a line of steel half surrounds the judges. The officer presents a paper to the President, requiring him, in plain words, to retire and close his court, rendering null and void all decrees issued by him, and to pay attention to this *at once, or*—! They turn from one to the other; the moment is supreme; the judges confer; resolution is on every face. They whisper; they are silent ; the heart of the officer beats heavily as he sees what a dread duty awaits him, *when, lo! they rise*—to do what? To protest, as one man, against the indignity? to resume their seats, to die if need be, but never to be driven from them? to commend their memory to France, and hurl defiance at the Usurper? No! simply *to walk out and shut the doors*! and the President of the Court has since applauded the act, and compared it to the greatest deed recorded by Tacitus !

Therefore, I say, let us not pity these men, for it is good feeling thrown away. They deserved treatment fifty times worse, if that were possible, and probably will in time receive it.

For myself, I fully believe that the intelligent body of the French nation are thoroughly ashamed of this universal swearing. They see clearly to what it leads— to general corruption, and that without having a single merit. They have only to turn over the pages of their past history to see the records of these oaths, their solemnity, *and their duration*, in order to judge of their present value. It is mere superfluous sin to swear.

The revolution of 1792 was ushered in by a great national oath, taken by King and people, and taken only to be broken; an oath of fidelity to that constitution, which in twelve short months was torn to pieces contemptuously by all, and thrown aside. From that

period to 1795 it is computed that more than *one
hundred times* the same oath of fidelity was renewed
and taken, with the only difference that it was for a
new object—the mistress having been changed; and so
on during the revolutionary period, men slid down to
the abyss on a road made slippery by fragments of
oaths. *

* See Carlyle, vol. ii. p. 5.

CHAPTER XVII.

UNIVERSAL SUFFRAGE IN FRANCE — DANGEROUS IF PEOPLE UNFIT
— AS IN FRANCE — SMALL MEANS OF POLITICAL INSTRUCTION
IN FRANCE — BALLOT A POOR SECURITY — THEORY AND PRAC-
TICE OF — HOW THE PEOPLE WERE DECEIVED.

THE advocates of universal suffrage in England
would do well to turn their attention towards
France, and study the working of the system there.
It is useless to argue the question of universal suffrage,
until the population in general is more *fit for it* than it
is at present, and I will not here discuss what *is the test*
of fitness for the exercise of the suffrage, or where the
limits should be placed; but will merely observe that to
grant the suffrage to unfit individuals is about as dangerous an experiment as to place torches in the hands
of children and send them to play in a powder magazine. France is a proof of this, and I have conversed
with few Frenchmen who do not trace their evils up
to this source, and devoutly wish that universal suffrage
were either abolished or restricted; but who dares
attempt it?

In France the suffrage is open to all, not being
minors, nor under judicial disabilities, i. e. not having
committed crimes or misdemeanours, political or other.
Now the great bulk of the French population is composed of peasants, or dwellers in the country; the town
population being comparatively small. Out of the
thirty-six millions, thirty inhabit the country. Among

this class ignorance prevails to a great extent,—an inconceivable extent when we consider that there is a system of Government education in practice. True that the education given is poor in the extreme, and of weak quality, being chiefly in the hands of the priests; still, with any system, the amount of ignorance prevailing is astonishing.

In Britanny, the general average gives seven hundred out of one thousand who *cannot read*, and from my experience, I should have thought the number even greater. Those who cannot read must pick up political knowledge as they may from those who can, but probably they derive the great part of it from the priests, in their Sunday discourses; and we may be sure that what is there given is not of a very enlightening character.

And what are the means of information to those who *can* read? The public press has ceased as a public instructor, and the only public means of this kind is the 'Moniteur,' the official organ of the Government, and its veracity is so well known, that ' to lie like the ' Moniteur,' is an old proverb. How is it possible, therefore, for them to form a correct, or anything approaching to a correct, judgement of passing events, thus deprived, as they are, of all fair means of acquiring that knowledge on which alone a correct judgement can be based? In truth, they form no judgement at all, but go as they are led; or, if crotchety and independent, pick up a *rumour* and act upon it. My servant said he voted ' oui,' for the Emperor, because he wished for *peace*, and was told that the question was peace or war, and added that all the world said Louis Bonaparte was a good man, and would tread in the steps of his uncle — which, truly, were not the steps *of peace*. Others were told that it was on the question of the republic, and that 'oui' meant voting *for* the republic. Many thought it was for the old Emperor *come again*; some that it was on the question whether the representatives were to be paid. Not one in one hundred really understood the matter, and there was no public press to set them right.

Only fancy if the opinion of Hodge or Jack, from the wolds or the fens, was asked on a political question —what a puzzle it would be to them; how they would scratch their heads, and stand on one leg! and, if the fate of the rest of the nation did not depend on their answer, it would be a good joke.

But in France, the learned, the wise, and the wealthy, who are numerically only a thousandth part of the other class, are in a great measure dependent on such as Hodge and Jack, are dragged along with them in their errors and blunders, and are at the same time denied the power of enlightening them. It is a false and dangerous position. Some one says that the instincts of a nation are always right—perhaps so, if they are the *natural* instincts; but if they are artificially created by interested parties, they cease being instincts, and become vitiated cravings or mere parrot-cries, repeating what is taught without understanding or feeling.

No one doubts, for instance, that the great body of the able and influential men of France were wholly opposed to the government of Louis Napoleon; yet, notwithstanding, they were overpowered by the horde of rustics, who could only tell a spade from a pitchfork, and their voices were drowned in the torrent. And yet this is called, forsooth, the voice of the people — that *vox populi*, which is almost equal to the *vox Dei!*

The government of Louis Napoleon, knowing its power over this mass, knowing the magic of the name

of '*The Emperor Napoleon*,' takes care to coax and
manage them with all possible skill. Préfets, sous-
préfets, maires (all appointed by the government),
harangue, address, stick up proclamations, make domi-
ciliary visits, speak of the paternal government which
is, by mere paper laws, to clothe the back and fill the
belly — invoke the name of the Emperor to the gaping
crowd — hint darkly at the possessors of property —
grant money for a church, a bridge, or a road — and
flatter the admiring throng that by their vote all things
will be put right for evermore.

And the voting, what a farce it was! what a mockery
of the free voting system. All over France millions or
'*Oui*' were printed, and not any '*Non*'— they were
forwarded and introduced everywhere by the officials,
accompanied by threats, wishes, and so forth; when the
voter arrived at the urn he was watched and scrutinised
closely, and if he had face enough to ask for a '*Non*,' he
was told to go and provide himself as he best could.

The *secrecy* of the ballot was a myth; it neither pre-
cluded intimidation nor canvassing, and was open to
the objection of calumnious assertion as to the vote,
which the voter had no means of repelling. Then *who
kept the ballot-boxes?* Does any sane man believe
that Louis Napoleon and his underlings, who rode
roughshod over Paris in December, and afterwards
imprisoned and exiled thousands of honourable and
innocent men, would hesitate a moment before the
trifling act of ordering the burning of the box containing an unfavourable vote, or adding a cipher or a
figure to the sum total? If anyone does think so, let
him at once get his head shaved, and a blister to the
nape of his neck, for depend on it he is in a state of
incipient softening of the brain. It is a mere matter

of arrangement whether the number of votes is to be recorded as 7,500,000 or 8,500,000. The order being given, the thing will of course be done.

Let a people be educated; let them understand their political duties; let them acquire a visible stake in the well-being of the country, and I would not object to universal suffrage; but until that period arrives, it is not only a delusion but a peril; and to incur that peril wilfully, to hazard the good we Englishmen undoubtedly *do* possess, for the sake of acquiring a *possible* extension of it, is more than folly, it is sheer infatuation. Property, in my humble opinion, should always be represented in some way; it is unjust that a man of property should have no more voice in the direction of his country's affairs than a man who lacks it; and how can this be provided for by universal suffrage, in which each man has a vote, and no man more? Let us take warning by France, and not rashly grant universal suffrage unless we wish to bring on the universal scramble. Events will soon show us that a nation which acts ignorantly, and without good sound motives, can change as easily as the lightest coquette; and ere long we may see the power to which Louis Napoleon has so successfully appealed, change its views, and either put him out, or be put out by him. Four governments in twenty years gives no great hope for the duration of the fifth.

The party which seems to me to gain most by universal suffrage is the priestly party. Their influence over the country people, who, as I have stated, constitute the great mass of the population, is still enormously great, and by working the confessional and the ballot-box together, and making one act upon the other, they do wonders for their cause.

It was amusing to see how they preached up the

Corsican St. Louis at one period. On the Sunday before
Nov. 21, the day of the voting on the Empire question,
nine out of ten priests in France delivered a political
harangue, exhorting their hearers by all means to support the chosen 'vessel' they had suddenly discovered.
The effect of this was immense, for the perfect organisation of the Romish Church enables it to give
such strokes as this with great effect. Knowing the
priests in general to be upholders of the 'Legitimists,'
the turn was curious; but the good men have their reasons, and know the force of the proverb, that 'A bird
in hand is worth two in the bush.' Many bishops published pastoral letters stirring up their clergy, and they
again wrote to their people, stirring *them* up; in fact,
France was like one great porridge-pot, and was all hot
and working from top to bottom.

Napoleon, of course, recompensed them for their services, and it was done at the expense of Protestantism.
Certainly the priests entertained the most exagge-
rated hopes that their day was coming, and anyone
who had eyes could see a change in their manner which
was very remarkable. They no longer bowed and
cringed, as in 1848, making friends with Mammon
against the time when they expected they should want
his help, but looked the world well in the face, and
treated Mammon very cavalierly when they met him.
Their tone towards Protestants was more and more rude
and overbearing, and all denoted that they thought
they saw from afar the day of their triumph, and were
already tasting its delights. But, after all, they have
only been *seers of visions!*

I wish some of our honest John Bulls, who shout so
loudly for 'Universal Suffrage' and 'Vote by Ballot,'
would come over to France, as I have before said. But

they should make haste. Things do not last long here; there will be a new system perhaps shortly, and the moment universal suffrage becomes hostile to the government *one of the two* will be abolished. I suppose that there are still herds of English *philosophers*, metropolitan and provincial, who think that the ballot is the general heal-all; that all the ills of humanity are to be cured by taking *only one* 'small box,' and that universal suffrage is but another phrase for universal felicity; but as human life has been disagreeably abridged since the Flood, we cannot spare time to argue such points, while there are others more pressing. Let such men, however, come here and open their eyes and ears; they will learn something I believe, — i.e. if so disposed, and not like the man who sacrificed all for his theory, and squared everything to suit it. For information on these subjects rains upon you; you need not seek it; if you only open your mouth and shut your eyes, you are filled immediately.

I am now in a commune where I believe it to be certain and beyond doubt, that more than 400 people voted '*Non*;' yet, strange to say, only some 30 are reported in the official list. I asked for information. 'Oh! it is easily understood; only a figure or two altered.' In another commune, no one was believed to have voted '*Oui*,' and lo! by a magical transmutation, no one was reported as having voted '*Non*.'

Meanwhile millions of '*Oui*' tickets were printed, and no one was allowed to print '*Non*.' These millions were distributed over the country, together with 'stirring up' circulars. The peasants were told that '*Oui*' meant 'Republic,' 'Henry V.' 'Orleans,' or anything else which answered; and sensible men *wonder* at the result!

I myself went, at this time, into a respectable book-

T

seller's shop at Morlaix. The counter was covered with
sheets of '*Oui*,' a universal affirmation; it was refreshing, in these times of discord, to see such general
agreement. The feeling seemed to have extended to all
around; the very apprentices, mere 'printer's devils' as
they were, smiled blandly upon me, an ink spotted
brotherhood of peace. I could almost have voted '*Oui*'
myself, and mechanically looked amiably at an old lady in
the corner of the shop. 'Who prints the "*Nons*"?' I
gently asked. 'No one,' replied the happy bookseller,
adding (what spoiled all in a moment), 'for no one is
allowed to do so.'

In some places other means were used. In a certain
commune of the *Yonne*, suspected of *negative*, but at
the same time dangerously *positive* tendencies, a pre-
liminary purgation took place, accompanied by bleeding.
Out of 500 voters 430 were arrested, and (strange to
say) the rest voted '*Oui*' to a man. In another commune in the *Loiret*, the same treatment was prescribed by
the prefectorial Sangrado, and with success: 497 having
been thus physicked, the remaining 142 voted '*Oui*;'
the cathartic having operated vigorously, and cleared
away all obstruction and inflammation.

In the town of Lille, the nephew of the representative
Aubrey having seen the agents of the préfet distribute
tickets with '*Oui*' in the great square, was so innocent (being a young man, and rather green) as to
distribute '*Nons*' also, and was immediately imprisoned
in the citadel. At Bonchamps, M. Parent, jun., Deputy
Juge de Paix, was arrested and shut up at Valenciennes,
for having advised certain persons, who asked him, to
vote '*Non*.' The unanimity was admirable; but it
reminds us of the unanimity at the public meeting in
'Martin Chuzzlewit,' 'The greatest harmony pre-

vailed.   The resolution was carried unanimously; only
one man said " No," and he was immediately *carried off
by a policeman.*'

And who believed that the 7,500,000 votes were
genuine ?   No one.   Let us hear Victor Hugo: —' Let
' us speak seriously.   Coup d'Etat gentlemen, nobody
' believes in your 7,500,000 votes.   Come, be frank for
' a moment; confess you are slightly *Greekish*; that
' you cheat a little.   How did you get the figure of
' 7,500,000?   Who counted?   *Baroche.*   Who exa-
' mined? *Rouher.*   Who checked? *Pietri.*   Who added
' up? *Maupas.*   Who certified? *Troplong.*   Who an-
' nounced? *Yourselves.*   In other words, servility
' counted, meanness examined, trickery checked, forgery
' added up, venality certified, and mendacity announced.
' Very good.   Whereupon M. Bonaparte ascends to the
' capitol, orders M. Sibour the Archbishop to thank
' Jupiter, puts a blue and gold livery on the Senate, a
' blue and silver livery on the Legislative Body, and a
' green and gold one on his coachman, lays his hands on
' his heart, declares that he is the product of universal
' suffrage, and that his legitimacy has issued from the
' ballot-box.'

I commend some of the above facts to the attention
of those who uphold the ballot and universal suffrage.
There may be some good points in their favor, and they
are conscientiously supported by many honest men; but
there are *cons* as well as *pros*, and with every disposition to form an impartial opinion, I think the contras
at present greatly predominate.

CHAPTER XVIII.

THE FRENCH PRESS—NEW LAW REGULATING IT — 'AVERTISSE-
MENT' — FRENCH IDEAS OF 'ORDER' — EFFETE STATE OF
JOURNALISM — A MODERN FRENCH PAPER, A SORT OF LIVING
SKELETON.

BUT what shall we say of 'the Press' in France?
To say that it does not exist is false ; but to say
that it *does* exist requires so many explanations, that
the assertion may be suspected of falseness also. Its
existence is painful and dishonouring to all, except to
those editors and writers who have flung down their pens
with disdain, and retired from their degraded profession.

It might naturally be expected that arbitrary power
would attack the press without delay ; that it would
endeavour to gag and bind the wakeful sentinel of
freedom before coming to open conflict with the main
army. And it *has* done so. By one of those thousand
decrees which issued from the teeming brain of Louis
Napoleon during the three first months of the Empire,
the press was put into *police* custody, from which it has
escaped only to be placed in solitary confinement on
the cellular system.

By the law of February 1852, it is provided that, if
any newspaper contain articles of a nature calculated to
do injury to public morality, or to weaken or offend the
institutions of the country, the préfet of the department in which the journal circulates should notify the

same to the principal editor. This is called an '*avertissement*' or warning, and after two such warnings, the
paper may be suspended by an order of the minister.
These warnings also are to be inserted in the first page of
the offending journal, without editorial note or comment,
and the warnings may be accompanied by such remarks
as prefectorial wisdom chooses to indulge in. For
despots don't like retort or even reply; it must be 'go
and he goeth,' and that without a word. Indignant
editors must not only feel but *kiss* the rod; as say the
Persians, they must eat dirt, and *do it diligently.*

Imagine the annoyance of a pert provincial editor, the
incarnate wisdom of a country town, who has long
launched without a check the popgun thunderbolt of his
weekly paper, at being thus obliged to swallow, with a
resigned face, a good scolding, and then to have to print
it in his paper! What would the Picwickian Pott of the
'Eatansville Gazette,' have done — how *could* he have
borne it? But the press being under the ferule of the
Imperial pedagogue, there is no resource but submission.

It is somewhat amusing to watch and see how despotism grows — how it extends itself into all quarters.
At first the prefectorial power of giving an *avertissement*
was only exercised for political reasons, then it extended
to matters of morality, at length to civility and good
breeding; in fine, there was reason to apprehend that
the very style and manner of the editor would be matter
of comment. And thus it ever is with tyranny — grant
the first step and you are led you know not where; for
who shall limit the vagaries of a capricious mind?
'*Obsta principiis*'— is the only safe rule; but France
seems to have lost her backbone for the present, and to
be made up chiefly of gristle and cartilage.

I will give a few instances, and, pray, remark the
lofty terms in which these high personages write. Their
pens must have been dipped into very uncommon ink,
of which, however, ' Moses and Son' and ' Holloway's
Pills' seem to be equally large consumers with them.

The *Courier of Verdun* is admonished 'for publish-
ing a copy of a letter to a sous-préfet, which involves
the administration in questions of individuality, to
which it wishes to remain a stranger.' This is really
autocratic, and might have proceeded from the Emperor of all the Russias, instead of from a quondam
clerk or lodging-house keeper now made into a préfet.

Another, *L'Union Bretonne*, is warned 'for not con-
ducting controversy *according to good manners*, and
afterwards for supporting the claims of a candidate who
had not taken the oath of allegiance.'

The *Journal de Bezières* is admonished for having
characterised certain proceedings of the local municipal
council as 'marked by irritation and small good
faith.' Happy Bezières! where nobody quarrels with
anybody! one would wish to live there, and I recommend it to the notice of 'quiet single gentlemen,'
seeking a residence.

Another receives a notice for having alluded to the
maire of his town as 'combining with others to oppose
a certain college, and having made *illnatured* remarks
upon him.'

Le Petit Courier de la Bretagne is warned for ' having
contested the truth of the official bulletins of the
President's journey to Strasbourg, and arrogated to
itself the right of *rectifying* them.'

A Paris journal is notified for discussing the principle
of hereditary succession, which is ' inopportune;' and
the *Presse*, the great liberal paper, is admonished,

and afterwards receives a second warning, for having
addressed to a scandalous writer who made unfounded
charges against that journal, the words ' you lie.'

These are a few specimens culled at random, but we
may imagine the harassing effect of such interference.
A mere warning would be no great matter—would, perhaps, be treated as warnings often are, and as they may
remember who have read the story of the ' Three
Warnings;' but a warning from the Préfet means something more, and that is *suspension of the journal.*
After a second warning the journal can be suspended
on the mere order of the Government. And suspension means that the editor and all his staff must be sent
adrift, some to ruin, others to grievous loss and trouble.
Many journals, too, belong to small companies, who
possess the journal in shares. Now, it is well known
that companies have neither conscience nor bowels,
save for themselves; and as ' suspension' means ' no
dividend;' they forthwith call a meeting, haul up the
unfortunate editor, and tell him forthwith to lower
his tone or resign his office.

We may therefore easily fancy the effect of this
law. The independence of the press is utterly destroyed
by it. Some few men of courage and principle hold
to their opinions, and proclaim them; but, overwhelmed
by the cowards and parasites, and the rest of the rabble
rout, they by degrees fall and disappear, or else are
struck down by the club of the law or the law of the
club, and die with honour. But the great mass obey the
word of command, and veer round more or less swiftly;
some making *volte face* in a day, others changing
slowly, and hoping to efface their traces as they change
their path little by little.

And so the great end of Louis Napoleon's party is

attained — 'order.' There is a magic in that word
'order;' it must have many faces, for all invoke it and
fight for it; if it be 'Heaven's *first* law, it is a Frenchman's
first *and last* also. Yet we must not be too severe upon
them. After their frequent 'disorder,' it is no wonder
some are misled by what *calls itself* the contrary.

But order produced by the pressure of despotism, and
that arising from well-regulated liberty, are two things.
In England, for instance, we have the latter kind —
where the policeman's staff is the emblem of the law;
in France it is of the former sort, and is represented by
the sword, which even mere policemen carry. Which,
good reader, is the most durable of the two? which is
the most conducive to the well-being of a nation?
which is the most congenial to a civilised people?
Therefore, when we speak of 'order' in France, let us
remember of what sort it is. Give any one force sufficient, and he will engage to produce 'order'; but
whether, when such order is produced, the world is
benefited, is another question. The end is not worth
the means. By a powerful machine you may compress
sawdust into an apparently hard block of wood; but the
pressure removed, it becomes sawdust as before, and
your pains are lost.

And when the great *summum bonum* is attained,
what is it but a sickly monotony, without life or spirit?
Once on a time, a friend of Paley was dilating to him on
the uninterrupted felicity of his married life: 'We've
been married thirty years, and never had a word between
us; what do you think of that?' 'Think,' said Paley;
'why, that it must have been *verra flat.*' And so with
'order.' No one must speak above his breath; all must
stand still in the first position, as you are placed by the
master; and if you grimace with your fellow, or look as

if you would like to pull another boy by the ear, down comes the fiddlestick upon your head without mercy.

And under this new law of the press, certainly there has been pressure enough. In Paris, forty journals have been extinguished; in the provinces, no less than two hundred! Only think of the misery inflicted in destroying these two or three hundred newspapers; the thousands of poor families deprived of a living, at a period when all trades have great difficulty to find work. Then think of the property sacrificed by a mere stroke of the official pen, given perhaps honestly, but probably spitefully.

And under this law, instead of offences against it being tried by the *civil* courts, they are placed under the jurisdiction of the correctional courts; i. e., the *police* courts. The press is treated as an association of rogues, and all are sent together before the police. This adds insult to injury. How well must the police sheet sound : ' No. 1. John Smith, alias " Wide-awake," for abusing the police; No. 2. Richard Grab and Bill Symes, for burglary; No. 3. *John Walter*, for an article in the *Times* reflecting on the Budget.' But it attains the object of lowering the standard of journalism; it accustoms people to speak in a breath of journalists and swindlers or pickpockets.

And what a wretched living skeleton is a French daily paper! It is like the figure of a man made up for a tailor's window — padded here, pinched or pared there, with eyes that see nothing, and a mouth that speaks nothing, and yet, withal, of a decent, not to say *modish*, exterior. Take the *Presse*, for instance, the most independent paper left in France, and one which has been ' warned ' twice. Girardin, the former editor, is a man of great talent, and has the pen of a great writer. He is remarkably epigrammatic and logical in style, and pitilessly fastens his opponents up in syllogisms and dilemmas from which there is no escape. His range of topics was wide as the world; he discussed freely, and all that he discussed he en-lightened. But the *Presse* belongs to a company, and Girardin must obey orders. It is useless to write what will not sell—especially what may, perhaps, suspend the journal; he must, therefore, moderate his ardour, and limit his selection of subjects, which is duly done, and again behold the poor *Presse*, 'the shadow of its former self.' Take a number now before me. A French novel or *feuilleton* occupies one quarter of the paper; another quarter is taken up by a treatise on the china manufac-ture—not from Girardin, of course—he could not handle such *earthy* materials, they are too sticky for him ; a third quarter is composed of the Paris Bourse and oldish news, and the remaining quarter is given to Government decrees and advertisements. There is very little bread to all the ' sack ; ' we may cease calling it a *news*paper. Fancy one-half of the *Times* being filled by a romantic and rather loose tale, and a history of porcelain ! What would London merchants and bankers say to that ?

The *Patrie*, the leading Government journal, for many weeks had long articles, of from four to six columns, on agriculture —not a practical treatise, for there would have been something useful in that, if not amusing — but a root and branch history of it from the beginning of all things under Abraham and Lot, and tracing it down through the middle ages; but the article was so very ponderous that it fell in of itself, or else perhaps the writer stuck fast in one of those heavy soils over which he used to drag and exhaust his readers. At another time the same paper entertained the world by a series of *lively* articles on *insects* of various kinds, and especially *domestic* and agricultural ones; and thence it acquired the title of the 'insect journal.' In fact, instead of politics, we have chiefly domestic information—a paper becomes a nursery guide—a housewife's complete manual—a receipt book. *Men must live*, and if they cannot fill up with one thing, they will do it with another. And such is the state of degradation of that press of which France was one day so proud!

And all this treatment is systematic. Louis Napoleon said, soon after his accession: 'My predecessors have been ruined by Parliamentism and Journalism. I shall abolish one, and starve the other;' and he is keeping his word. It may be difficult to admire the man, but one can but admire the tenacity with which he pursues and holds to his purposes. According to Carlyle, it constitutes one quality of heroism, and, if in a good cause, is the sign of a great man; but a great virtue lies in that *if*.

If a stranger, a visitor from another planet for instance, were to alight upon France, and take his ideas of the state of the country from the tone of *its journals*, he would say, 'What a strange country is this! I am surrounded by evidences of past greatness — splendid buildings, useful and noble institutions, polished manners, eminence in the arts and sciences, and yet the mind of the people seems vegetating; I see no indications of its present exercise. They must have passed their culminating point, and must be in the stage of debility and decay. There seems no interest taken in politics; there are no discussions on the *res publica*; all is tranquillity and peace, but it is the tranquillity of a very low order of the animal creation. Doubtless

the mind of France is in its dotage, yet it seems a happy
and contented dotage.'

But how erroneous would be this judgement! Beneath the apparently calm surface is the molten and
glowing lava — the boiling temperament of France —
swelling all the more violently from the outward compression. Let the pressure be removed, even though
for a moment, let a fissure be made in the mountain
side, and in a moment we should see the fiery torrent
rush forth with its ancient impetuosity, and the peaceful paradise of the planetary visitant would be converted
into a smoking scene of destruction. But all great
operations of nature are terrible in process, though
beneficent in result.

In France they are now brought back to the middle
ages, when laborious monks multiplied books by manu-
script. A book, for instance, is proscribed by the censor
— good! its best parts are immediately extracted and
copied; and the process, and the extra value given by
proscription, engrave their meaning doubly upon the
mind.

Victor Hugo's book, from which I have quoted, was
rigorously pursued everywhere; the police scented it
out with the skill of bloodhounds, caught a trace of a
copy here and of another there, watched, took notes, perhaps at last seized and confiscated it.   And what then?
Why, that ten read it for one who *would* have read it,
and by passing it from hand to hand with mystery and
fidelity, the readers baffled the pursuers, and increased
its interest ten-fold.   The copy that I saw, and read
behind a door with a candle while the owner kept
watch, had a charmed life.   The police were frequently
in the act of seizing it, when *presto! pass!* and lo! it
vanished into another house, and the web had to be spun

anew. I never saw the game of hunt the slipper made political before.

The various letters of the Count de Chambord (Henry V.) were treated in the same manner. No one was allowed to sell the *printed* copies. *Eh bien!* men and women made *written* copies, which were doubly valuable. I made several copies for French friends of the letters, taken from English papers, and these were re-translated into French, not without loss probably, and thus the French news came from England.

Not much march of intellect and civilisation in all this! Nature abhors a vacuum, but there is at present a great one in France. It is the Empire *of nothing*— you take up a daily newspaper, which should be the mirror of the world and show you what is saying, doing, and thinking, and you find *nothing*. Great is the praise, and much the do about nothing! '*Oh! puissance de vide*,' as Emile Girardin exclaims in one of his spirited articles, instead of a '*Presse periodique*,' we have a '*Presse pneumatique*,' in which, as in an exhausted receiver, a very mouse would die from want of air to breathe.

It is the intention of the Government to create a strictly Government press, by circulating the *Moniteur* at a very low price. This will complete the process, and effectually shut out the light from the people. Henceforth they will be fed on such nourishment as the Government chooses, and in such quantity as *to it* seemeth good, and, as may be easily imagined, the quality will not be of a superior kind. Milk diet is mild, but *very tasteless*, does not make muscle; but I suppose the Emperor thinks that meat makes blood too fast.

And how will the public mind be enlightened by this process? Will it not rather be vitiated and lowered? For the essential quality of the Press is its independence; when that is lost, it is worse than useless, it is dangerous. Unless the Press is the faithful record of public events, it is valueless and does harm; instead of the friendly beacon, it becomes the wrecker's light.

Henceforth we shall read such sentences as the following, which are probably kept in stereotype, so as to be always ready, and avoid trouble: — 'The Emperor 'took his usual drive on the Boulevards to-day, accom- 'panied by his Staff. The cries of "Vive l'Empereur!" 'resounded along the whole line of his route. It was a 'veritable ovation. His Majesty seemed in excellent 'health.' Or, 'An interesting incident occurred as the 'Emperor was entering the Palace. A young woman, 'of a charming exterior, threw herself at his feet, ex- 'claiming, "Oh! thanks, Sire! for the mercy you have '"extended to my father. May Heaven preserve your '"Majesty!" The Emperor was visibly affected, and 'raised her up, with words of comfort. The crowd was 'moved at this additional proof of his benevolence.' Or, 'At the review, yesterday, the Emperor approached 'an old veteran who stood near him, and who, leaning 'painfully on his staff, was attentively regarding him, 'and said, "Ah! vieux moustache, and so you are here! '"I have not forgotten your services at Leipsic and in the '"hundred days; take this as my remembrance!" pre- 'senting him with a purse containing 500 francs. The 'old man faltered, almost falling from emotion, "At last '"I die happy! Vive Napoleon l'Empereur!"' and so forth. Real incidents such as these are worthy of record, and well deserve a place in public journals; when true, they give useful light to the world: but here they are manufactured by a poetical clerk in the office of the *Moniteur* who does the romantic articles for so many francs per week. And as the public generally know this, and disbelieve what they read, the effect is a general mistrust of all news whatsoever, which at last grows into a general indifference and apathy, *the great end of a despot.* ' He makes a solitude, and calls it peace.'

Who that saw the revolution of 1848, could have believed the state to which a few short years have brought the Press of France?

One Paris journal publishes each day a few chapters from ' Uncle Tom's Cabin.' Of course it is impossible to give the nigger idiom and pronunciation, and therefore the wit of Sam and Topsey, and the rest of our black brethren who figure so conspicuously there, is all lost; but the translator goes on as gravely and seriously as possible, without suspecting that he is all the while in the condition of the person who tells the story without the point. Quotations from English journals are very rarely seen, because too free for this close atmosphere, so that the contents of the paper may be set down as *nil.* They have in fact got as far as the single straw per day, and therefore we may soon expect the death of the animal; and its death would be preferable to the zoophytic life in which it at present lingers.

The general state of literature corresponds with the state of the Press. The censorship over the one is as severe as that over the other. No books worth reading are published; for thought is sympathetic, and the repression of it in so important a direction as politics weakens it elsewhere. The result is a general stagnation. For, thought forbid, expression naturally grows weaker. As Cowper says, ' Thoughts shut up want air, and die like plants, when brought into the sun.'

In 1848 the mind of France was in prodigious activity. The press teemed with works of all kinds, doubtless good *and bad*; but when the human mind is in vigour and activity, and casts off its ideas on all sides, although the chief part may die speedily, yet some reach the undersoil, take root and flourish, and future ages benefit thereby. And as we have the firm belief that the good will outlast the evil, we would encourage as much as possible the free public expression of thought. But now all is dead; it is the winter of the mind, and the few shoots which appear here and there on the waste are either poison bearing or stunted. And the minds of men grow cramped as does their position. They grow content with less mental food than formerly, making a virtue of necessity, and their minds shrink in size and power, like unexercised and poorly nourished muscles.

And all this has been gradually brought about by the efforts of *one man*. We may therefore be sure that he has *a power* in him. The man who mounts an unbacked colt, sits him firmly in his furious plungings, restrains him, curbs him down, makes him come and go, and finally reduces him into the passive instrument of his will, is one who has at least the merit of a strong will and of riding well. And Louis Napoleon has *power*, let us be certain of that — innate individual power — power self-relying and self-exercised. Up to his accession his page had been almost a blank; but now it is filled with many characters both good and bad — and will yet receive many more. He has played one part, but he has others yet to perform; we are only at the first acts yet. But the *dènouement* may not be far off; and let all look out lest that *dènouement* should involve themselves.

IT must be difficult to find a magnanimous despot.
The character itself is unhappily not unusual, but
it is the qualification superadded which renders it so.
Such a man, triumphing over the sustained resistance
of a noble-minded people, would be visited, one would
think, by continual remorse in seeing their brave but
useless efforts. While scourging and oppressing, he
must still admire them, and every act of rigour must
keenly wound his own bosom, although legally due according to his Draconian code.

Napoleon III. is spared much of this. He need have
few regrets for virtue trampled upon, freedom subdued,
honour thrust aside ; for few such qualities have been
exhibited. On one side severity, on the other servility ; such are the two chief features of the picture.
And it is better it should be so, to complete the lesson
and abridge the sympathies of the rest of mankind.
Life is short ; sympathy, when sincere, is too valuable
to be expended hastily, and as yet we have only just
passed the commencement: the end is to come.

When I consider the estimate in which Louis Napoleon was held by his own countrymen until he came
into power, when I call to mind the abuse lavished
upon him for his youthful escapades, the ridicule since

U

showered down upon him for his ideas of government, the general contempt and dislike of him even when called by the ignorant mass of the people to rule over them ; and when I find him now at the head of affairs, a sovereign despot, beflattered and befooled in such an outrageous manner by the very people who once so treated him, I shake myself and rub my eyes, and imagine that I must have been dreaming. If they were right then, they must be very wrong now; and if right now, they have only reached the right after half a generation of error. In either case, their judgement would seem to be worth little.

In the society with which I was acquainted before his accession, there were men of all parties — Orleanists, Legitimists, Republicans Red and Pink, but Napoleonists none or next to none; no one would hoist *that* flag. A hundred times have I heard men pretending to good judgement and looked up to by their fellows, pronounce dogmatically, and as if it were an axiom of Euclid, that *he* had not a chance, that it were folly to discuss it; and all around said *Amen.* A hundred times have I heard so-called well-informed people say with a Burleigh nod, ' Oh! he stops the gap — acts as a warming pan if you will — it is all very well; but as to anything more permanent, should he attempt even to be re-elected as President, he would be put out of doors in an hour.' And even when those who had eyes, and could use them, saw plainly in what direction the current was running, and that, successful or not, it was evident that ere long something dynastic would be attempted, these self-possessed blunderers only replied, ' *Eh bien !* — and what then ? — only let him try.' And he did try; set aside without hesitation or scruple the constitution he had sworn allegiance to, acted with ability and determination, and succeeded. And then where were our *constitutional* friends? They had disappeared from the scene — you saw *them* no more; but they soon reappeared as staunch Napoleonists in the Imperial uniform, and it required the lapse of time and a clear vision to recognise in them your former dogmatists.

For there is a magic in success, it changes and distorts most things; and through this wonderful prismatic lens all France commenced looking, with exclamations such as only proceed from Frenchmen; and apparently with a belief that *the whole human race* had substituted the same lenses for their natural eyes. Party seemed annihilated, you heard nothing of Orleanists, Legitimists, or Republicans—all praised and all voted for the foundation of a new dynasty; after which they would smooth down their beards as though they had performed a great moral act, and would recommence talking, in secret but with fervour, of their respective champions Chambord and Co., and their chances and means of success.

For the voting shows that nearly the whole male population of France supported Napoleon, although it is certain that a large and influential body in their hearts hated him.

Only the other day, in talking to a naval officer, who was or had been a strong Legitimist, and had ranted violently against Louis Napoleon, he said, speaking of the rumoured attempt to shoot him at Marseilles, ' What on earth should we have done, had it succeeded? It would have been a dreadful blow to France ;' forgetting for the moment that he had a score of times called him ' imbecile,' ' idiot,' ' usurper,' and so forth.

I do deliberately say, that the want of political

sincerity and principle then exhibited in France sur-
passed all of which we can form an idea; nor do I see
much hope of the real regeneration of the country during
the present generation. There seems no faith, no determination, no belief in principles, no independence of
thought; all *that* seems sunk under the temporary pressure of circumstances, and not a trace is left behind.

But what an encouragement is this to usurpation! It
seems to consolidate, but at the same time it takes
away real support from usurpation, by giving hope to
anyone bold enough to attempt it again. It says in
effect, 'Only succeed — no matter what are your means
— only get into the throne — no matter by what atro-
cities, and all the world will salute you, and keep you
there.' It consecrates the doctrine that 'might makes
right,' and opens wide the door to future troubles. It
produces the chaos of politics.

Meanwhile the Count of Chambord protests, and many
of his friends vote '*Oui*' for another Louis than *Louis
Capet*; the Republicans publish their manifesto, which
men read and smile at as too late; and vote, notwithstanding, '*Oui*' for Louis. Louis looks coldly and
grimly upon all, despising them doubtless in his heart,
and expecting the time when he will scourge them well
for their meanness. As Bacon remarks, the meanness of
mankind is best seen from high places; and both Louis
Napoleon and the Count of Chambord must have seen
a good deal of it by this time.

As for the latter, all people speak well of him, as a
man, and he seems to possess every kind and amiable
quality; but he has been born a hundred years too
late. His stiff, rusty notions of hereditary succession
and Divine right have long ago been put by, and meet
with little response now-a-days. By his address, pub-

lished some time ago, in which he expressly stated that he would enter France by Divine right or not at all, and that he rejected all call *by the people*, he committed political suicide; and so long as that address exists in force he is dead beyond resuscitation. And probably he feels this, or instead of protesting by parchment, he would have protested by his sword, against the re-founding of this modern dynasty. He feels that the theory of Divine right has no echo in the people's hearts, and disdaining to change or sully his principles, he lets the current run on, like his unfortunate ancestor, Louis XVI., and bides his time.

Labitur et labetur in omne volubilis ævum.

But this is bad policy for a King—this do-nothing, bide-my-time policy. It is a virtual surrender of his claims, and a release of his followers from their allegiance. It is the policy of the oyster, and nothing more; and in so acting, the Count of Chambord puts the seal to his own abdication.

One of the numerous offerings to the vanity of the Emperor struck me as worth preserving, together with the name of the inventor; for the man must have had an original genius to have thought of it, and deserves a patent. In a proclamation to his commune, Monsieur de Calvimont (*a noble* be it observed), *Maire* of Perigeux, after giving to Louis Napoleon all possible varieties of virtue, terrestrial and celestial, sums up by saying, as a proof undeniable of his greatness and high origin, 'God made Napoleon, and rested!' as though his excellences were so numerous, his powers so vast, that Providence was exhausted in the effort, and after the creation was obliged to seek repose. *God made Napoleon, and rested!* Did courtly incense ever go so far before? But, as was remarked by a friend, he omitted the words 'and saw that it was good.' Nor did the efforts of this Biblical pilferer go unrewarded; for the municipals of the town were so enchanted with the novelty of the idea and the eloquence of their *maire,* that they shortly afterwards presented him with a sword of honour, though it should properly have been made of lath, like the one flourished by Harlequin in the pantomime.

Another eminent writer, the Abbé Damas, speaking of the services rendered to the cause of religion by Napoleon III. (meaning the help and countenance afforded by him to the priests), remarks, ' After all, God is *not ungrateful* to the French nation.' As much as to say, ' Considering the signal piety and virtues of the French nation, and that God has now done us such a high service, we may really say, whatever we might before have thought, that God is *not* ungrateful. For 'twixt man and God we must keep the balance even; it being an account of service rendered on *each* side. Providence does something for *us*; we must do something for *Him*; at least it is only fair that we should, though we may do as we like; but, considering all things, we may really say, and we are happy in the opportunity of saying it, that God is *not* ungrateful to the French nation, to whom he owes *so much.'* It would be a second slaughter of the innocents to comment further on this.

The ' Patrie,' the Government newspaper, in recording the solemn service at Nôtre Dame, when Louis Napoleon had the standards blessed, and when a great mass was performed, enlarged upon the same idea. ' Hitherto God has rendered to Cæsar, has rained largely upon him all His favours; now Cæsar *returns* the debt, and renders his homage to God.' As if it was an interchange of compliments between *equals,* or a benefit to the Deity *bestowed by man.* What mad stuff is this! what an appreciation of the relations between the Omnipotent Creator and the worm He has created from the dust, and who must soon return to it! Will similar language be used when the worm, stripped of those accidental trappings, Imperial or other, which perish in the using, and do but weigh down the wearer under an accumulated responsibility, stands, naked and trembling, before the bar of God?

And thus drearily close my ' Notes on religious and civil liberty in France.'

Perhaps they should more properly have been called notes on the *absence* of liberty; for the amount actually existing is so infinitesimally small as to escape analysis, save of a very minute and searching kind.

It is marvellous indeed, the straw a day to which the French animal is reduced, and he once so spirited and high bounding — it is marvellous that he has not burst through the ropes and fetters about him, and recovered the freedom he has been cheated of; but I suppose his low diet has weakened and soddened him; and it is marvellous to think that all this change has been brought about *by one man.* We have recently wondered at the feats of Rarey the horse-tamer; but he sinks into nothing compared with Napoleon the man-tamer, the political Rarey of his time.

And yet people are to be found who call him an imbecile, and attribute all to his Ministers!

Time will one day solve the problem of the necessity and wisdom of all this—how far France could be governed on the principles of moderate liberty, how far she was fit for more than she now gets; but meanwhile

History is best served by presenting facts as they actually exist, and storing them up for future use.

Let Englishmen fervently thank Providence for their insular position and character, and for the ' little ditch ' which separates them from Gaul, and like a *cordon sanitaire* prevents the contagion of their moral and political disorders reaching us.

With these securities moral and physical, we can philosophise in peace, and look with comparative tranquillity on the *dénouement* of the political drama now passing before the people of France, strengthening ourselves for the future, and taking warning from their example.

And so the curtain falls, for the present.

CHAPTER XX.

IN '*The Bible in Britanny*,' I give at some length
my ideas on the then political state of France, and
on the probable action of Louis Napoleon as to Europe
generally, and as to England in particular; and I therein
add certain cautions and predictions on the subject,
with respect to England and the dangers to which she
then seemed exposed.

Ten years have since elapsed, and my opinions have
been in some respects modified by facts which have
since occurred, and I think it only an act of justice and
fairness to state those modifications and their causes.

Certainly at the period when I last wrote (in 1851),
not only England, but Europe generally, was filled with
apprehension as to what would be the political movement of France under Napoleon, and the future was
regarded with gloom and anxiety. Every well-wisher
of England exhorted her to gird herself up, and be
ready for a struggle, for it seemed near at hand, and
many discourses were preached on the text of ' Trust
in Providence, and keep your powder dry.' And, sooth
to say, the powder that has been kept dry, in readiness

for a war with France, must now be so dry as to be highly
dangerous to its possessors; and we should advise them
to get rid of it without delay, for fear it should explode
spontaneously and blow them all up.

Louis Napoleon, instead of the sworn foe, has *proved
himself* the firm ally of England; and whatever may have
been his secret and deep intentions as to us, on which
his opponents are so fond of dilating, we are entitled to
say, speaking from fact and history, that they have been
so *very* secret, and kept so *very* deep down in the re-
cesses of his heart, as never yet to have seen the light
at all, or to have been seen or heard of by any man.
And this during the double *lustrum* of ten years—a
period of some duration in a man's life.

Looking, therefore, at events by the light of experience and actuality, I think it is impossible to deny
the fact, that the conduct of Louis Napoleon as to
England has turned out quite otherwise than was expected by the British public in general.

I am not going to be the apologist of the Emperor
as to the *coup d'état.* History will give her verdict upon
that point in due time, as she has done upon all other
great events; but it will hardly be in *our* time. History
waits a long period before pronouncing her verdict,
and requires a great body of impartial evidence; as we
may see by the fact that it is only now, after the lapse
of 200 years, that her verdict is being delivered upon
Cromwell; a verdict, too, which reverses the decisions
of many inferior courts of that so-called equity which
is administered by the accredited Scribes and Pharisees
of historical literature; and History's verdict possibly
leaves out of view many circumstances which used to
be considered of great moment in the times of party
strife, and takes into its consideration many others

which, at the period when the events occurred, were not thought of at all. I say, therefore, that we cannot, as yet, give a really correct and impartial judgement as to the *coup d'état*, either as 'to the act itself, or the individual who was the chief actor in it.

Let us think of Cromwell, and avoid a hasty judgement. Fifty years back, and Cromwell, viewed under such light and by such evidence as then prevailed, was only called 'hypocrite,' 'liar,' 'regicide,' 'religious buffoon,' and so forth. Now we hear him styled 'the great Englishman,' 'the most powerful ruler England ever had,' and ere long, perhaps, his statue will be in the Palace of Westminster.

Nor will I now speak of Louis Napoleon and his system of governing *France*, so different from our own. I will leave that to be dealt with by others, when time enables them to take a full view of it as a whole. At present we see only the outsides of things — the bare acts — we must wait for the evidence of the various contemporary actors, given truly and without fear or favour, and that is seldom done by men in their lifetime. Time alone will show us the secret strings and pulleys of the machine, of which at present we see only the movements.

But as to the relations of Louis Napoleon *with England*, we can speak of *them* with the actual experience of the past ten years, and the events of that period justify us in saying that he has been the most faithful and enlightened ally of England who ever filled the French throne. From Lord Palmerston and Gladstone to Lord Derby and D'Israeli, from Lord Brougham and Lord Shaftesbury to Cobden and Bright, all join in asserting and repeating this; and as it is totally different from what was expected and confidently predicted

by many, it would, I think, be the height of injustice
to refuse the expression of an altered and more favourable opinion upon this point, now that circumstances show
that we were once mistaken in our judgement.

It is evident that, from the very commencement of
his reign, he has made the maintenance of the alliance
with England the keystone and master-principle of his
policy, and has allowed nothing to cause him to deviate
from or infringe it. He has had the good sense and
sagacity to see that that alliance would be his chief support, and that his own real interests were bound up in
maintaining it intact.

What matters to him a good or bad understanding
with Russia, Prussia, or Austria, so long as he possesses
the good-will of England, worth more than all the
others put together? The moral support that good-will
gives him is incalculable. He must feel it in all things,
and profits by it, and is too wise a man to do aught to
risk it. England's support given to a somewhat doubtful dynasty, like that of the Bonapartes, which lies
under a political ostracism (for their resumption of
power is forbidden by an express article in the Treaty
of Vienna of 1815, which I believe has never been repealed), is like that of a good, stiff-backed, wealthy and
worthy uncle of high character to a needy but well-
meaning nephew, who has had his ups and downs in
life, and finally gets into his place again, a sadder and
wiser man than he ever was before.

English gold is far better than English lead and iron
cast into balls, and Napoleon III. knows it well.

The other day the Bank of France was short of
cash — what then? They draw upon their sister in
England, the ' old lady in Threadneedle Street,' and
get out of their troubles; and French commerce is re-

lieved, and the relief to the circulation extends to the
remotest point in the French body politic; and helps
even the poor artisan in Paris, who is as it were the
little toe-nail of the giant, to get his daily bread as
usual, and a trifle cheaper.

The solid advantages conferred by Uncle John are
more than equal in value to the traditionary glories of
Uncle Nap; with the additional advantage of giving
the much-wanted '*as in præsenti.*' French commerce
wants relief, and must have 'primary commodities'
cheaper, and therefore comes the treaty of last year ; and
our iron and coal and 'woollens,' and other things, get
into France at a lower duty ; and, in exchange, their wine
flows in upon us tenfold, so that we can drink claret as
cheap in England as in Paris, and the trade between
the two countries mounts *in one year* from 2,000,000*l.*
to 6,000,000*l.*, and helps us powerfully in our present
time of distress.

Is this not better for French interests, and those of
Napoleon in particular, than an infinitesimal chance of
acting Falstaff and seeing London from Gadshill; and
a tolerable certainty of an allied occupation of Paris
shortly afterwards, as a natural consequence ?

I therefore maintain that, chiefly (if you like it so)
from regard to his own interests and also from regard to
those of France, he has made the '*entente cordiale*'
between the two countries the leading point in his
general policy, and *has steadfastly adhered to it* through
good and through evil report. Yes ! certainly through
evil report; for no man has had such floods of abuse
poured upon him by the English press as he has.
Turn by turn each journal, whether 'leading' or led,
has bespattered him ; though '*en revanche,*' turn by
turn each has flattered and bepraised him ; and I suppose

he has sufficient good sense to let one neutralise the other, and care for neither.

It has been well for the world and himself that he has been an easy-tempered man, with an unusually thick 'epidermis;' had it been his uncle, to whom nature had given a very thin skin indeed, and who continually winced under the stings of that buzzing gadfly, the press, we should have had a war long ago; and produced chiefly by the unbridled style of writing in which our newspaper writers often indulge, when they think the public wants something strong. But even making every allowance for his thick skin, he must have been sorely tempted now and then, one would imagine, when reading the vocabulary of abuse showered upon him; for I am much disposed to think that there is not a crime in the Decalogue of which he has not been accused by some portion or other of the English press during the past ten years; of that free press, supposed by innocent philosophers fresh from Eden to be conducted by grave and serious men, under a deep sense of responsibility; instead of, as in many cases, by paltry scribes, who write 'sensation' articles for party purposes, or saleable ones for daily bread.

And he has had good opportunities, too, of doing us an evil turn, and has made very strange use of them for a man with the 'deep' and 'secret' determination against us which some of the very 'deep ones' attribute to him. For instance, when the Indian mutiny broke out — in what a low state was England at that moment! India in the flames of rebellion, and scarce any regular troops in England; for within a month after the news arrived every available man was sent to quell the mutiny, and, save the Guards, few regulars were left behind. And what did the Emperor do? Did he hold aloof, plot with

Russia, accumulate forces at Cherbourg and Boulogne without any avowed purpose, and make us keep our army at home, in which case India had been lost? On the contrary, he offered to aid us with troops, if required, and would have permitted us to send our men through France viâ Marseilles, to save time!

And during that dreary winter before Sebastopol, when by the negligence of our own administrative authorities our noble army was reduced to the strength of a division, and that chiefly of skeletons, and the prestige of England as a military power was at a lower ebb than it had been since Walcheren ; why did not Louis Napoleon take advantage of our distress, patch up a peace with Russia, and fall upon us ; instead of taking part of our work in the trenches, and supplying us with great coats, ambulances, and necessaries of all kinds and descriptions? Where were his 'deep' intentions then?

And lately, in the dispute with America about the Trent, when all was trembling in the balance, and when war between England and America seemed most imminent, what did the Emperor do? Instead of a line of policy encouraging the Americans by doubtful words, without tangibly offending us; or merely doing *nothing* — a very safe policy at least, and costing nothing and involving nothing—he spoke out at the earliest moment when things were in suspense, and spoke clearly and strongly, and told America, whether she liked it or not, that in the opinion of France and himself she was clearly wrong, and should give way: and no one can doubt but that the excellent and straightforward despatch of Thouvenel contributed very materially to the maintenance of peace between America and ourselves.

Are these facts to count as nothing in the balance? Are English people to go on still with the same cuckoo

note of 'deep hostile views against England,' 'revenge
for Waterloo and St. Helena,' &c. &c., as if the good
offices I have above alluded to had never been rendered?
I much fear that many of them will, because prejudice
and not reason first influenced, and probably still influences them, and prejudice disdains facts; but fairness
and justice would not act so.

I have not the least wish to ignore any evil acts he
may have done; but I say, let us *discriminate* in our
censure, and give him credit for good ones where they
really and palpably exist.

Of course the Emperor looks at things chiefly *from a
French point of view* and not an English one, and considers French interests chiefly, and not English ones;
and of course he acts in the way which he considers best
for France, and also best for the permanence of his own
dynasty; and he is also obliged to consult in some
degree the current of French public opinion; and is
there anything passing strange that he, the *French*
Emperor, does this?

But John Bull *will* have everything fashioned upon
the English model, and is never satisfied unless all the
other people of the world wear clothes *of London
make,* whatever may be their national costume, or even
if they prefer wearing none at all.

Therefore he finds continual fault with the Emperor
for the way he rules in France, 'unconstitutional,' 'arbitrary,' 'despotic,' and so forth—in short, *un-English.*
Well! of course France is not England, we all know
that; and yet in these few words lies a great part of the
matter. France is *not* England, and never will be, and
will not be in a state to enjoy and make a reasonable
use of the political liberty which England enjoys, for a
generation or two; and even when she *is* in that happy

state, she will, probably, from the difference in the national character, use that liberty in a very different way from what we do.

Only look back on the past two centuries, during which England has been gradually, but by *very slow* degrees, winning her liberties and gaining her capacity to use them—think how many struggles between the rulers and the ruled the page of History records, since the time of the first Stuart — how the great conflict has wavered, now advancing now receding, so that progress has often seemed to have become retrogression — consider the naturally reasonable and practical character of the Englishman, disposed, as History shows, to settle great questions by instalments, instead of trying for all or nothing — consider this and much more of the same sort, and remember that France has never had any such training or any such advantages, and differs from us totally in national tone and temperament; and then say whether she is likely to be yet in a condition to accept and make a proper use of liberty on the London model?

The history of France for the same two centuries, how it differs from ours! For the first century and a half, or nearly so, we see an unlimited tyranny and oppression of the French people, grinding them down into the earth and extracting their very vitals for the advantage of a privileged few, hardly a ten thousandth part of the whole. Then we see a violent volcanic eruption, bursting all restraints and ties, and devastating everywhere—the great revolution. Then despotism again, though of a comparatively enlightened kind, holding aloft the flame of glory and dazzling the people, so as to make them either forget or be reconciled to the chains reimposed on them; then short fitful intervals of liberty soon extinguished, and now freedom emasculated and subdued; in courtly language, called the liberty of order — or rather, as I should say, of being ordered.

How, under these circumstances, is it possible that the political self-education of France can have made progress? To give to any people so situated full liberty at once, would be as likely to succeed as to harness a set of unbroken thoroughbred four-year olds to a carriage, and expect them to pull well together; and yet this is what John Bull would require, with his universal London-made suit.

The problem of governing France is a most difficult one, as History abundantly proves. I have frequently heard enlightened and liberal Frenchmen discourse on the subject, and all have agreed that at present the nation is *not fit* for self-government, and that they must be governed, though on liberal principles, *par une main de fer, gantée de velours* — a hand of iron in a glove of velvet.

On the Italian question Englishmen are equally determined to view all things only through the light of English spectacles, and those (softly be it spoken) strongly tinged with green. It seems quite clear, to me at least, that, but for Louis Napoleon and his efforts, Italy would probably still be under the rule of the Bourbons and Dukes, and tyrannised over by Austria. It was he who, with the view to set Italy free, put that stone in motion which stirred all from the Alps to the Adriatic. The movement of Italian liberty dates from his speech of Jan. 1, 1859, followed by his war with Austria, and his victory of Solferino; and despite all *tracasseries* and vexatious delays, Italians cannot but feel this, and be grateful to him for it.

It is true that he did not obtain what he desired in

Italy—namely, a union of confederate states, under the patronage, so to speak, of France; that is, France having the chief influence among them — that he strove hard, and by all means, to carry out his project, and was only beaten by the current of events being too strong for him; and that even now he resigns himself to the current unwillingly, like a strong swimmer who still casts lingering glances on the bank he wishes to reach. But these wishes have been defeated, happily for the world, and he succumbs, and yields to the disagreeable necessity, and has not had recourse to violence to secure or further his object, as many despots would have done.

I am not at all surprised at his reluctant acquiescence in the principle of the *unity* of Italy, if I regard the subject *from a French point of view*. There can be little doubt but that it is contrary to all French traditions and opinions, and that it will materially check, for the future, the power of France as a disturber of Europe. Instead of having on her frontier a sort of border territory, or debateable land, which has so often been the battle-ground of Europe — and into which France could, from time to time, make incursions so agreeable to the spirit of the young Gaul, or *la jeune France*, and return laden with glory and spoil—she will henceforth have a powerful and united kingdom of 26,000,000 of men, soon I hope to have more weight in the ' balance of power ' than Austria or Prussia ; and, above all, banded together by a constitutional form of government, and all the deep love of ancient liberty, the more profound from having been only recently regained after the struggle of ages. The reestablishment of a free government over Italy is a powerful addition to the ranks of freedom everywhere, and will,

I hope and believe, give to England, in any future
conflict, a firm friend and ally.   I can, therefore, easily
see why it has been acquiesced in *reluctantly* by France
and by the Emperor.

As to Rome, also, and its occupation by French
troops, I think we do not make sufficient allowance for
the great difficulties the Emperor has to contend with
in regard to that question.   John Bull, who is sick of
the subject, and hates the Pope, and reads the ' Times '
every morning as the finish to his breakfast, goes into
a passion, and would send all the cardinals and priests
to the right about, as he would order off trespassers
from one of his fields; but though this may be easily
done by him, it is not so easy to the Emperor.   With
him it is not only the question of Rome, but of France;
and whenever he recalls his troops from Rome, he flings
down his glove to the Romish priesthood in France, and
declares open war with them.   And who shall say how
that struggle would end?   They lifted him to power—
who shall say if they have not power to depose him
also?   And how can he do battle with them, save with
the help of the Republican party, and *how about that?*
He may, therefore, be excused for hesitating before
taking the step.

Then the Empress is a *dévote,* and is, of course, the
grand *point d'appui* of the Romish party.   They work
upon her in every possible way, and make her wretched,
I dare say, and she, in her sphere, works upon her
husband; and this, though a domestic and private
matter, adds not a little to his difficulties, we may be
sure.

Then the Legitimists and high people, the func-
tionaries who are well placed and getting rich, and *wish
to remain so,* all these scheme and influence as much as

they can, and surround the Emperor with innumerable cobwebs.

And, above all, he has to contend with *Rome*, with that system of subtlety which has unlimited resources of intrigue and power, with those long-robed *diplomates* and casuists whose heads and pens never sleep. Are all these difficulties nothing?

And if the French troops retire, what would happen between Austria and Italy? Would Austria, the eldest daughter of the Church, stand by and see Italy possess Rome? or would she make a last great effort to prevent it, seconded, perhaps, by Spain, and certainly by Catholic opinion in France? And who can say whether Italy, as yet unconsolidated and unsettled, is able successfully to cope in the field with Austria, who has a well-organised military system lately proved to be so powerful?

Italy would, doubtless, do all that could be done, but she might, as yet, be '*impar congressus Achilli;*' and suppose it *should* prove so? And after a second battle of Novara, suppose the Bourbon should reappear at Naples, the Grand Duke at Tuscany, and things be again 'as they were,' and all the blood, treasure, suffering and trouble of the last five years go for nothing?

And let us remember that France, being divided, could not act *in favour of Italy* with decision. In fact, were the Pope *in extremis*, and to cry aloud to Catholic France for succour, such is the magic of old names and influence, that no one can say what answer might not come from that impulsive and wayward nation. And suppose France rushed *en masse* to the rescue?

I insist that these are not mere wild suppositions and fancies, but are quite within the limits of *the probable.*

And meanwhile, England, bound by the ' non-intervention' principle, would probably look on and do nothing!

With all these difficulties around him, I can therefore understand why Napoleon hesitates before making the final move in the Romish question. The next move *may* be checkmate, but it may be *stalemate* instead; whereas, if Italy makes good use of the present time, every month adds to her chances in that war with Austria which will, in all probability, follow the evacuation of Rome by France.

It seems to me, therefore, that the delay in the evacuation of Rome by France, if it agitates and distracts, yet, on the whole, will produce good results for the new kingdom of Italy, and is a safe and more certain course of policy.

I sympathise sincerely with the Italians, and with that noble Garibaldi, under their numerous disappointments and trials, hard to bear; but I believe that their best ally is Patience, and that their strength is to get ready and wait, while the inevitable current of events does its work and washes away obstacles from before them, as it has already so wonderfully done.

But while I thus express my humble opinion as to the real friendly feelings of Napoleon towards England, I do not say that we should therefore at once disband the regular army, break up our fleet of 'ironsides,' bid the volunteers adieu, and look upon the Millennium as having commenced. Nothing of the kind.

Napoleon will not be on the throne of France for ever, and may not be there to-morrow; and what may come after him, he must be a far-seeing man to say. I am much inclined to think that the Bourbons will have the next turn of Fortune's wheel in *their* favour, and in that case let us all beware. Bourbons and Romanists in conjunction bode evil to Old England; but, thank God, she is not afraid even of *them*.

As to the Republican party, they played their part so ill and clumsily the last chance they had, that I don't think France will try them again soon, and I doubt if France is as yet sufficiently enlightened in political duties to be fit for a republic; but I quite think that the republic would be friendly towards England, and would be pacific, as republics, when let alone, generally are. It is only despots who make offensive wars.

But let the Bourbons return to France, and we should soon regret Napoleon, and acknowledge our injustice towards him. And in view of this possible event, it is wise and prudent to keep ourselves in a proper state of defence, and to avail ourselves of all the improvements in warlike implements which science can produce.

And let us make much, too, of our noble Volunteers! Ah! *there* is a force which England alone of all nations of the earth could produce, and of which she may be justly proud; an unpaid army of 150,000 of the *élite* of her sons, animated by no motive but patriotism, and assembled for 'defence and not defiance,' the true justification of all armies. They are the real peace-makers and peace-preservers, and have been, and will yet be, the means of saving us from many a war. Long may they flourish, and live in the hearts and respect of their fellow-citizens; and may England never lack, and never cease being grateful to, her brave Volunteers!

I trust the effect of what I have written may be to induce some persons to review their opinions as to Louis Napoleon. I am but a plain man, and have no pretensions to see farther into the political millstone than other plain people, or to speak other sense than common sense. But considering what I wrote on the subject ten years ago, in 'Britanny and the Bible,' I have felt bound to write as I now do, in common justice, judging by the *new light* of experience and fact.

Certainly *Englishmen* have small ground for complaint of his personal conduct towards *them.* In all respects *they* have been not only fairly, but most liberally and courteously treated by him. I believe that no Englishman with wrongs to be redressed, has ever made a personal application to the Emperor in vain. In fact, other nations complain that undue preference is given to us by him. He has reformed his tariff to suit us; he has abolished passports, that perennial nuisance which worried Paterfamilias out of his life; he has opened many Exhibitions and places to *us* on that mere assertion of nationality, '*civis Romanus sum;*' and lately he has so far modified his customs' regulations, those wearying formalities which ryle John above all else, that anyone who chooses to travel in light marching order may land in a French port as he would in an English one, and walk in a direct line from the steamer to ' mine inn,' with that cherished palladium of liberty, an unviolated carpet bag. Is all this nothing to Paterfamilias ? Should not the unprotected female, and the erratic bachelor, make sweet union, and join in a tuneful chorus of thanks and gratitude ?

And yet some people talk of ' deep designs,' and ' St. Helena,' and the rest of the drove bray a loud assent !

There is a popular story, current and very slippery, of Louis Napoleon having said that it was his fate to invade London and be killed there. I often wonder who invented it, for that it *was* invented I feel sure. I wish some one would own it, and show its pedigree; and I believe we should see that it was of pure English blood, without a cross. I once took some pains to discover its paternity. It had been told by a Mr. Overend, who contested a place in Yorkshire, at an election dinner, and I wrote, through the 'Daily News,' asking its origin, but received no reply. I wish Mr. Overend would give his authority for it, and enable us to trace the poetic figment to its source. The bare idea of Louis Napoleon — the silent and prudent man, *par excellence* — who seldom speaks at all, and who in all his works has never breathed a word against England, ' coming out strong' with such a *boutade* as this! 'Tis rather too absurd. If he really thought it, he would never have said it; and if he did not think it, he would not have been so foolish as to have said it, for it is a poisonous remark.

But I will conclude these observations, which will, of course, be judged differently by different people, but which I make in all sincerity. Probably, however, they may, and I hope they will, find an echo somewhere. They are directed towards the promotion of peace and good-will among nations, which principles are happily taking a more and more lasting root among us. And in the train of Peace comes Freedom civil and religious, enlightenment and improvement social and moral, of which every onward step secures a farther advance in the path. And Peace is the handmaid of the Gospel, and its best product.

'Tis a glorious cause, and one worth labouring for, both individually and socially, for blessed are the peacemakers! And if each man would only add his mite, like the pilgrim adds his stone to the heap in the desert, the temple would soon rise and show its fair proportions to the world, and enclose a goodly and ever increasing crowd of worshippers.

When travellers can pass between London and Paris

in twelve hours, or send a message from one city to the other in ten minutes, it is time for the two nations to regard each other as members of one family, and to look old worm-eaten prejudices steadily in the face. And if they do so those ancient and (to some) imposing looking Figures will soon show their ghostly nature by vanishing into thin air.

And in the hope that the observations I have made, and the sentiments I have expressed, may contribute in some small degree to this most desirable and excellent result, I bid a long '*adieu*' to my readers, and close this political postscript to 'Lower Britanny and the Bible.'

' LONDON ·
PRINTED BY SPOTTISWOODE AND CO.
NEW-STREET SQUARE

www.ingramcontent.com/pod-product-compliance
Lightning Source LLC
Chambersburg PA
CBHW060521030726
47498CB00004B/1030